Martina Leeker, Imanuel Schipper, Timon Beyes (eds.)
Performing the Digital

Martina Leeker, Imanuel Schipper, Timon Beyes (eds.)

Performing the Digital

Performativity and Performance Studies in Digital Cultures

[transcript]

Supported by the Niedersächsisches Vorab Program

VolkswagenStiftung

Niedersächsisches Ministerium
für Wissenschaft und Kultur

An electronic version of this book is freely available, thanks to the support of libraries working with Knowledge Unlatched. KU is a collaborative initiative designed to make high quality books Open Access for the public good. The Open Access ISBN for this book is 978-3-8394-3355-3.

Bibliographic information published by the Deutsche Nationalbibliothek
The Deutsche Nationalbibliothek lists this publication in the Deutsche Nationalbibliografie; detailed bibliographic data are available in the Internet at http://dnb.d-nb.de

Cover layout: Kordula Röckenhaus, Bielefeld
Cover illustration: Jörg Baumann, 2013, Situation Rooms,
Rimini Protokoll & Ruhrtriennale
Proofread by Hana Yoosuf, Janet Leyton-Grant, Anna Königshofer
Typeset by Julia Choutka, Sophie Köster, Inga Luchs, Vincent Rieger
Image editing: Tobias Schulze
Printed and bound in Great Britain by Marston Book Services Ltd, Oxfordshire
Print-ISBN 978-3-8376-3355-9
PDF-ISBN 978-3-8394-3355-3

Contents

Introducing

Performativity, performance studies and digital cultures
Martina Leeker, Imanuel Schipper and Timon Beyes | 9

Historicizing

Performing (the) digital. Positions of critique in digital cultures
Martina Leeker | 21

Annotating

Making digital choreographic objects interrelate: A focus on coding practices
Scott deLahunta and Florian Jenett | 63

Affecting

Speculation about 1:0. On the productive difference of the interval
Marie-Luise Angerer | 83

Trading

The noisy motions of instruments: The performative space of digital finance
Ann-Christina Lange | 101

Encrypting

Performing encryption
Susan Kozel | 117

Protesting

Mobile phone signals and protest crowds: Performing an unstable post-media constellation
Oliver Leistert | 137

MAPPING

Mapping invisibility: Surveillance art and the potential of performative cartography
Sigrid Merx | 157

TAGGING

The big urban game, re-play and full city tags: Art game conceptions in activism and performance
Margarete Jahrmann | 171

CO-PRODUCING

From flâneur to co-creator: The performative spectator
Imanuel Schipper | 191

INSTITUTING

Performing institutions: A catalogue of performative practices
Melanie Mohren and Bernhard Herbordt | 213

ORGANIZING

'The machine could swallow everything.' *Satin Island* and performing organization
Timon Beyes | 229

CRASHING

Performing the economy, digital media and crisis. A critique of Michel Callon
Jens Schröter | 247

DEMOCRATIZING

Performance and democratizing digitality: StudioLab as critical design pedagogy
Jon McKenzie | 279

Notes on contributors | 297

Introducing

Performativity, performance studies and digital cultures

MARTINA LEEKER, IMANUEL SCHIPPER AND TIMON BEYES

Performing the Digital seeks to map and reflect registers of performance and techno-social layers of performativity in today's digital cultures. The book's basic proposition is that the ubiquity and pervasiveness of digital media and their networked infrastructures profoundly influence the ways and styles in which performativity appears and is enacted. Contemporary technological apparatuses and media provoke new forms of 'intra-action' between what is usually considered to be either human or machinic agency, to use Barad's terminology of posthumanist performativity (Barad 2003).

In this sense, digital cultures are performative cultures. They condition and are shaped by techno-social processes and agencies, and they afford new possibilities for performative practices and interventions. It follows that the study of performativity in its heterogeneous dimensions cannot afford to ignore the agential forces and effects of digital technologies and their entanglements with human bodies. Accordingly, investigations of social, economic and political processes conducted in and across other disciplines have to reckon with the performativity of digital devices and algorithmic organizing. The book's genesis and development – and, we hope, the discussions it will instigate – were therefore informed by two guiding questions: How is performativity shaped by contemporary technological conditions? And how do performative practices reflect and alter techno-social formations?

In proposing answers to these questions, *Performing the Digital* offers a double contribution. First, we see the book as part of the wider 'performative turn' in the cultural and social sciences (Bachmann-Medick 2016; Thrift 2008), contributing to an understanding of how techno-social performativity – or perhaps a regime of digital performativity – effects the world we live in. More specifically, this collection seeks to map and thus make visible the relations between distinct approaches, overcoming the usual boundaries of focusing either on the performativity of affect (see Angerer, Leistert, this volume), or of markets (see Lange, Schröter, this volume), or of organization (see Beyes, McKenzie, this volume), or of critique (see Kozel, Leeker, this volume), etc. In its manifoldness and malleability, the notion of performativity emerges as a powerful concept to explore and reimagine digital cultures.

Second, we aim to contribute to and further develop recent engagements with technological developments and media-theoretical concepts in the field of performance studies itself (Auslander 2005; Bay-Cheng et al. 2010; Salter 2010). By relating questions and issues of performance and performativity to the broader empirical and conceptual landscape of digital cultures, the notion of performance is not limited to art-, dance- or theater-based practices but is seen as encapsulated in wider processes of techno-social emergence, production and control (McKenzie 2001).

Conceived as an explorative venture into territory of performativity (studies) and digital cultures, *Performing the Digital* brings together scholars from different disciplines – performance studies, media theory, sociology, organization studies – and practitioners of performance. Arranged according to the 'doings' that are in the focus of the respective chapters, the book's map of themes, concerns and concepts of 'performing the digital' as well as the interrelations between them presents a timely, promising and, we believe, exciting field of research.

In the remainder of this introduction, the collection is contextualized with a short discussion of its two guiding themes: the performativity of digital cultures, and performance studies' encounter with digital technologies. Based on this, the book's outline and the sequence of notions and chapters are briefly presented.

DIGITAL CULTURES AND PERFORMATIVITY

If we were to assume that digital technologies were merely tools, conveniently on hand and ready for human deployment, then this book would be superfluous. Yet perhaps now more than ever, such an image of technology seems patently absurd. As the prevalence of the terms 'ubiquitous' and 'pervasive' in conjunction with technologies, media and computing indicates (Ekman 2013), life is embedded in, and interwoven with, technological environments (Hörl 2013; Engemann/Sprenger 2015) – from the fiber-optic cables of the Internet to the omnipresence of intelligent artifacts that can, in part, communicate with one another without the intervention of human subjects. As a result, the book is framed through the notion of 'digital cultures'. Digital technologies now widely, perhaps even invariably participate in the 'making' of culture (Deuze 2006; Gere 2008; Stalder 2016).[1]

Correspondingly, the understandings of performativity and performative practices need to be rethought. To put it somewhat crudely, digital devices and infrastructures perform, and they make humans (and non-humans) perform. 'Smart things' profile and categorize, foresee and predict, propose and delete, charm and become dubious. Such ascriptions would have been perceived as suspect forms of anthropomorphization only a few years ago (Tholen 1994); now they come across as matter-of-factly descriptions of what technological objects and software do. And the consequences are serious. Consider the financial markets and their algorithms of high frequency trading (see Lange, this volume), the everyday organization of affect (see Angerer, this volume), the simulations of climate change research or the dressage of the quantified self and its self-optimization devices (Baxmann et al. 2016). Yet this is not merely a technological or medial a-priori of cultural forms and processes. In what amounts to techno-social interplays, human bodies also make digital technologies perform, through, for instance, embodied movements, gestures and habits, and the practices of streaming, updating, capturing, uploading, linking, saving, sharing, trashing, trolling etc. (Chun 2016).

Now, traditional or conventional notions of performativity and performance are grounded in the distinction between human and technological performance (see Leeker, this volume). Human performativity is linked to intentionality, reflexivity and sense-making, to embodiment, repetition and transgression. The technological, one the other hand, refers to deterministic operations without semiotic or affective qualities. This neat separation of human agency and non-human 'procedurality' has become untenable. Human bodies and technological apparatuses enter instead into a relation of performativity, a redistribution of agetial constellations towards a techno-social 'mangle of practice', to use Pickering's term (Pickering 1995) (and it is by no means clear that, in this mangle, 'performing devices' are necessarily cooperative, as Schröter (2015) has pointed out). In digital cultures, we might then say, the 'performative turn'

1 As Baecker (2007) argued, media revolutions, such as the invention of the printing press, are accompanied by new cultural processes, practices and forms that emerge to make the ensuing excesses of words, images and affects 'manageable' (Baecker 2007: 7). What Baecker called the 'next society' is negotiated in today's discussions on 'digital cultures'. We opt for 'cultures' in the plural, since these processes, practices and forms are multiple, heterogeneous and partly contested.

(McKenzie 2001; Fischer-Lichte 2004) needs to embrace its own 'technological turn'. The following essays explore different forms, registers and understandings of technological cum social performativity.

PERFORMANCE STUDIES AND DIGITAL CULTURES

For an investigation of performativity, performance studies is likely the first discipline brought to mind. In this context, *Performing the Digital*'s transdisciplinary set-up echoes the development of this relatively young field, which emerged in the 1980s. While there are various schools and branches of performance studies (see Pelias/VanOosting 1987; Madison/Hamera 2006; Powell/Shaffer 2009),[2] they share certain similarities. First, they can be characterized by a lively symbiosis between "aesthetic practices and the study of them" (Kirshenblatt-Gimblett 2008: 46), i.e. by a strong linkage between artistic practice and reflective analysis. Second, there is a marked tendency across the different schools towards the inclusion of a variety of research fields and approaches. As befits its 'object' of analysis and practice, performance studies both draws on methods and theories of a range of disciplines and contributes to their respective discourses (as is manifested by the wider performative turn in the cultural and social sciences). Third, performance studies explores bodies, identities, events, and narratives in terms of "the myriad ways in which meaning is created and social life is shaped" (Pearson/Shanks 2001: xiii). As Schechner (2006: 40) wrote, "[a]ny behavior, event, action, or thing can be studied 'as' performance".

Reflecting the circumstances under which something is considered to be 'performance' and exploring how performativity takes place and unfolds is therefore more important than a-priori definitions of what performance 'is' or might be. This is precisely why influential scholars (e.g. McKenzie 2001; Jackson 2004; Bay-Cheng et al. 2010) called for the field to distance itself from what currently defines the education and professional activities of performance workers, from Western concepts of theater and dance, and from the understanding of performance as an art form. Instead, performance studies should regard itself as a "means of understanding historical, social, and cultural processes" (Schechner 2008: 9); and "[p]erformance must be construed as a 'broad spectrum' or 'continuum' of human actions ranging from ritual, play, sports, popular

2 Indeed, performance is "an essentially contested concept, meaning that its very existence is bound up in disagreement about what it is, and that the disagreement over its essence is itself part of that essence" (Strine et al. 1990: 187-188).

entertainments, the performing arts and everyday life performances to the enactment of social, professional, gender, race and class roles, and on to healing, the media and the internet" (Schechner 2006: 2). Similarly, Fischer-Lichte proposed that what she called "performative studies" would denote the study of culture through the perspective of the performative; it thus stands for a "specific interdisciplinary approach to different subjects, which are analyzed from the perspective of the performative" (Fischer-Lichte 2012: 134; our translation).[3]

Clearly, then, researching and intervening into the present and performativity of digital cultures call for the sensibilities and approaches of performance studies. To do so, however, the field is challenged to more fully embrace and grapple with today's technological condition and the human/non-human or perhaps 'posthuman' performances that shape social and cultural processes (Bay-Cheng et al. 2010). This collection and its respective contributions seek to help push the field towards a more sustained engagement with performance and performativity 'after' digital media.

AN ASSEMBLAGE OF DOINGS

The book's structure seeks to reflect and, yes, perform its aims and rationale. As the outcome of an explorative, transdisciplinary endeavour into the messy and complex sphere of relations of digital cultures, performativity and performance studies, it constitutes "the beginnings of a map, or, more accurately perhaps, a map of beginnings" (Pile/Thrift 1995: 2) – an assemblage of phenomena, cases and concepts through which we can begin to chart and further explore the performative makings of and in digital cultures. After all, and contradicting the

3 We here use the notion of transdisciplinarity (and not inter- or crossdisciplinarity). A contested term, of course (Osborne 2015), 'transdisciplinarity' pragmatically entails an orientation towards and alongside phenomena or spheres of phenomena that require the reflexive mobilization of different and diverse theoretical contexts and methodical practices. As Osborne (2015) recently pointed out, the potential of transdisciplinarity – against its restriction to practical rationality and technocratic problem-solving – resides in the construction of a problem and the definition of a joint field of research, which harbors the potential of unexpected twists and of the problematization of established concepts and methods. In this sense feminist theory, for example, and gender studies and media studies can all be regarded as transdisciplinary research contexts par excellence – as well as, we would add, performance studies or performativity studies.

tropes of transparency and participation that seem to befall the jubilant discussions of technological progress, the techno-social relations and procedures of 'performing the digital' are largely invisible, obscure and opaque, cloaked in secrecy and incomprehensibility (Beyes/Pias 2014) or 'black boxing' and obfuscation (Galloway 2014). Under these conditions, the strategies and tactics of conducting research, of doing theory and of scholarly representation are open to debate and experimentation (e.g. Galloway 2011).

How, then, to perform 'performing the digital' through the time-honored medium of the book? Rather than structuring this collection according to different theoretical approaches, pre-given aspects of performance studies or social spheres or systems, we have opted for a non-hierarchical and 'flat' way of ordering the chapters – manifesting a 'map of beginnings' and perhaps a kind of queering of dominant registers of scholarly book production. The contributions are framed through 'doings'; they thus enter into and engage with the complexity of digital cultures by way of specific processual notions. We have sought to lend the sequencing of the 'doings' a certain narrative coherence or flow:

To begin, there is ***historicizing***: **Martina Leeker** inquires into the parallel trajectories of performance theory and media technologies up to the present, and in this context discusses the possibilities and limits of critique in digital cultures. From there, **Scott deLahunta** and **Florian Jenett** delve into a concrete performance in and on digital cultures through the notion and practice of ***annotating*** in the enactment of digital choreographies. This is one way of ***affecting*** human bodies by way of coding; the following chapter by **Marie-Luise Angerer** enlists affect theory, in particular the notion of the 'affective interval', to ponder the performative effects of digital 'co-processing' between media technology and human bodies. Such digitally produced 'involuntary moments' have taken on a particularly serious and quite uncanny role in the financial markets, as **Ann-Christina Lange** demonstrates in her investigation of the algorithmic exploitation of time-delays in financial ***trading***.

That the affective landscape is increasingly shaped by mobile media technologies leads to new forms of surveillance as well as to new ways of performing with and through such media. In her contribution, **Susan Kozel** reflects on ***encrypting*** as a performative counter-practice to control and 'dataveillance'. That ***protesting*** is reconfigured through digital devices such as mobile phones and the ways such reconfiguration occurs is explored in the subsequent chapter by **Oliver Leistert**. Drawing upon Guattari's notion of post-media, Leistert examines the problems for collective enunciations that the modulation of affect via mobile devices poses. Perhaps, however, the digital possibilities of performative cartography offer alternative and emancipatory forms of ***mapping***, as

Sigrid Merx studies by following a concrete artistic intervention in Amsterdam. Such performances thus have to deal with urban topographies that are marked through tags. Relating Lefebvre's 'triadic' notion of space to digital ***tagging***, **Margarete Jahrmann** studies the gamification of urban space for commercial and activist purposes. Such urban art changes the role and practices of audience and spectators from watching and listening to ***co-producing***. Discussing works by Ligna and Rimini Protokoll, **Imanuel Schipper** analyzes the turn towards 'the performative spectator'.

Beyond temporary interventions, there is the performative labor of ***instituting***. **Melanie Mohren** and **Bernhard Herbordt** reflect on their own artistic practice of 'performing institutions'. From here, it is a small step to apprehending processes of ***organizing*** as performative. **Timon Beyes** reads Tom McCarthy's novel *Satin Island* (2015) as a novel on intersecting layers of 'performing organization', in particular with regard to a posthumanist performativity. And the markets? They are prone to ***crashing***. Taking issue with Michel Callon's influential work on the performativity of economic thought, **Jens Schröter** shows how this kind of performance theory lacks a notion of crisis and seems thus incapable of thinking and exploring alternative forms of organizing. Perhaps, such forms can be experimented with in education. Inquiring into the relationship of performance and ***democratizing*** digitality, **Jon McKenzie** discusses the potential of 'critical design pedagogy'.

As this brief tour through the contributions shows, mapping different ways of exploring and theorizing performativity in digital cultures is a critical project. It is critical in at least two ways: For one, we need to learn to think and apprehend how techno-social performativity – as a kind of actualization or further development of the regime of performativity analyzed by McKenzie (2001) – inscribes human and non-human actors into what can for instance be called affective (Angerer 2014) and governmental (Rouvroy 2011) regimes. Second, especially the interventionist and practice-based chapters in this book demonstrate the possibilities of queering and at least temporarily reconfiguring such regimes. In digital cultures, too, performance theory thus offers a two-fold agenda of critique: to investigate the intricate relation of power and performativity, and to insist on the openness and changeability that is immanent to performative processes. It is up to scholars and practitioners (and scholar-practitioners) of performativity to further pursue and interweave both trajectories.

ACKNOWLEDGEMENTS

This book grew out of the symposium on "Performing the Digital", held in January 2015 at the Digital Cultures Research Lab (DCRL) of Leuphana University Lüneburg. The symposium was jointly organized by DCRL, the Institute for Design Research at Zurich University of the Arts and Copenhagen Business School's Department of Management, Politics and Philosophy. We are very grateful to the symposium participants for the inspiring talks and discussions that informed this collection, and of course to the individual authors for their contributions.

A big 'thank you' goes out to Julia Choutka, Inga Luchs, Sophie Köster and Vincent Rieger for their work on typesetting and formatting the manuscript (and for patiently dealing with editorial interventions) as well as to Tobias Schulze for taking care of the images. Moreover, we are indebted to Hana Yoosuf, Janet Leyton-Grant and Anna Königshofer for their invaluable proofreading. Finally, we thank Ina Dubberke, Samantha Gupta and Armin Beverungen for their support in organizing both symposium and publication; they and our other colleagues at the DCRL enable endeavours such as this one by collectively enacting, and caring for, a truly transdisciplinary space of scholarship.

REFERENCES

Angerer, Marie-Luise (2014[2007]): Desire After Affect (N. Grindell, trans.), London: Rowman & Littlefield.

Auslander, Philip (2005): "At the Listening Post, or, do machines perform?" In: International Journal of Performance Arts and Digital Media 1/1, pp. 5-10.

Bachmann-Medick, Doris (2016): Cultural Turns: New Orientations in the Study of Culture. Berlin: de Gruyter.

Baecker, Dirk (2007): Studien zur nächsten Gesellschaft. Frankfurt am Main: Suhrkamp.

Barad, Karen (2003): "Posthumanist performativity: toward an understanding of how matter comes to matter." In: Signs: Journal of Women in Culture and Society 28/3, pp. 801–831.

Baxmann, Inge/Beyes, Timon/Pias, Claus (eds.) (2016): Social Media – New Masses, Berlin: Diaphanes.

Bay-Cheng, Sarah/Kattenbelt, Chiel/Lavender, Andy (2010): Mapping Intermediality in Performance, Amsterdam: Amsterdam University Press.

Beyes, Timon/Pias, Claus (2014): "Transparenz und Geheimnis." In: Zeitschrift für Kulturwissenschaft 8/2, pp. 111-117.

Chun, Wendy Hui Kyong (2016): Updating to Remain the Same: Habitual New Media, Cambridge, MA: MIT Press.

Deuze, Mark (2006): "Participation, remediation, bricolage: Considering principal components of a digital culture." In: The Information Society 22/2, pp. 63-75.

Ekman, Ulrik (ed.) (2013): Throughout. Art and Culture Emerging with Ubiquitous Computing, Cambridge, MA: MIT Press.

Engemann, Christoph/Sprenger, Florian (eds.) (2015): Das Internet der Dinge: Über smarte Objekte, intelligente Umgebungen und die technische Durchdringung der Welt, Bielefeld: transcript.

Fischer-Lichte, Erika (2004): Ästhetik des Performativen, Frankfurt am Main: Suhrkamp.

Fischer-Lichte, Erika (2012): Performativität, Bielefeld: transcript.

Galloway, Alexander (2011): "Are some things unrepresentable?" In: Theory, Culture & Society 28/7-8, pp. 85-102.

Galloway, Alexander (2014): "The cybernetic hypothesis." In: Differences 25/1, pp. 107-131.

Gere, Charlie (2008): Digital Culture (2nd ed.), London: Reaktion Books.

Hörl, Erich (2013): "A thousand ecologies: The process of cyberneticization and general ecology." In: Diedrich Diederichsen/Anselm Franke (eds.), The Whole Earth: California and the Disappearance of the Outside, Berlin: Sternberg Press, pp. 121-130.

Jackson, Shannon (2004): Professing Performance: Theatre in the Academy from Philology to Performativity, Cambridge: Cambridge University Press.

Kirshenblatt-Gimblett, Barbara (2008): "Performance Studies." In: Henry Bial (ed.), The Performance Studies Reader, London: Routledge, pp. 43–55.

Madison, D. Soyini/Hamera, Judith (eds.) (2006): The SAGE Handbook of Performance Studies, London: Sage

McCarthy, Tom (2015): Satin Island, London: Jonathan Cape.

McKenzie, Jon (2001): Perform or Else: From Discipline to Performance, London: Routledge.

Osborne, Peter (2015): "Problematizing disciplinarity, transdisciplinary problematics." In: Theory, Culture & Society 32/5-6, pp. 3-35.

Pearson, Mike/Shanks, Michael (2001): Theatre/Archaeology, London: Routledge.

Pelias, Ronald J./VanOosting, James (1987): "A paradigm for performance studies." In: Quarterly Journal of Speech 73/2, pp. 219–31.

Pickering, Andrew (1995): The Mangle of Practice: Time, Agency and Science, Chicago: Chicago University Press.

Pile, Steve/Thrift, Nigel (1995): "Introduction." In: Steve Pile/Nigel Thrift (eds.), Mapping the Subject: Geographies of Cultural Transformation, London: Routledge, pp. 1-12.

Powell, Benjamin D./Shaffer, Tracy Stephenson (2009): "On the haunting of performance studies." In: Liminalities: A Journal of Performance Studies 5/1, pp. 1–19.

Rouvroy, Antoinette (2011): "Governmentality in an age of autonomic computing: Technology, virtuality and utopia." In: Mireille Hildebrandt/ Antoinette Rouvroy (eds.), Law, Human Agency and Autonomic Computing, London: Routledge, pp. 119-139.

Salter, Chris (2010): Entangled: Technology and the Transformation of Performance, Cambridge, MA: MIT Press.

Schechner, Richard (2006): Performance Studies: An Introduction, London: Routledge.

Schechner, Richard (2008[1988]): "Performance studies: The broad spectrum approach." In: Henry Bial (ed.), The Performance Studies Reader, London: Routledge, pp. 7–9.

Schröter, Jens (2015): "Das Internet der Dinge, die allgemeine Medienökologie und ihr Ökonomisch-Unbewusstes." In: Christoph Engemann/Florian Sprenger (eds.), Das Internet der Dinge: Über smarte Objekte, intelligente Umgebungen und die technische Durchdringung der Welt, Bielefeld: transcript, pp. 225-240.

Stalder, Felix (2016): Kultur der Digitalität, Berlin: Suhrkamp.

Strine, Mary S./Long, Beverly Whitaker/ Hopkins, Mary Frances (1990): "Research in interpretation and performance studies: Trends, issues, priorities." In: Gerald Phillips/Julia Wood (eds.), Speech Communication: Essays to Commemorate the 75th Anniversary of the Speech Communication Association, Carbondale: Southern Illinois UP, pp. 181-204.

Tholen, Georg Christoph (1994): "Platzverweis." In: Norbert Bolz/Friedrich A. Kittler/Georg Christoph Tholen (eds.), Computer als Medium, München: Fink Verlag, pp. 111-135.

Thrift, Nigel (2008): Non-Representational Theory: Space, Politics, Affect, London: Routledge.

Historicizing

Performing (the) digital

Positions of critique in digital cultures

MARTINA LEEKER

Digital cultures[1] are performative cultures. This assumption is illustrated by the ubiquitous and invisible infrastructures that constitute them, which are interstratified by so-called 'smart things'[2] (Engemann/Sprenger 2015; Günel/Halpern 2016), creating a socio-technical environment, in which performances of the technological come about. While human users may not be able to comprehend the entire technological performance, they are without a doubt intertwined with it. The digital performs, the human reacts to the agency the technologies suggest, and vice versa: "Performing (the) Digital".[3]

1 The usage of a plural implies that digital cultures are constituted through a variety of simultaneously existing cultural configurations, which are molded by digital objects and operations. Cultures and technologies are inseparable and constantly and mutually influence each other. For further information on research to the topic of digital cultures see "DCRL Questions: What are digital cultures?" – a research interviews video series, Digital Cultures Research Lab, Leuphana University Lüneburg, available at http://www.leuphana.de/en/research-centers/cdc/digital-cultures-research-lab/projects /dcrl-questions.html.

2 The notion of 'things' highlights the new status of 'objects' as performative. If the notion 'objects' is used, it refers to the new context.

3 The following is therefore not an analysis of artistic performances, which employ media (cf. Leeker 2001), but much rather a contextualization of the same.

There is a considerable genealogical background to this assumption, which needs to be reconstructed. It is founded within a 'discourse history of performativity',[4] which has been taking place across scientific disciplines concerning technology and the humanities since the 1950s. It is through this history that the reciprocity of performance between humans and technology was established. As a result, technical things and computational operations could be understood as performative, while at the same time relieving human agency from mere intentional and representational action.

The expanded definition of performativity allows consideration of a 'dispositif of the performative within digital cultures', which corresponds to the scenario above. This dispositif is constituted by an ensoulment[5] of technical things up to the point of having agency that is not entirely relatable or controllable by humans. The result is a 'technological wonderland'[6] that functions autonomously and (mostly) without friction in the metaphorical backrooms of society, thereby fascinating its inhabitants and inviting them to linger and loiter (Pflüger 2008). Simultaneously, this dispositif does not conceal its precarity: it is constantly at risk of technological failure and the revelation of its ensoulment and magic as pure illusion. This ambivalent relationship between control and loss of control does not, however, reduce its fascinating power of seduction; on the contrary, the ambivalent game only increases its appeal. Performativity therefore implies not a simple expression of action, but a complex amalgam of a performance and production (mis-en-scène) history of unrestricted, ensouled technologies. As outlined below, their purpose is to create a politics and an economy of 'self-illusion'

4 This historic analysis of discourse does not intend to identify a 'correct' definition of performativity. It aims instead to decipher which concepts of performativity are generated within which contexts, what their effects are, and how they are separated and combined with other conceptualizations of the same.

5 Current theoretical conceptions of animism and ensoulment differ from the spiritual traditions of the 19th century (Hagen 1999), which informed notions of performances with technology up until the 1960s (Leeker 2016b). The latter depended on explaining technological worlds with inexplicable phenomena, such as ghosts or ethereal conceptions. Contemporary animism however is purely operative, which makes it all the more fascinating.

6 'Wonder' in this case refers to occurrences that cannot be understood and are therefore processed only through illusions, as would be the case in a magic trick. In this translation, wonder and enchantment are used interchangeably [note from translator]. As the magic happens on the technological side, a power divide is established between technical things and human users.

(Leeker 2012; 2016b) of human actants, which can be understood as a form of governmentality (Foucault's notion of governmentality, cf. Lemke 2001). There is a specific way of generating a self[7] in digital cultures, which is linked to their dependency on data and interaction. Only when something is present can it be mined for data and be engaged with. It is only under these conditions that socio-technological environments produce a self. This self is an illusion, as it is pure invention and it is not relevant in itself, but only within its functionality – a principal obscured by the self-illusion mechanisms of the technological wonderland.

'Ubiquitous computing' marks a paradigmatic manifestation of discourse and dispositif in the context of performativity. This concept plays a central role within a genealogy of current digital cultures and is therefore a vital component in deciphering the realities they produce as dispositif of the performative. Their constitution and effects will be elaborated upon, exemplified through the manifestos and technological things by the artist and engineer Rich Gold,[8] one of the leading researchers at the Xerox Palo Alto Research Center (Xerox PARC). The essay follows the hypothesis that Gold's inventions were essential to the creation of the narrative of fascination and enchantment (cf. Sprenger 2016)[9] of a technological being within digital cultures, thereby mysteriously binding them to the human user.

Art – specifically performance art – has traditionally prevailed as a method of gaining the distance necessary for a reflection and critique of techno-cultural conditions (McKenzie 2001; 2005; 2013). Within 'performing (the) digital' however, this is complicated by an appropriation of technological seduction. The scholarly analysis of the dispositif of the performative more often than not is merely descriptive rather than analytical.[10] How then can performative methods

7 At this point it is vital to clarify that the text does not share the assumption of an existence of a self prior to technological conditions and environments, which is endangered by the same. Instead, the underlying premise is that these conditions produce a self, which is specific to the logic of digital cultures.

8 Gold, Rich: Official Homepage, July 26, 2016 (http://web.archive.org/web/20040223013202/http://www.richgold.org/index.htm)

9 Florian Sprenger (2016) has instigated a seismic shift in seeing ensoulment and wonder as constituents of digital cultures in ubiquitous computing. He has graciously provided his text prior to publication for this analysis.

10 Critique in digital cultures is therefore always constitutively and inescapably self-referential. Its explorations necessarily employ digital tools, as is e.g. necessary for the evaluation of big data. This constitution influences the understanding of science itself, to a point that self-reflexive scientific research is being postulated as an essential

engage with these cultures on a critical level? Methods and epistemology of so-called artistic research (Gramelsberger 2009) may hold an answer to this question.

1. PERFORMATIVITY THROUGHOUT THE DISCIPLINES: A HISTORIC OUTLINE OF A DISCOURSE

An outline[11] of the discourse history of performativity (Wirth 2002b; Seier 2007) shows the performance of machines becoming more human, and inversely, the becoming-operational of human agency. From this venture, the narratives of an unleashing of technology become apparent. It materializes an alignment of human and technology, the creation of agencies of action between humans and technological objects, as well as the (re-)enchantment of the world through human and technological performances.

1.1 Austin Cybernetic

This discourse history of performativity has its origins with John Austin's speech act theory,[12] which the British philosopher presented in twelve lectures as a visiting professor at Harvard University in 1955. Published posthumously in 1962 under the title *How to do Things With Words* (Austin 1975), it became the primary authority on speech act theory, developing a fundamental repositioning of the status of speech. Speech was no longer seen as a description of reality, it no longer functions solely as an expression of something that can be true or false. Rather, it develops agency, as words directly produce the actions they are expressing. Austin calls these words (verbs) that have an illocutionary force 'performative' and the circumstance of creating this agency 'performativity'.

methodology of digital cultures research analyzing the governmental effects and affects of the same.

11 Instead of offering an all-encompassing history of performativity, the intention is to focus on central systemic aspects involved in constructing a certain dispositif of the performative.

12 This starting point was chosen because relevant theorists of performativity mostly refer to Austin in their work. However, the interrelation of semiotics, theater/ performance and computational history reach as far back as the early 1900s, for example within Frege's logic of language, Hilbert's self-referential mathematics and Edward Gordon Craig's symbolic theater (Leeker 2013a: 87-106).

Once triggered, the 'performative turn' grows throughout the decades, undergoing modifications by social sciences, technology studies and the humanities, as well as computer engineering, which lead to a re-definition and conceptualization of culture and technology as performative.

This transfer induces a cultivation of the epistemological conditions of the performative turn, which coincided with a realization that language/media have gained their own driving force and power. As they gain agency, they become self-referential. This means that they produce the things they articulate and their articulations are never about something that exists outside of them. However, this seemingly emancipatory condition leads to a precariousness of the relationship of language/media, as well as that of their users to the world. As speech acts are dependent on a variety of factors, some of which are beyond the user's control, the possibility of a failed speech act is prevalent. Attempting to contain and minimize this risk, Austin embeds speech acts in a system of social conventions and institutional ties, creating an extensive list of 'doctrine of infelicities' (e. g., abuse, misfires), which prevent unsuccessful speech acts (Rolf 2009: 26-36). He also excludes insincere speech acts, such as utterances on the stage of a theater from felicitous or successful speech (Austin 1975). These precautions will later reappear in computational engineering and programming language, as well as in a re-orientation of the human and human performance within cultural sciences. For it is exactly those infelicitous speech acts that will later cause an intense critique of autonomous subjectivity (Derrida 1988). Arguing that language/media has its own driving force, an intentional media user is radically put to question. The biggest effect of speech act theory however, is the merge of the symbolic level and action. This effect, spreading through disciplines and cultures, is reminiscent of the magical conditions[13] that every utterance may become reality.[14]

It is, therefore, essential for the dispositif of the performative within digital cultures to note that the performative turn has facilitated an approximation and equalization of medial, technological and human performances. Although Austin

13 Hartmut Winkler (2004: 215-230) has explicated the power of the merge of the symbolic and the practical sphere and as a result advocates for a strict differentiation of performativity according to their degree of practical reference.

14 Austin later reformulated his speech act theory to include locutionary, illocutionary and perlocutionary acts. This differentiation dissolved the difference between constative (related to truth) and performative (related to action) utterances, so that every utterance would become an act, thereby universalizing the performativity of language (cf. Wirth 2002: 9-60).

did not reference media history,[15] the relevance and detonating force of speech act theory fully develops within its contextualization in the development of the computer and cybernetics throughout the 1950s.[16] For the unleashing of language, the collateral subversion of traditional concepts of subjectivity and the coinciding of symbolic representation and action, all run parallel to a practical-productive phase of cybernetics (Kline 2009; 2015), following the heated theoretical discussions on cybernetics in the 1940s (Pias 2002). Since then, speech act theory and computational coding have formed strong ties, or as Inke Arns puts it:

> "In code, 'saying' and 'doing' merge in so far as these speech acts are not descriptive or representational, they instead directly affect, move or create their effects [...] Ultimately, performativity results in the magical merging of the signifier and the signified [...]." (Arns 2001: n. pag.; my translation)[17]

In addition, the performativity of code is put to use in cybernetic machines and systems (Mindell 2000). Not only do they begin to operate autonomously via feedback loops, information processing and closed circuits (Pias 2004), they also begin to have agency within the world (Lettkemann/Meister 2004). The crucial point in this performative turn is therefore the direct human integration into this systemic self-organization as one of many data processing operators (Mindell

---

15 It can be assumed that Austin was aware of the automatization and formalization of human language. During his time at Harvard, he was closely associated with Noam Chomsky, who was working on the formalization of language at M.I.T at the time. Bernard Geoghegan (2011: 96-126) has laid out a plausible exploration that Claude Shannon's information theory and Norbert Wiener's cybernetic theorems in the 1950s strongly influenced Roman Jakobson's concepts and practices of formalization of language, as well as impacting on Levi-Strauss' ethnographic work. In effect, it is a viable assumption that changes in media relations and technological conditions challenge different scientific disciplines in similar ways and are therefore implicitly or explicitly dealt with in an interdisciplinary manner.

16 Further research would be required to assert whether this happened simultaneously or if speech act theory only became possible within the technological conditions of the computer and the epistemological framing of cybernetics.

17 "Im Code fallen 'Sagen' und 'Tun' zusammen, insofern diese Sprechakte keine Beschreibung oder Repräsentation von etwas sind, sondern diese direkt affizieren, in Bewegung setzen, Effekte zeitigen. [...] Performativität läuft so letztlich auf die magische Ineinssetzung von Zeichen und Bezeichnetem hinaus [...]." (Arns 2001: n. pag.)

2001; 2002). The conception and recognition of speech act theory is consequently contemporaneous with the becoming-performative of the computer. From a perspective of media epistemology and history, the performative turn can therefore also be read as enabling a narrative of unleashed technology, as well as an alignment of a technological and human-centric conception of performances. The result of this genesis and transmission history is that the different forms of performativity are no longer separate. Performativity represents an inevitable techno-sociality with magical omens.

1.2 Immigration of speech acts to the computer

The interaction of performativity of language and the computer brought about a new model of techno-human relationships in the 1980s and 1990s. Through the developing 'workplace studies', speech act theory migrates into the systems and programming of "Computer Supported Cooperative Work" (CSCW) (Knoblauch/Heath 1999). Here, programs are implemented to facilitate workflows in conference and meeting systems. Formalized speech act theory becomes a key player in multi-agent regulations and communication processes (Schulz-Schaeffer 2000), as well as in electronic transaction processing (Elgass 1996). At this stage, the infelicitous speech acts described by Austin become relevant to the development of programs regulating computers and human-machine interactions, as well as mediated communication between humans or between machines respectively. These infelicitous speech acts serve as a framework for translating philosophical models of language into algorithmic speech acts. These should be successful as long as human and technical 'fallacies' about the fixed allocation of performative verbs to certain actions are excluded as much as possible.

Within the discourse history of performativity, this produces the crucial point that technological performances become 'more humane'. Drawing upon disappointments in scientific research on artificial intelligence, technical accidents and human error in interaction with technological systems, Terry Winogard develops a modest "Language/Action Perspective", and demands consideration of social factors when working with computers (Flores/Winograd 1986; Knoblauch/Heath 1999: 165). Because communication and action are not arranged rationally, they are highly dependent on contingent occurrences within social contexts (Suchman 1987; 1993). This means that human actors are merely partners or counterparts that enable technological performances to become more humane, allowing for the situatedness and processual character of technology to become a factor for labor, organization and economy (Knoblauch/Heath 1999: 166).

This new condition allows for the dispositif of the performative within digital cultures a positive discursive reassessment of the precarity of performative speech acts, which Austin had deemed to be problematic. While they are modularized through the technological level, the level of human communication unchains them. This leads to a consolidation and ennoblement of performativity of technology, which is nonetheless an illusion, as code cannot be noise (Arns 2001). It would then lead to a systemic breakdown. This mise-en-scène of performativity results in a discursive belief of supposedly inevitable socio-technological systems (Suchman 1983; 1993; Knoblauch 1999), which is nurtured by the interdisciplinary work of engineers, computational and information scientists, sociologists, as well as ethnographers and anthropologists. The more their work interacts, the more technological and anthropological systems are approximated and engage in permanent and mutual influence.[18] These socio-technological systems are less a fact, however, than an invention through which digital cultures, deeply rooted in technological forms of cooperation, can come into existence.[19] Orit Halpern (2014) even describes technology as having become a permanent demo or testing ground (test bed) since the 1970s. To continuously develop in a recursive process, this demo needs crisis, accidents, catastrophe and human deficiency. Interactions and a lust for catastrophe and emergence thereby become virulent as factors for the discourse history of performativity, which is accompanied by illusion and the occlusion of technical operations.

1.3 Operationalizing the performative in cultural and theater studies

Contrary to the performative becoming-more-humane of technologies, the discourses on performativity in cultural and theater studies result in an operationalization of concepts of performativity, which inserts itself into spaces, where

18 Heath/Knoblauch give an example of this mutual influence: "dass die Patienten die Schilderung ihrer Beschwerden und Symptome sehr genau darauf abstimmen, wie der Arzt die Daten in das Computersystem eingibt." (Knoblauch/Heath 1999: 170) ("...that patients, when speaking of their grievances, react to the data the doctors retrieve and feed to their computational systems"; my translation)

19 Against this media historic backdrop it would be necessary to investigate the discourse on techno-ecologies, as well as the rediscovery of Gilbert Simondon as a part of euphorically welcomed socio-technological liaisons of the human and the technological.

speech acts/performativity develops its own power, a third force next to human and media.[20] This third entity is generative in accordance with non-comprehensible laws, creating something where there was previously nothing. According to Jacques Derrida (1988), language is generative through self-referential iterations and repetition.[21] Consistent with Judith Butler (1998), performatives produce gender, identity and subjectivity. Finally, Sybille Krämer (2002: 345) clarifies that media need embodiment in operations such as writing, reading and interpreting; therefore voices, for example, can disturb utterances and actions when words have been lost to the wind.

The conception of performativity outlined in theater studies (Fischer-Lichte 2004) in and throughout the mid-1990s (Fischer-Lichte/Kolesch 1998)[22] shows an affinity towards the technological as well. Even if it went by almost unnoticeably, there are deep structural similarities to the performative turn of technology. That is, the notion of autopoiesis is introduced, which of course describes cybernetic feedback (Beniger 1986). Within autopoiesis, cultural and artistic performances complete the coincidence of signs and actions, as well as the resulting self-referentiality of performance. This is demonstrated by the emphasis on so-called 'co-presence' as constituent to artistic performance (Fischer-Lichte 2004).

20 "Media anthropology expeditiously retaliates this operationality with de-anthropomorphization: „Damit sieht sich so […] geforderte Medienanthropologie auf einmal […] in der Verantwortung, allerhand von dem, was sie eigentlich bloß verwerfen wollte, wie Bewusstsein und Intention, zu analysieren, und zwar in ihrer realitätsbegründenden Funktion als Operatoren der Komplexitätsreduktion, als Formen der Verdichtung oder des Blackboxing im komplexen Feld der Medienanthropologie" (Engell/Siegert 2013: 9-10) ("media-anthropology, challenged in this way, suddenly has the responsibility of analyzing everything it attempted to dismiss, e.g. consciousness and intention, and attempt an understanding of these functions as constitutional operators, reducing complexity, increasing consolidation or black-boxing within the complex field of media anthropology" [my translation]).

21 Sybille Krämer emphasizes the possibility of finding successful speech acts through re-iterations and performances in the theatrical sense even in Austin's theories. According to Krämer, every execution of a speech act is a re-iteration of the same, which includes the power of iterability and alteration. Speech acts function the same way rituals do, manifesting themselves upon their repetition.

22 The following refers especially to the work on performativity in theater studies through the collaborative research of the *Sonderforschungsbereich* "Kulturen des Performativen" (cultures of performativity) at Freie Universität Berlin (cf. Fischer-Lichte/Kolesch 1998).

Co-presence implies that the bodily presence of the actors and the audience mutually produce the roles, as well as the performance. Performance itself, then becomes a speech act, producing what it enacts: subjects, bodies, spaces, enactment, but also a designation of performativity as liminality (Fischer-Lichte 2004: 305-314) of transformed humans.

This background makes it even more surprising that theater studies tend to disapprove of the notion that technology can perform (Otto 2013: 55-67). The performances of technical things and their regulatory algorithms are seen as sheer and reductive 'performance' (German: *Performanz*), as opposed to human performance, which is open, unpredictable and emergent (McKenzie 2001). However, computational sciences and engineering practices have recorded a jolt towards performativity (Suchman 1983; 1993), which positions it in a discursive field of emergence, unpredictability and contingency. Where the becoming-performative of the computer was meant to bind it into humane structures, the humanities ultimately dispose of the human in the performative.

The denial of performativity of technological performance in some areas of theater studies, sorting it into a system of mere operationality, seems to have a specific cause. The discourses in theater studies constructs itself in this way, so as to hide the effects of their own performativity, which parallels a transformation of human performances into a chain of operations. The genealogy of performativity emerges as an amalgam of affirmation, contradiction and occlusion. From this, the initial scenario can emerge as a performance of technological things and environments in which the human still plays a role, even if it is small and precarious.

1.4 Performance as enchantment

The assertion of the re-enchantment of culture through the power of performativity (Fischer-Lichte 2004: 315-362) is the most important contribution from analysis of artistic performances in theater studies in favor of the dispositif of the performative. According to Erika Fischer-Lichte, performativity corresponds with a renunciation of "comprehensive ability" (Fischer-Lichte 2004: 362), which results in re-enchantment and an "embodied mind" (ibid.). It is the duty of human agents to act in life, as enactment would take place in art (cf. Fischer-Lichte 2004: 362). The unleashing through performances is accompanied by an enchantment of culture, which, according to Fischer-Lichte, parallels "modern society" (Fischer-Lichte 2004: 360):

> "Increasingly, they mediate the conviction that the world is indeed criss-crossed by invisible forces, which influence us in secrecy. Although we sense them physically, we cannot see or hear them. It is the assumption that in nature and society emergences occur that are beyond intentionality, planning and prediction; that everything is connected." (Fischer-Lichte 2004: 360; my translation)[23]

Through this enchantment, the world becomes "just as inaccessible as the autopoietic feedback loop that is effective in performances" (Fischer-Lichte 2004: 361).[24]

Performativity as a magical power thereby determines that recognition is suspended and is replaced by the merging of human agents with their technological environment. A condition of non-knowing, emergence and unpredictability becomes the basis for existence. The coinciding of speech and action through speech act theory turns into a gateway for ontological and inherent magic and enchantment. As Sybille Krämer (2002: 323) has lucidly noted, the principle of representation necessary to overcome this magic is thereby extinguished. The human, technology and media converge, so that an over-identification of human agents is delineated, with which they succumb to the illusion of digital omnipresence and omnipotence. This only promotes the unleashing and autonomy of the technological, as well as commitment to it.

23 "Zunehmend vermitteln sie die Überzeugung, daß die Welt in der Tat von unsichtbaren Kräften durchzogen ist, die auf uns einwirken, ohne daß wir sie zu sehen oder zu hören vermöchten, obwohl wir ihre Auswirkungen körperlich erspüren können; daß in der Natur und in den Gesellschaften Emergenzen auftreten, die sich jeglicher Intentionalität, Planung und Vorausberechnung entziehen; daß alles mit allem verknüpft ist [...]." (Fischer-Lichte 2004: 360) There are distinct similarities between these concepts of performativity and the discourse on techno-ecologies (Hörl 2011). For instance, Mark B Hansen (2011: 365-409) has also explored the invisible forces that operate within media ecologies.

24 "[...] ähnlich unverfügbar wie jene autopoietische feedback-Schleife, die in Aufführungen wirkt." (Fischer-Lichte 2004. 361)

1.5 From performativity discourse to a dispositif of the performative

The variety of discourses emerging within the different disciplines can be bundled to form a discourse history of performativity in light of a dispositif of the performative. Foucault's conceptual framing of the dispositif offers an understanding of the latter, which he describes as following:

> "What I'm trying to pick out with this term is, firstly, a thoroughly heterogeneous ensemble consisting of discourses, institutions, architectural forms, regulatory decisions, laws, administrative measures, scientific statements, philosophical, moral and philanthropic propositions – in short, the said as much as the unsaid. Such are the elements of the apparatus. The apparatus itself is the system of relations that can be established between these elements." (Foucault 1980: 194)

Accordingly, the dispositif of the performative within digital cultures creates a setting in which material formations, practices and discourses are immersed into a network of relationality. It can be added that it "has at its major function at a given historical moment that of responding to an urgent need" (Foucault 1980: 195). It will be necessary to analyze which needs the dispositif of performativity within digital cultures responds to, and what solutions it offers.

All of the above point to a situation in which human and technological performances have become compatible with a dispositif of the performative within digital cultures on the basis of a heterogeneous discursive field of performativity. It is a hypothesis that this unclear collective arrangement, impossible to homogenize, should enable a place for the uniqueness of human performance with the result that human agents can produce a self within socio-technical environments.[25] These environments could be strongly dependent on a self, as the production of human agents in the discourse on performativity in all its contradictory concepts suggests. In comparison to the autonomous and intentional self, this is a new concept. Because this new self is fundamentally linked to technology in the socio-technological discursive field, but at the same time suggests self-dependency of agency to a limited extent. This is demonstrated in the interaction with programs as it happens within CSCW, just as it is shown in cultural performances. At the same time, the self is confronted with the obscuring of technology through enchantment. Due to these configurations it is a hypothesis that the

25 The concept of the self has been perpetuated in spite of it's permanent swan song (cf. Derrida 1988; Butler 1998).

production of self within digital cultures now relies on a self-illusion, which obscures its technological operations, while at the same time binding the human to them. The generation of a self has to be analyzed within the framework of the dispositif of the performative within digital cultures and their governmental effects (Lemke 2001).

With this prefix the discourse turns into a dispositif, illustrated and exemplified by the magical world of ubiquitous computing created by Rich Gold at the beginning of the 1990s. It is not by chance that great similarities appear in the descriptions of Erika Fischer-Lichte (2004) when she talks about the enchanting performativity of artistic performances.

2. RICH GOLD'S UBIQUITOUS MAGICAL TOY WONDERLAND – INTO THE DISPOSITIF OF PERFORMATIVITY WITHIN DIGITAL CULTURES

Ubiquitous computing of the 1990s has made joint performances of technological and human agents common practice. The performativity of technological performances, once regulated and ensured by speech acts, can now wander from the CSCW systems out into space and back into technological things. Through this, these things are assigned agency and begin to 'speak' and 'answer' to humans, albeit to a limited extent in Weiser's days.[26] The performatives live within the things, which serve as agential callings to their users.

In this manner, the performances satisfy the conceptual framework of the dispositif, laid out here according to Foucault (1980). In the following section, it will be clarified which necessities ubiquitous computing responds to according to the dispositif of performative, and which effects of governmentality it educes.

26 Mark Weiser (1991) imagines the subservient spirits as foresighted and proactive and underlines his theorem with a short anecdote: "Sal awakens: she smells coffee. A few minutes ago her alarm clock, alerted by her restless rolling before waking, had quietly asked 'coffee?', and she had mumbled 'yes.' 'Yes' and 'no' are the only words it knows."

2.1 Ubiquitous Computing and the Arts

In 1988, the inventor of ubiquitous computing (Rogers 2006), Mark Weiser[27] began working on this new project, which he described as: "Ubiquitous computing is the method of enhancing computer use by making many computers available throughout the physical environment, but making them effectively invisible to the user" (Weiser 1993: 75). It marks the dawn of a new world "in which each person is continually interacting with hundreds of nearby wirelessly interconnected computers" (ibid.). This circumferential and mundane socio-technological situation "penetrate[s] all groups in society" (Weiser 1991) and Weiser believed that "sociologically, ubiquitous computing may mean the decline of the computer addict" (ibid.). For him, the effects of addiction materialize within the constant need to be with one's technological things. "Its highest ideal is to make a computer so exciting, so wonderful, so interesting, that we never want to be without it" (Weiser 1996: n. pag.). Simultaneously, "[…] its highest ideal is to make a computer so embedded, so fitting, so natural, that we use it without even thinking about it" (Weiser 1996). In summary, this constitutes the following: Large and immobile computers migrate into small mobile technological things, which form an environment within which they themselves become invisible. This situation allows for human users to engage with technologies without reflecting on them, as they become increasingly obscured. This leads to an ongoing and increasing addiction, which pervades the whole of society. The user is *in* the technological world, which is omnipresent, commonplace and indispensable.

One of the main accomplishments of Weiser's transdisciplinary task force may have been making this ambivalent world more palatable to the user. Over a period of four years, Rich Gold was an important member of the force. He joined the Palo Alto Research Center (PARC) by XEROX in 1991. Gold was a musician, composer, performer, writer, designer, comic-strip artist, game developer, toy maker and a multitalented all round inventor. These qualities allowed him to develop ubiquitous computing into a children's magical wonderland, in which technological objects are animate (cf. Sprenger 2016), function in the backrooms of society and enter into agential relations with humans.[28]

27 Cf. Mark Weiser's homepage (http://pubweb.parc.xerox.com/weiser/weiser.html)

28 Of his function within the lab, Gold says: "But the other task was to construct a philosophy. A Ubi-Comp Cult. My ubi-philosophy was based on Weiser's formulations, but also divergent from it (he was enough of a genius to know that sub-cults were a good thing.) My formulation of Ubi-Comp started with Ubi-Comp product genres […]." (Gold 2002: 66)

Rich Gold's ubiquitous worlds can be seen as performative (McGonical 1999: 8), when applying the criteria laid out in the previous chapters. Firstly, the technological performances bring about liminal experiences (Fischer-Lichte 2004). Secondly, the action they constitute is always a repetition (Krämer 2002), in Gold's case, repeated actions with commonplace objects and toys, and lastly, the symbolic and practical levels collapse into one.

With this, ubiquitous computing can be seen as a dispositif of the performative, demarcating the determining basis for contemporary digital cultures and their seduction. As will be shown in following passages, it is a world in which consciously constructed mis-wiring, enchantment and seduction become strategies, binding the users and operating through their self-illusion. This production or generation of the self is highly strategic and is encouraged incessantly. For technological things and their infrastructures require a self with human agency, to be operated and developed. A person or individual however, is of no importance (Rouvroy 2013).

2.2 "Little Computer People" – less equal agencies

Figure 1: Little Computer People

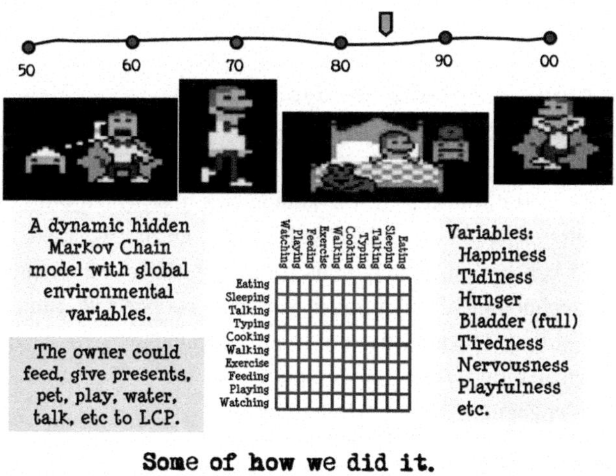

Gold, Rich (2008): The Plenitude: Design and Engineering in the Era of Ubiquitous Computing, Cambridge: MIT Press, p. 50.

The esprit which feeds the dispositif of the performative within ubiquitous computing can be channeled through a computer game, “Little Computer People” (1985), which Gold developed in the 1980s when working for Activison (Gold 2002: 130-132). The aim of the game was to nurture a little computational figure inhabiting a virtual dollhouse, keeping it fed, active and groomed with the help of the keyboard and joystick.[29] The programmers claimed that these small inhabitants were responsible for bugs within the computational systems (Höltgen 2011).

In this belief, they ascribe an independent existence to the computer, as it interacts with the user in the form of the little computer people (ibid.), while the users are responsible for the well-being of the technological object. What is decisive within this scenario is that the computer no longer needs to be anthropomorphized. Instead, the technological history of the human is transformed into a new model. The circuits and codes within the computer receive their own form of agency, whereby the human user enters the agential community via the small figure. The specificity of this community is that the power structure is hierarchic, because bugs could develop within the system should the little figure not be taken care of appropriately. Gazing upon this situation from contemporary digital cultures, the metaphor within “Little Computer People” couldn’t have been more fitting. These days, human agents are data generators who feed technological things with data that keeps them up and running.

2.3 Technological objects as toys. Repetition and transformation

The playful seduction intrinsic to the computer game, which didn’t lead to entirely cooperative agential ensembles with technological things, are carried forth in Rich Gold’s conception of ubiquitous computing. Here, the method of binding users to the technological environment through cooperative strategies is preserved and modified. The modification is compounded through the emergence of the technological things from the computer and the performances are located within entities engaging with the toys in the room.

“My formulation of Ubi-Comp started with Ubi-Comp product genres, a carry over from my toy days. Each product category genre had its own history, metaphor, shelf space, use

29 The game has been categorized as the predecessor for the tamagotchi, as well as the computer game ‘the SIMS’ (Höltgen 2011).

in the world, sales method, manufacturing technique, aesthetics, dependencies and other products dependent on it." (Gold 2002: 66)

This recourse to a toy universe trivialized the essence of these objects, but also offered an advantage. As things we are familiar with from our childhood, they are easily accessible and interaction is intuitive.[30] As Gold put it: "Lastly, they are *colonizing* in that they take the forms of already existing, historically-determined, objects of the Plenitude. There are Ubi-pens, Ubi-cars, Ubi-T-shirts, Ubi-walls, Ubi-notepads, Ubi-Shoes" (Gold 2002: 207). Gold's techno-social universe is inhabited by commonplace objects, which are nonetheless fascinating, as they have been made animate. As Gold says: "Many of the objects about us seem alive, or as I often say, 'enspirited'" (Gold 1993b).

Figure 2: Artist's kitchen

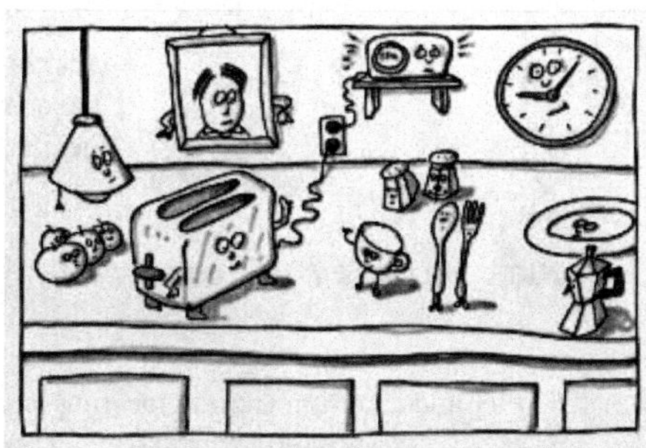

An Artist's Conception of a Ubiquitous Computing Kitchen

But Weiser said:
"I don't want to argue with my car about where to go."

Gold, Rich (2002): The Plenitude: Design and Engineering in the Era of Ubiquitous Computing, Cambridge: MIT Press, p. 208.

30 Gold's technological objects are more appealing and fun than the reality of ubiquitous computing would turn out to be. Weiser created small, mobile devices for collaborative work processes, like tablets, pads, and boards. These functioned through the logic generated by ubiquitous computing within workplace studies (Friedwald 2008; Bell/Dourish 2011) and tended to be counter-intuitive.

Gold himself states: "So what kinds of toys did I design? I guess the simple answer is that I tried to design computer toys that didn't look like computers. I wanted the mysterious effects of computation, but I wanted it in non-mysterious objects" (Gold 2002: 137).

Figure 3: Colonization

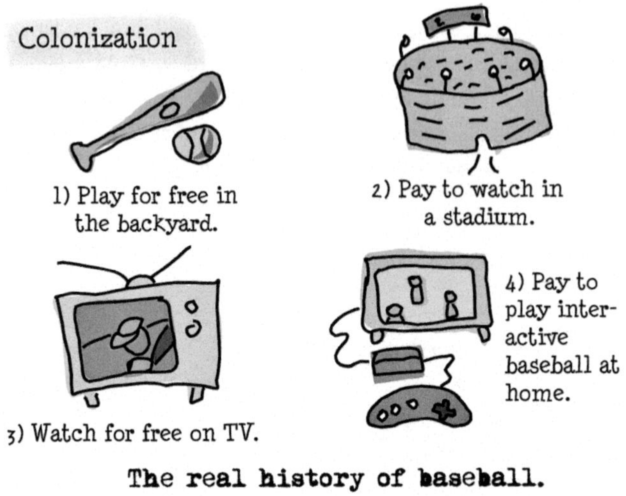

Gold, Rich (2002): The Plenitude: Design and Engineering in the Era of Ubiquitous Computing, Cambridge: MIT Press, p. 117.

Within this colonization it is essential that the things are not only occupied, but involved in an artistic-performative process of transformation through the designer, as well as the user. A chain of translations occurs, through which the new form and function of the familiar toy is reassessed intuitively. The technological objects repeat a cultural context, transforming it through their iterations. The result is that one feels familiar and at home within technological worlds, and also creatively challenged. However, the creative achievement does not lie within subversion of the familiar, but rather in the consolidation of appearances, inscriptions and agencies.

2.4 Dancers in the dark

The technological things are not only familiar, they are now also enspirited and magical. Gold compares ubiquitous computing with a children's bedroom late at night, when the toys begin to dance as soon as the grown-ups have turned off the lights: "This new augmented reality is perhaps a little like the enchanted village, in which common objects have magically acquired new abilities, a village where toy blocks really do sing and dance when I turn out the lights" (Gold 1993a).

The things are easily accessible; there is a specific attitude to engaging with them. One should approach and act with them like in a children's magical wonderland. Things will guide the way, once the user has opened all channels of perception. As Gold says: "In my sophistry, all things in the world have tiny personalities, little 'selves', small consciousnesses. These enlivened objects help and hinder, collude and conspire, whisper and talk with each other and with us" (Gold 1993b). Things are therefore performative here, as it were, in the sense of the speech act, because they carry calls for action (Gibson 1979) within them. They provide guidence on how to manage them and which actions are appropriate. With Gold, things remain in the shadows; they are dancers in the dark. In this way, the call for action manifests more in the form of seduction, inclinations, fumbling experimentation rather than through cognitive performance. It is more of a felt and experienced action that creates performative artistic and aesthetic practice. The power divide between technological objects and the user that was established within Gold's "Little Computer People" is continued. However, threat is not manifested in the technological thing; it lies within the dark environment surrounding its existence. Embodiment through an environment makes it increasingly difficult to escape looming threat and ambiguity.

Jane McGonical (1999: 29-32) has related Gold's scenario of ubiquitous computing in the children's darkened bedrooms to Winnicot's theory of transitional objects (Winnicott 1971). This theory describes a child's compensatory transfer of affect to e.g. a stuffed animal after the loss of the omnipotence present through symbiosis with its mother. While this may seem far-fetched, it does resonate with Gold's depiction of a darkened nursery – his ubiquitous computational universes are enchanting and seductive. Users alternate between emancipation and disempowerment. In interaction with technological objects, users are omnipotent. At the same time, they are harassed, seduced and led into darkness. Here is the first glimpse of governmentality within the dispositif of the performative within digital cultures. They arise from the constant oscillation between empowerment and disempowerment, which creates and maintains the self-illusion while repeatedly destroying it. The result is a self-reliant interplay of destruction and re-generation of the self (Moser 2013).

2.5 Ubicomp. Theater with mis-wiring

Within Gold's explanations of the nursery tales as masquerade, he specifies the governmental effect and its methods as follows:

> "The everyday objects themselves become a kind of ruse: a baby doll (or toy block) might look like a familiar remnant of childhood but it is really only one of a thousand distributed nodes which control the functioning of the whole house. Likewise, the baby doll itself activates its own mechanisms, behaviors and charms based partly on the comings and goings of its adopted (organic) family, and partly on digital discussions with other objects in the house." (Gold 1993a)

Things are not only performative, they also play a theatrical part, equivalent to Austin's un-serious speech acts on stage. Gold's magical wonderland then becomes a history of mise-en-scène of the performative, in which it performs something other than it is, while keeping this circumstance hidden. What this 'other' is made of can be deciphered with the help of the objects. They are not mere things, but intersections, which could control e.g. an entire house. This exemplifies that the performance lies within technological environments and not within the thing itself. Ubiquitous computing does not correspond with things, but rather the environments they are embedded in. The likeable objects are mere distractions from the regulatory and controlling operations. It is necessary to take a closer look, to define what their calls to action are actually obscuring. In Rich Gold's words:

> "Ubiquitous Computing is a new metaphor in which computers are spread invisibly throughout the environment, embedded and hiding as it were, within the objects of our everyday life. Each of these computers can talk with any of the other computers much like chattering animals in a living jungle, sometimes exchanging detailed information, sometimes just noting who's around." (Gold 1993a)

The new objects, now computers, obscure their function as nodes and intersections of technological operations and grids, where they exchange data taken from human agency and transform them in their own logic. What emanates is a doubly structured performativity: The unleashing of technological objects into the performative is accompanied by the performance of a history of mise-en-scène, in which technological performances are obscured.

These mise-en-scènes rely on interaction with technological objects and cunningly implement the mis-wiring Gold supposes are in the human brain. "Our brain thinks that it's fun", Gold (2002: 137) says of the interaction. However:

"Interactivity exploits one of the mis-wirings of our minds: if something moves and reacts based on invisible forces (like the calculations of a small computer chip) we think it is alive. Our economy is now based on this mis-wiring." (Gold 2007, 53)

That humans blithely participate in the technological environment is an effect of their enchantment, seduction and circumvention and also due to an exploitation of neurological conditions. These form the basis of an inescapable data economy as subconscious levels of perception and processing of human agents are put to use. The techno-ubiquitous universe is therefore a perfidious and ambivalent game, a positively techno-neurotic theater. Interactions and affordances are the interfaces of a ubiquitous wireless connection, as Weiser (1991) has correctly noted, which challenge the users on a psycho-neural level. Users are deliberately misguided, deceived, bedazzled and duped to enable and uphold the technological ecologies. This theatrical play corresponds with the technological conditions in digital cultures.

2.6 Lazy spirit

The effects of this ubiquitous magical wonderland are not mitigated by this doubled performativity. As Gold states: "Our pattern-matching mechanisms seem to make only a lazy distinction between the symbol and the symbolized. This is surely what allows advertising to work, not to mention art, literature, painting, erotica and of course, language itself." (Gold 1993a)

Enabled since Austin, the collapse of differentiation between the symbolic level and agency blossoms within technological performances. A positioning outside of these structures has become just as impossible as a position of critique. Caught in the magical wonderland, one can perform solely for the sake of economic players (e. g., Amazon, travel agencies or health insurance companies), or original data politics in the sense of data behaviorism (Rouvroy 2012), which inserts surfaces to obscure its own interests and technological processes. The magic spell takes effect and temptation wins. A lack of differentiation is no longer the exception – just as Austin had explicated through the conception of 'action language' – but has become the status quo. The magical wonderland of theatrical sciences and artistic performance respectively (in the opinion of Erika

Fischer-Lichte, 2004), as well as the world of ubiquitous computing, undergo a joint venture and, in doing so, promote and enable each other.

2.7 The necessity and use of the dispositif of the performative within digital cultures

Within the dispositif of the performative that paradigmatically came to light through Rich Gold's visions, a technological and humane performance of a life with and in socio-technological environments can be designed and regulated. It is constituted from fascinations such as (a) playing with of control and loss of control, (b) enspirited things and opaque technological environments, (c) the completely imbalanced cooperation with technological things and the dissolution into agential communities with the same, (d) the insecurity of evidence and unforeseeable technological and cultural processes, and finally (e) technological seduction. The independence and restricted intelligibility of technological environments refer to the Foucauldian plight (1980 [1977]), to which the dispositif of the performative responds. With regard to the independence of technology, the socio-technological performativity produces a new highly dubious cooperative configuration of the relationship between technology and the human. This differs strongly from the traditional model of an instrumental relationship between the two. In this model the technological was a secondary object to an autonomous subject. In breaking with the old paradigm through the socio-technological performance, human agency, subsumed within agential communities, still has a place in informational technological systems and infrastructures. Furthermore, socio-technological explanatory models allow for redefinitions of the 'human' and 'technology', which in theory should allow for a differentiated engagement with complicated historical formations of technology and culture. These should then react to technological environments and their capacity to process complex data. In effect this leads to a black-boxing of technology, which cannot be grasped through traditional methods of theory generation and understanding (cf. Beyes/Pias 2014).[31]

Finally, the dispositif described creates a specific form of becoming self and self-governance, which, as exemplified by Rich Gold's infantile magical wonderland, feels secure within these new environments. The strategy of self-illusion takes place in performance within the agential communities, where actually the

31 However, Rich Gold's work exemplifies how non-comprehension and non-knowledge are mostly an effect of smart exploitations of mis-wiring, as well as intellectual laziness.

desire to cooperate with the human agent is lacking. The self is an illusion in the sense that it is created solely to entertain the operations of technological objects and infrastructures, without substantiating itself or receiving attention for anything other than its function. To secure these operations, the illusionary self is continuously 'addressed' and thereby perpetuated. This generation of self is methodologically grounded in the enchantment and seduction of enspirited things, as well as psycho-neuronal mis-wiring, through which it becomes self-illusion. This way of producing and simulating a self is constitutive for the condition, function and preservation of digital cultures. The illusionary, conjured self, once generated, begins to resist the exposure of its precarious existence, thereby securing the data flow necessary for the politics and economy of these infrastructures (Günel/Halpern 2016). From a governmental angle of digital cultures, this self is a huge asset, as it governs itself for the sake of keeping up the illusion and is automatically piloted by technology. This makes it impossible, or at least deeply difficult, to reach an awareness of the magical enchantment and mis-wiring it is subjected to, just as it obscures the real political and economic structures.

Looking into this history of performativity might help to define how digital cultures make their human agents give away their data and feel at home in technological environments. A contradictory 'regime of nevertheless' develops, in which, despite all insecurity, despite insight into the doubly performative constitution, and with all knowledge of the obscurity of technology, as well as its enchantment and seduction, thought and action nevertheless succumb.

3. Performing the performing the digital. Positions of critique

The question arises, how positions for observation, reflection and critique can be found in the situation of performative ubiquity? When the symbolic level and agency merge and create a reality beyond mere representation, when performances that were previously considered methods of subversion (Butler 1998; McKenzie 2005, 2013) are constitutive for digital cultures, there seems to be no possibility of escaping or even undermining these structures.

3.1 Performance as critique, according to Foucault

According to Foucault (1992), critique is not a critique of the possibilities and conditions of knowledge and awareness, nor does it constitute judgment. Critique of knowledge/epistemology is transformed into the search for the genesis of knowledge/epistemology, as well as the power structures, which enable them or which they produce. Instead of passing judgment, the aim is exposure to e.g. reveal functions and effects of categorizations and interpretations, even one's own attitudes and assessments in an attempt to suspend them (Seier 2011). This is what Florian Sprenger calls a "genealogical critique" (Sprenger 2014: 12), which "tells the story of a becoming and confronts what has become with its contingency: It is possible that everything may have been different and it is possible that everything will be different. This applies especially to the genealogists themselves. Critique is therefore the creation of space for the non-essential and the annulment of common sense" (Sprenger 2014: 12-13; my translation).[32]

Based on this methodological and systematic understanding, a critique of the dispositif of the performative requires an understanding of how governance, deduced from Foucault's understanding of governmentality, functions in this scenario. This is the basis to steer a practice, which enables – to paraphrase Foucault – not to be governed by an identifiable constellation of power in such a way. Critique is never the suspension of power structures, but always the other side of this coin. Hence, power itself, as well as one's own part within power structures, have to be understood in order to undermine them (Raunig 2008; Seier 2011; Sprenger 2014). Critique within the dispositif of the performative means recognizing the seduction, enchantment, the psycho-neuronal occupation, as well as the self-illusion, so as to be able to subvert them. It is then a strategy to develop a performance of 'performing (the) digital'. To do so, the following section will present methods of a 'discursive aesthetic', as well as forms of knowledge and existences within artistic research (Busch 2009). Within theory and practice of the latter, the focus will be on the epistemological power to question and subvert knowledge structures in particular. In this way, critique can become a practice, exploiting the notion of genealogical critique that everything is, to an extent, contingent.

32 [...] erzählt die Geschichte eines Gewordenseins und konfrontiert das Gewordene so mit seiner Kontingenz: Es wäre möglich, dass alles anders gewesen ist, und es ist möglich, dass alles anders sein wird. Dies betrifft insbesondere den Genealogen selbst. Kritik heißt demnach, einen Raum für das Nichtnotwendige zu schaffen und Selbstverständnisse auszuhebeln (Sprenger 2014: 12-13).

3.2 Queering through performance

Jon McKenzie (2001; 2005; 2013) has developed helpful theoretical and practical research to specify reflexive performance. He has elaborated upon performativity as a competitive display of technology and the self, replacing discipline in "becoming the central dispositif of power and knowledge of our times" (McKenzie 2013: 44). He also investigates its subversions, as seen with, e.g., the Design Lab of the University of Wisconsin-Madison. Its task would be "to democratize digitality" (McKenzie, this volume). At the same time, the following will explore McKenzie's entry point and approach, so as to suggest a modification of the same.

For McKenzie, the problem with a critical performativity lies within the vast scope of the dispositif of knowledge and power of the performative that it is difficult to elude. It ranges from the system-optimizing performance within neoliberal organizational structures – "perform, or else" (McKenzie 2001) – to high-functioning performances of technology, as well as cultural *and* artistic performances (McKenzie 2013). This combination makes it difficult to view performances solely as instruments of resistance of contemporary constellations of power, as would be often assumed within performance and theater studies (McKenzie 2005: 23). McKenzie (ibid.) suggests three categorizations of performances (organizational, technological and cultural), seeing them to be part of a socio-technological machine of production and organization, which allow for a differentiated view. He calls these categorizations of "machinic performance" (ibid.), where the components of this 'machine' can be distinguished from each other through the degree and the quality of their effects and values and in this sense: performance. McKenzie distinguishes between "efficiency" (organizational performance), "effectiveness" (technological performance) and "efficacy" (e.g., cultural performance) (ibid.: 24), whereby each performance can turn into the named effects and values. It is therefore a continuous tightrope walk, whether artistic performances are suitable for intersecting, or queering societal power structures and technological norms, as they can only happen 'within' socio-technological arrangements (ibid.: 28), "[...] seeking out and making connections with mutant elements already at work within them, while at the same time guarding against the microfacsisms that inhabit activist groups of the Right and even, at times, the Left" (ibid.: 28-29).

The subversive mutations within artistic performance may however, so also McKenzie, lead to an affirmation of a technological self, when its characteristics – namely transgressiveness, resistance and liminality – collide with technological or organizational performativity. This problematic turn may come up in

McKenzie's experiments, perhaps due to the effect of the performative in digital cultures. If, for example, technological performativity is evaluated positively and develops into a description of the situation within digital cultures, just as if within these, knowledge of complexity and unpredictable conditions would determine the state of the art, then artistic performance can no longer queer the system of normative and efficient performativity. It would engage in cooperation and repetition of the same nature, instead of intervening (Leeker 2015). This tipping point is present even in McKenzie's work, when he states:

> "My guiding premise is that the traditional distinction between active and contemplative lives is collapsing in our own digital moment, and turning into a new, mixed performative life that is bringing with it new modes that are more networked than hierarchical, more collaborative than individual, more ecological than humanist, more affective than theoretical, more holistic than specialized, more fragmented than unified. I call these post-ideational modes of thought and action, since they move us away from Western culture's most fundamental assumptions about thinking, the image of distinct ideas, specialized disciplines, stable subjects and objects of knowledge, and clear distinctions between theory and practice, argument and rhetoric, writing and media. New performative modes of 'thought-action' draw instead from such areas as experimental arts, indigenous media, neuroscience, and recombinant culture, mashing up practices of orality and literacy, stability and plasticity, mythic and dialectical thought, visual and aural forms, contemplative and active lives." (McKenzie n.d: 1)

3.3 Perspectives on discourse-analytical aesthetics and permanent observation

To prevent the constitution of cultural performances from becoming mere repetition of the dispositif of the performative, an altered form of critique will be explored. Due to the equiprimordial sense of the discourses on performativity, a performative configuration may not be the most suitable. Hence, the 'performing of performances' of the dispositif will be the focus. It is considered an applied critique with performative methods, informed by media history and media epistemology. Instead of formulating a specific discourse, it is necessary to register the discursive formations, reconstruct their genesis and analyze them. Subsequently, an aesthetic can be carved out, which makes these analyses visible and experienceable, foregrounds their ability to change, while at the same time reflecting upon their effects. Based on genealogical critique, a discourse-analytical aesthetic can be produced (Leeker 2013b; 2014a; 2014b). This aesthetic may form statements, but also substantial and creative suggestions (re-design), which nonetheless differ from McKenzie's ideas. An essential factor would be the observation of their productivity. Based on the discursive productivity, which is more difficult to pinpoint within digital cultures due to the consolidation of symbolic and practical levels, while simultaneously being increased by these same factors, constant observation is the crucial silver bullet in the barrel of critique. "Queering" would then consist not of designing or creating performativity, but rather in intersecting its discursiveness.

In the following, two examples are introduced, with which this discourse-analytical aesthetic was tried and tested. The examples consist of student projects the author devised within the transdisciplinary field of 'Complementary Studies' at Leuphana University Lüneburg. Both projects theoretically engaged with contemporary socio-technological discourses and had the task of visualizing and thereby enabling a critique of their effects. On the one hand, this includes the examination of the problematic positioning of human agents within unleashed technological environments. On the other hand, the students engaged with methodologies to critically deal with the non-knowledge and not-comprehension intrinsic to digital cultures.

3.4 You can never be too paranoid!

Paranoia will be elaborated as an appropriate method and epistemological attitude of providing critique for the dispositif of the performative within digital cultures that can be realized and tested through performance. As Marie-Luise Angerer has claimed, you can never be too paranoid (Leeker 2013b). Digital cultures are increasingly non-transparent, directing human agency on an affective level (affective computing) and are implemented for operations in the dark. Paranoia is no longer a pathological condition, but has become an indispensable modality for knowledge creation and an epistemological machine.

This insight was explored through a video installation performance on "Media and Paranoia" (2014) (Leeker 2014a).[33] Film clips about paranoia produced by RFID or webcam hacking were confronted with paranoia arising due to the interventionist activist group 'Anonymous' or the 'darknet' (Leeker 2014b). This range of paranoid fields is symptomatic for the ambivalent status of paranoia, as its focused usage has already been taken up within contexts of the political left

33 The project developed from a seminar in the winter semester of 2014/15. The installation was made up of film clips covering the project theme, as well as faked vlogs the students produced thematically. A final presentation gathered all films into one live composition.

as well as by groups aiming at resistance or political education (c.f. McKenzie as quoted above). Consequently, paranoia is necessary and yet problematic. Not only does it level political camps, it is also involved in cultural production processes, creating the fear it is meant to overcome. In this way, paranoia is a strategy of governmentality, which Eva Horn identifies as a "political style of digital cultures" (Horn 2012: n. pag.).

The installation, which serves as a showcase for a methodology of critique in digital cultures, aimed to clarify these ambivalences of paranoia – being at the same time an instrument of knowledge and governmental discourse – and still put its reflexive potential to use as a behavioral pattern and a form of knowledge production. A contradictory situation is created, which is just as paranoid as its object of study, so that paranoia, resurfacing as a form of knowledge production, can be implemented against the paranoia of governmental discourse, without absorbing or reinstating the latter. The performative installation transpired to be a suitable aesthetic method, for it created a situation that was both immersive and reflexive. Visitors of the installation were drawn into the paranoid environment, while at the same time being forced to critically question the often contrary contributions presented.

In this way, educated paranoia comes to be an essential method of performing the performing in digital cultures and could be implemented in different contexts, institutes and projects.

3.5 Owlglass pranks with disabled things

A second method of critically performing within the dispositif of the performative is the engagement with 'owlglass pranks'. Discourses are taken seriously and exaggerated to a point of over-affirmation. This pointed and exaggerated embodiment probes its governmental consequences and epistemic effects, thereby considering modalities of change.

Through this critical method, the exhibition/performance 'Versehrte Dinge' (disabled things)[34] assessed the contemporary plane of discourse within digital cultures 'after' ubiquitous computing. The current situation is embossed by a 'techno-ecologism' (Hörl 2011), which acts on the observation that singular media entities have dissolved into a techno-social environment, which is inhabited by smart things (Engemann/Sprenger 2015) that intend to engage and cooperate

34 This project took place within a student seminar in the winter semester of 2015/16. An audiovisual and textual documentation and analysis of the project is in preparation (Leeker 2016c).

with human users (Latour 2001; Gießmann/Schüttpelz 2015). Here, things would gain an emancipated status, equitable to other entities (Latour 2001) within symmetric agencies. The socio-technological environment is translated into a hyper-nervous system of existences, which addresses, affects and appropriates the human on a preconscious level (Hansen 2011).

Owlglass pranks raised the question of whether things and technological environments then have their own agency and rights. For example, can damaged things simply be disposed of within these new conditions? If not, what does that mean for human agents, surrounded by broken technical things? The exhibition created a parallel universe in which a Magna Carta of things was presented as a daycare center with psychological support for broken things. The over-affirmation presented 'Siri' as a fairy godmother of mediated knowledge production. The delivery and circulation of data became a right, as they are equal to human agents. This over-affirmation intentionally induced a reflection of the unleashing of objects, which visitors could experience within the exhibition and its performances.

Within this form of artistic research with discourse-analytical aesthetics, another method was an incessant ambivalence meant to drive visitors into an alternating state of emotions and thought, which was induced by guides leading them through the exhibition. These guides prompted euphoric, as exemplified in Weiser and Rich Gold's work, and critical views of the given situation. In the case of the latter, the critique was grounded in analyses of contemporary discourses on techno-ecologies and things from media- and cultural studies, which engage with their utilization for capitalistic chains of valorization (Schröter 2015) and the phantasm of techno-totality (Engemann/Sprenger 2015: 58).[35]

It is here that the circle comes to a close. The narratives of the dispositif of the performative are simultaneously a foundation for a critique of the same within artistic performance with discourse-analytical aesthetics. The performance of owlglass tales deconstructs the performativity inherent to digital cultures from a position of media history and epistemological critique, without directly suggest-

35 As Engemann and Sprenger put it: „Die Totalitätsfigur der Ubiquität und ihres Anspruchs eines totalen Einschlusses in eine Welt der Adressierbarkeit verweist auf historische Formationen von Allwissen und Weltschließung, die in ihren theologischen, aber auch geschichtsphilosophische Dimensionen bislang kaum reflektiert wurden" ("the figurative totality of ubiquity and its claim to a total enclosure into a world of addressability points to historical formations of omniscient and foreclosed worlds, which have hardly been reflected upon within dimensions of theology and philosophy of history") (Engemann/Sprenger 2015: 58, my translation).

ing alternative worlds. Contrary to Jon McKenzie's suggestions, different design models can only prosper through a reflection and recognition of the governmentality of the dispositif of the digital. The problematic situation, in which scholarly disciplines describing and analyzing digital cultures will always reproduce the things they are describing, is diverted to a certain extent, as the over-affirmation of discourses of things and techno-environments allows the altering of designs by divesting them of discourse.

3.6 Artistic research as critical practice

In closing, artistic research will be described as a critique of the dispositif of the performative within the unique conditions of digital cultures. This leads to an understanding of critique as a practice that creates alternatives to a problematic democratizing configuration, which follows performative maelstroms (cf. McKenzie). This 'praxeological turn' is essential, as Gerald Raunig (2008) has explained, as critique is only effective when it does not stagnate as an attitude, but leads to an alternative conception of living. A necessity within this process, as Raunig explores, is the doubled figure of critique as "suspension and recomposition". The particular task of suspending a judgement is to create spaces for new composition and practice. Raunig clarifies that this practice of recomposition relates to a manipulation of "textual machines" and "social machines" (Raunig 2008). It is imperative to not only appropriate texts and interpretations, but also actual habits of living. It should be stressed that this recomposition as critical praxis lies within an affirmation of a techno-social 'have-become'; hence the goal is the claim that the modes of living are not manifest and could always be different.

Raunig (2008) exemplifies this critical practice through a scenario of resistance. The Beguines were female members of a Christian denomination in the 13th century, who took no vows and did not live in confinement, thereby leading a life outside of the regulations of a pastoral community as a practicing critique. The reconfiguration of textual machines takes place through, according to Raunig (ibid.: n. pag.), "the attempt to intensify, reinterpret and rewrite them, the excessive application and outdoing of the rule, the over-affirmation and exaggeration of the regulations: to the extent that Beguines exercised ecstatic practices". Concerning social machines, Raunig goes on to say: "[…] Beguines […] lived unmarried and in poverty, or more strongly formulated: in the rejection of the marital dominance of men and in the rejection of wealth, which was also understood at the time in the sense of a rejection of power and higher position" (ibid.: n. pag.).

The suggestion here and within the two projects "Media and Paranoia" and "Disabled Things" is that they can be seen as examples of artistic research formulating a critical practice within digital cultures. The projects fulfill Raunig's criteria of critique as a practice. Within artistic practice the textual machine is subverted, especially in the form of a discourse-analytical aesthetic. For example, when meaning is suspended through over-affirmation or exaggeration and knowledge can be re-configured. Furthermore, Raunig (2008) hints at the textual work of the Beguines to be "ecstatic practice", creating non-biblical messages, such as performative practices of knowledge production, building a basis from which knowledge can be re-configured. Within the project "Media and Paranoia", the paranoid status of the 'Anonymous' collective and the 'darknet' was only discovered through the performance within the installation. From here, knowledge and the production of it could be reconfigured as a form of enlightened or educated paranoia. A contestation of the social machine happened when the protagonists of artistic research began falling out of each of their various disciplines and reconfiguring the same.[36] For they are not generally accepted within an artistic context, nor within academia, but reconfigure their life and work within academic contexts from a marginalized position. Fittingly, Raunig writes of the Beguines: "This means that the Beguines were border-crossers, who were always and from the start in danger of being thrown into the outside of ecclesiastical immanence" (ibid.: n. pag.).

Finally, artistic research can represent a practice, which develops in the tradition of the Beguine practices as a model for critique. This transfer is especially useful within the specific conditions of the dispositif of the performative within digital cultures, for both engage with knowledge, understanding and the drawing up of boundaries.[37] Because of the mentioned self-referentiality of digital cultures and the irritation of conceptions of reliable knowledge due to the significance of illusions (Gramelsberger 2009; Pias 2011), the current situation makes knowledge itself unreliable and inaccessible (Beyes/Pias 2014). In this context,

---

36 This includes the foundation of institutes for artistic research or the creation of PhD-programs at art academies, which, despite all just critique, have managed to question and reconfigure traditional knowledge regimes (cf. Busch 2009: 141-158).

37 At this point, artistic practice is not understood as its own or different, non-rational knowledge (Mersch 2009: 27-47; Badura et al. 2015). From a discourse-critical point of view, these concepts should be viewed within their productive effects, e.g. in the way they produce knowledge. Through articulation of a different, aesthetic knowledge, the same is produced and commissioned to consolidate or discredit knowledges from within rational sciences.

artistic research targets the borders and evidence of knowing and non-knowledge, understanding and non-comprehension, as well as the borders between the human and the technological, acting as theory and practice to question these concepts.[38] Artistic research can therefore be seen as a critical practice within digital cultures,[39] which collects and negotiates spectrums of unsettling knowledge and pushes thresholds in a specific manner.

The constant observation of the dispositif of the performative within digital cultures, as it is cultivated within discourse-analytical aesthetics, can at least sporadically become a 'practice of critique' through the constitution of artistic research.

Translated by Sara Morais

REFERENCES

Arns, Inke (2001): "Texte, die (sich) bewegen: zur Performativität von Programmiercodes in der Netzkunst", lecture at the "Kinetographien" conference, European Academy Berlin, July 20, 2016 (http://www.netzliteratur.net/arns/performativ-code.html)

Arns, Inke (2007): "Read_me, run_me, execute_me. Code als ausführbarer Text: Softwarekunst und ihr Fokus auf Programmcodes als performative Texte." In: Medien Kunst Netz, June 22, 2016 (http://www.medienkunstnetz.de/themen/generative_tools/software_art/)

Auslander, Philip (1999): Liveness: Performance in a Mediatized Culture, London: Routledge.

Austin, John Langshaw (1975 [1962]): "How to do things with words." In: The William James Lectures delivered at Harvard University in 1955, Oxford: Clarendon Press.

Badura, Jens/Mersch, Dieter et al. (2015): Künstlerische Forschung. Ein Handbuch, Berlin/Zurich: Diaphanes.

Bell, Genevieve/Dourish, Paul (2011): Divining a Digital Future: Mess and Mythology in Ubiquitous Computing, Cambridge, MA: MIT Press.

Beniger, James (1986): The Control Revolution. Technological and Economic Origins of the Information Society, Cambridge: Harvard University Press.

38 Thanks to my colleague Andreas Bernard for pointing this out.

39 Further research will be necessary to analyze in what way, if any, artistic research is also a product of technological and discursive digital cultures.

Beyes, Timon/Pias, Claus (2014): "Transparenz und Geheimnis." In: Zeitschrift für Kulturwissenschaft 8/2, pp. 111-117.

Bourdieu, Pierre (1990 [1982]): Was heißt sprechen? Zur Ökonomie des sprachlichen Tausches, Vienna: Braumüller.

Busch, Kathrin (2009): "Wissenskünste. Künstlerische Forschung und ästhetisches Denken." In: Elke Bippus (ed.), Kunst des Forschens. Praxis eines ästhetischen Denkens, Berlin/Zurich: Diaphanes, pp. 141-158.

Butler, Judith (1998): Haß spricht. Zur Politik des Performativen, Berlin: Berlin Verlag.

Derrida, Jacques (1988): "Signature Event Context." In: Jaques Derrida, Limited Inc, Evanston, IL: Northwestern University Press, pp. 1- 23.

Elgass, Petra (1996): Teambasierte Geschäftsprozessplanung: Konzeption und prototypische Umsetzung eines computergestützten Planungsmodells, Wiesbaden: Deutscher Universitäts-Verlag.

Engell, Lorenz/Bernhard Siegert (2013): "Editorial." In: Zeitschrift für Medien- und Kulturforschung 1/2013, Schwerpunkt Medienanthropologie, pp. 5-10.

Engemann, Christoph/Sprenger, Florian (2015): "Im Netz der Dinge. Zur Einleitung." In: Christoph Engemann/Florian Sprenger (eds.), Internet der Dinge. Über smarte Objekte, intelligente Umgebungen und die technische Durchdringung der Welt, Bielefeld: transcript, pp. 7-58.

Fischer-Lichte, Erika (2004): Ästhetik des Performativen, Frankfurt am Main: Suhrkamp.

Fischer-Lichte, Erika/Kolesch, Doris (eds.) (1998): Kulturen des Performativen. In: Paragrana: Internationale Zeitschrift Historische für Anthropologie 7/1.

Foucault, Michel (1980[1977]): "The confession of the flesh." [Interview], In: Colin Gordon (ed.), Power/Knowledge: Selected Interviews and Other Writings, New York: Pantheon, pp. 194-228.

Foucault, Michel (1992[1978]): Was ist Kritik? (W. Seitter, trans.), Berlin: Merve.

Friedewald, Michael (2008): "Ubiquitous Computing: Ein neues Konzept der Mensch-Computer-Interaktion und seine Folgen." In: Hans Dieter Hellige (ed.): Mensch-Computer-Interface: Zur Geschichte und Zukunft der Computerbedienung, Bielefeld: transcript, pp. 259-280.

Geoghegan, Bernard Dionysius (2011): "From information theory to french theory: Jakobson, Levi-Strauss, and the cybernetic apparatus." In: Critical Inquiry 38/1, pp. 96-126.

Gibson, James Jerome (1979): The Ecological Approach to Visual Perception, Boston: Houghton Mifflin.

Gießmann, Sebastian/Schüttpelz, Erhard (2015): "Medien der Kooperation. Überlegungen zum Forschungsstand." In: Navigationen 15/1, pp. 7-54.

Gold, Rich (1993a): "This is not that pipe." July 30, 2016 (http://web.archive.org/web/20040305153117/; http://www.richgold.org/PIPE/pipe.html)

Gold, Rich (1993b): "Art in the age of ubiquitous computing." In: American Art 7/4, pp. 2-11, June 30, 2016 (http://web.archive.org/web/20040318231033; http://www.richgold.org/UBI-ART/HTML/slide7.html)

Gold, Rich (2002): "The plenitude: Design and engineering in the era of ubiquitous computing." June 30, 2016 (http://hci.stanford.edu/dschool/resources/ThePlenitude.pdf.)

Gold, Rich (n.y.): "No information without representation." June 30, 2016 (http: //web.archive.org/web/20040305153039; http://www.richgold.org/inform/information6.html)

Gramelsberger, Gabriele (2009): "Epistemische Praktiken des Forschens im Zeitalter des Computers." In: Elke Bippus (ed.), Kunst des Forschens. Praxis eines ästhetischen Denkens, Berlin/Zurich: Diaphanes, pp. 91-108.

Günel, Gökçe/Halpern, Orit (2016): "Demoing unto death: Smart cities, environment, and 'apocalyptic hope'." In: The Fibreculture Journal, forthcoming

Hagen, Wolfgang (1999): "Der Okkultismus der Avantgarde um 1900." In: Sigrid Schade/ Georg Christoph Tholen (eds.), Konfigurationen. Zwischen Kunst und Medien, München: Fink, pp. 338-357.

Halpern, Orit (2014): "Inhuman vision." In: Media-N: Journal of the New Media Caucus, Special Issue Art and Infrastructure, June 30, 2016: (http://median.newmediacaucus.org/art-infrastructures-information/inhuman-vision)

Hansen, Mark B. (2011): "Medien des 21. Jahrhunderts, technisches Empfinden und unsere originäre Umweltbedingung." In: Erich Hörl (ed.), Die technologische Bedingung. Beiträge zur Beschreibung der technischen Welt, Berlin: Suhrkamp, pp. 365-409.

Höltgen, Stefan (2011): "Vom Bug-on-a-chip zum House-on-a-Disc. 'Little Computer People' und die Archäologie des Computerfehlers." In: RETRO Magazin 21, pp. 12-14.

Hörl, Erich (2011): "Die technologische Bedingung. Zur Einführung." In: Erich Hörl (ed.), Die technologische Bedingung. Beiträge zur Beschreibung der technischen Welt, Berlin: Suhrkamp, pp. 7-53.

Horn, Eva (2012): "World Trade Center Paranoia. Politische Ängste nach 9/11." July 7, 2016 (https://germanistik.univie.ac.at/fileadmin/user_upload/inst_germanistik/Aktuelles/Horn_WTC_Paranoia.pdf)

Kline, Ronald (2009): "Where are the cyborgs in cybernetics?" In: Social Studies of Science 39/3, pp. 331-362.

Kline, Ronald R. (2015): The Cybernetics Moment. Or Why We Call Our Age the Information Age, Baltimore: Johns Hopkins University Press.

Knoblauch, Hubert/Heath, Christian (1999): "Technologie, Interaktion und Organisation: Die Workplace Studies." In: Schweizerische Zeitschrift für Soziologie 25/2, pp. 163-181.

Krämer, Sybille (2002): "Sprache, Stimme, Schrift. Sieben Gedanken über Performativität als Medialität." In: Uwe Wirth (ed.), Performanz. Zwischen Sprachphilosophie und Kulturwissenschaften, Frankfurt am Main: Suhrkamp, pp. 323-346.

Latour, Bruno (2001): Das Parlament der Dinge. Für eine politische Ökologie, Frankfurt am Main: Suhrkamp.

Leeker, Martina (ed.) (2001): Maschinen, Medien, Performances. Theater an der Schnittstelle zu digitalen Medien, Berlin: Alexander press.

Leeker, Martina (2012): "Just do it. Mimesis in technischem und künstlerischem Systems Engineering." In: Friedrich Balke/Bernhard Siegert/Joseph Vogl (eds.), Mimesis, Archiv für Mediengeschichte 12, pp. 153-166.

Leeker, Martina (2013a): "Theater – Raum – Medien: Optionen für einen reflexiven Umgang mit Medienkulturen." In: Kristin Westphal/Benjanim Jörissen (eds.), Vom Straßenkind zum Medienkind: Raum- und Medienforschung im 21. Jahrhundert, Weinheim/Basel: Beltz Juventa, pp. 87-106.

Leeker, Martina (2013b): "Die Projekte der Messe der Medien." May 16, 2016 (http://projects.digital-cultures.net/dcrl-experiments-interventions/wissensordnungen/messe-der-medien/projekte-mm/#InnerDCRLhollangerer and: https://vimeo.com/94499178)

Leeker, Martina (2014a): "Medien & Paranoia. Eine Live-Installation zur Fortbildung in Paranoia." May 16, 2016 (http://projects.digital-cultures.net/dcrl-experiments-interventions/wissensordnungen/medien-paranoia)

Leeker, Martina (2014b): "Die Projekte zu Medien & Paranoia." May 16, 2016 (http://projects.digital-cultures.net/dcrl-experiments-interventions/wissensordnungen/medien-paranoia)

Leeker, Martina (2015): "Yes Men und die Barbiehaare. Künstlerische Interventionen in technologischen Bedingungen digitaler Kulturen." May 16, 2016 (http://projects.digital-cultures.net/dcrl-experiments-interventions/politische-oekonomie/yes-men-barbiehaare)

Leeker, Martina (2016a): "Medienästhetik und implizites Wissen, 1964/ 1991/2011." In: Anja Kraus et al. (eds.), Schweigendes Wissen in Lernen und Erziehung, Bildung und Sozialisation, Weinheim: Juventa-Beltz, forthcoming.

Leeker, Martina (2016b): "Theater and Engineering. Kontrolle und Macht in medialen Umwelten in den 1960er Jahren, und heute?" In: Friedrich Balke/Maria Muhle (eds.), Räume und Medien des Regierens, München: Fink, pp. 198 – 217

Leeker, Martina (2016c): "Versehrte Dinge. Eine Ausstellungs-Performance im Übergang zum Technosphärischen." In: Martina Leeker, Experiments and Interventions. On Methods for Digital Cultures (http://projects.digital-cultures.net/dcrl-experiments-interventions/), forthcoming.

Lemke, Thomas (2001): "Gouvernementalität." In: Marcus S. Kleiner (ed.), Michel Foucault. Eine Einführung in sein Denken, Frankfurt am Main: Campus Verlag, pp. 108-122.

Lettkemann, Eric/Meister, Martin (2004): "Vom Flugabwehrgeschütz zum niedlichen Roboter. Zum Wandel des Kooperation stiftenden Universalismus der Kybernetik." In: Jörg Strübing/Ingo Schulz-Schaeffer/Martin Meister/Jochen Gläser (eds.), Kooperation im Niemandsland. Neue Perspektiven auf Zusammenarbeit in Wissenschaft und Technik, Opladen: Leske + Budrich, pp. 105-136.

McGonical, Jane Evelyn (1999): This might be a game. Ubiquitous play and performance at the turn of the twenty-first century, Diss., University of California, Berkeley, July 13, 2016 (http://www.avantgame.com/McGonigal_THIS_MIGHT_BE_A_GAME_sm.pdf)

McKenzie, Jon (2001): Perform or Else: From Discipline to Performance, New York: Routledge.

McKenzie, Jon (2005): "Hacktivism and machinic performance." In: Live Ends. Performance in the Information Age. Performance Paradigm 1, pp. 22- 30, July 13, 2016 (http://www.performanceparadigm.net/wpcontent/uploads/2007/06/mckenzie.pdf)

McKenzie, Jon (2012): "Smart media at the University of Wisconsin-Madison." In: Enculturation: A Journal of Rhetoric, Writing, and Culture, June 11, 2016 (http://enculturation.net/smart-media)

McKenzie, Jon (2013): "Performativitäten, Gegen-Performativitäten und Meta-Performativitäten." In: Erika Fischer-Lichte/Kristiane Hasselmann (eds.), Performing the Future. Die Zukunft der Performativitätsforschung, Munich: Fink, pp. 141-159.

McKenzie, Jon (n. d.): "Practicing the Vita performativa." May 16, 2016 (http://www.labster8.net/wp-content/uploads/2015/09/McKenzie-Vita-Performativa-abstract.pdf).

Mersch, Dieter (2009): "Kunst als epistemische Praxis." In: Elke Bippus (ed.), Kunst des Forschens. Praxis eines ästhetischen Denkens, Berlin/Zurich: Diaphanes, pp. 27-47.

Mindell, David, A. (2000): "Cybernetics: Knowledge domains in engineering systems." July 26, 2016. (http://web.mit.edu/esd.83/www/notebook/Cybernetics.PDF.)

Mindell, David A. (2001): "Automation's finest hour: Radar and system integration in World War II." In: Thomas P. Hughes/Agatha C. Hughes (eds.), Systems, Experts, and Computers. The Systems Approach in Management and Engineering, World War II and After, Cambridge, MA: MIT Press, pp. 27-56.

Mindell, David A. (2002): Between Human and Machine: Feedback, Control, and Computing before Cybernetics, Baltimore, MD/London: The Johns Hopkins University Press.

Moser, Jeannie (2013): Psychotropen. Eine LSD-Biographie, Constance: Constance University Press.

Otto, Ulf (2013): Internetauftritte. Eine Theatergeschichte der neuen Medien, Bielefeld: transcript, pp. 49-84.

Pflüger, Jörg (2008): "Interaktion im Kontext." In: Hans Dieter Hellige (ed.), Mensch-Computer-Interface. Zur Geschichte und Zukunft der Computerbedienung, Bielefeld: transcript, pp. 323- 389.

Pias, Claus (2002): "Die kybernetische Illusion." In: Claudia Liebrand/Irmela Schneider (eds.), Medien in Medien, Köln: DuMont, pp. 51-66.

Pias, Claus (2004): "Zeit der Kybernetik – Eine Einstimmung." In: Claus Pias (ed.), Cybernetics – Kybernetik. Die Macy-Konferenzen 1946-1953 2: Dokumente und Reflexionen, Zurich: Diaphanes, pp. 9-42.

Pias, Claus (2011): "On the Epistemology of Computer Simulation." In: Zeitschrift für Medien- und Kulturforschung 2/1, pp. 29-54.

Raunig, Gerald (2008): "What is ciritique? Suspension and recomposition in textual and social machines." July 26, 2016 (http://eipcp.net/transversal/0808/raunig/en)

Rogers, Yvonne (2006): "Moving on from Weiser's vision of calm computing: Engaging ubicomp experiences." In: Paul Dourish/Adrian Friday (eds.), UbiComp 2006: Ubiquitous Computing, Heidelberg/Berlin: Springer, pp. 404-421.

Rolf, Eckard (2009): Der andere Austin. Zur Rekonstruktion/Dekonstruktion performativer Äußerungen – von Searle über Derrida zu Cavell und darüber hinaus, Bielefeld: transcript.

Rouvroy, Antoinette (2012): "The end(s) of critique: data-behaviourism vs. due-process." July 26, 2016 (https://www.academia.edu/7754445/The_end_s_of_critique_data-behaviourism_vs._due-process.)

Rouvroy, Antoinette (2013): "Gouvernementalité algorithmique et perspectives d'émancipation: le disparate comme condition d'individuation par la relation?" In: Politique des algorithmes. Les métriques du web. RESEAUX, 31/177, pp. 163-196.

Schröter, Jens (2015): "Das Internet der Dinge, die allgemeine Medienökologie und ihr ökonomisch Unbewusstes." In: Christoph Engemann/Florian Sprenger (eds.), Internet der Dinge. Über smarte Objekte, intelligente Umgebungen und die technische Durchdringung der Welt, Bielefeld: transcript, pp. 225-240.

Schulz-Schaeffer, Ingo (2000): "Vergesellschaftung und Vergemeinschaftung künstlicher Agenten. Sozialvorstellungen in der Multiagenten-Forschung." In: DFG-GZ: MA 759/2-2, Technikbewertung und -gestaltung Research Reports 3, TU Hamburg.

Seier, Andrea (2007): Remediatisierung. Die performative Konstitution von Gender und Medien, Munster: LIT press.

Seier, Andrea (2011): Elend der Kritik? Bruno Latours Kritik an Diskursanalyse und Dekonstruktion. In: Wolfram Breger/ Jürgen Link/ Rolf Parr (eds.), Kulturrevolution. Zeitschrift für angewandte Diskurstheorie 60, pp. 59-63.

Sprenger, Florian (2014): "Die Kontingenz des Gegebenen. Zur Zeit der Datenkritik." In: Mediale Kontrolle unter Beobachtung 3/1, July 26, 2016 (http://www.medialekontrolle.de/wp-content/uploads/2014/09/Sprenger-Florian-2014-03-01.pdf.)

Sprenger, Florian (2016): "Handlungsmächte und das Zaubern ohne Zauberer: Von der Beseelung der Dinge zum Ubiquitous Computing." In: Jan Müggenburg et al. (eds.), Trick 17. Mediengeschichten zwischen Zauberkunst und Wissenschaft, Lüneburg: Meson press, pp. 87-114.

Suchman, Lucy (1987): Plans and Situated Actions: The Problem of Human-Machine Communication, New York: Cambridge University Press.

Suchman, Lucy (1993): "Technologies of accountability: On lizards and aeroplanes." In: Graham Button (ed.), Technology in Working Order, London: Routledge, pp. 113-126.

Weiser, Mark (1991): "The computer for the 21st century." In: Scientific American 265/3, pp. 94-104.

Weiser, Mark (1993): "Some computer science issues in ubiquitous computing." In: Communications of the ACM 36/7, pp. 74-84.

Weiser, Mark (1996): "Ubiquitous Computing." July 26, 2016 (http://www.ubiq.com/hypertext/weiser/UbiHome.html)

Winkler, Hartmut (2004): Diskursökonomie – Versuch über die innere Ökonomie der Medien, Frankfurt am Main: Suhrkamp, pp. 215-230.

Winnicott, Donald W. (1971): Playing and Reality, London: Tavistock Publications.

Winograd, Terry (1987): "A language/action perspective on the design of cooperative work." In: Human-Computer Interaction 3:1, pp. 3-30.

Winograd, Terry/Flores, Fernando (1986): Understanding Computers and Cognition. A New Foundation for Design, Norwood, NJ: Ablex.

Wirth, Uwe (ed.) (2002a): Performanz. Zwischen Sprachphilosophie und Kulturwissenschaften, Frankfurt am Main: Suhrkamp

Wirth, Uwe (2002b): "Der Performanzbegriff im Spannungsfeld von Illokution, Iteration und Indexikalität." In: Uwe Wirth (ed.), Performanz. Zwischen Sprachphilosophie und Kulturwissenschaften, Frankfurt am Main: Suhrkamp, pp. 9-60.

Annotating

Making digital choreographic objects interrelate

A focus on coding practices

SCOTT DELAHUNTA AND FLORIAN JENETT

Dance is a field of artistic practice(s) commonly associated with bodily movements and with the concept of a choreographer making certain kinds of decisions about where and when these movements will be performed in front of an audience on a stage. There is plentiful evidence for this understanding of dance even though there is little consensus within the field itself about things like the physical training of dancers, the education of choreographers or even if choreography needs to include dancers. Still a large part of the dance field pays deep attention to human movement and a host of associated and evolving practices experienced through and with movement. And as with experience, dance can be understood as something continuous, ephemeral, i.e. disappearing from moment-to-moment and difficult if not impossible to document. However, this conception of dance as impossible to document has been thoroughly challenged, first by artists and then scholars exploring how ideas and concepts occurring in movement and in choreographic creation can be recorded, analysed and shared. Instead of focusing on ideas about movement or about dances, these approaches have concentrated on forms of logic occurring intrinsically in movement and movement making. Results of this research have been and continue to be published for further study and engagement, testing the impact such "choreographic ideas" might have on the world outside of the rehearsal studio (cf. deLahunta 2013).

In the discussion to follow, we will draw attention to some dance artists who have been amongst the first to explore alternative approaches to the documentation and transmission of movement ideas. The relevance for digital cultures is that these artists and their collaborators embraced digital media as the most effective means of doing this work, to render the "complex spatial-corporeal-temporal relationships involved in dance [...] visible, accessible and comprehendible to a reader" (deLahunta 2013: 174). We will show how this basic interest on the part of choreographers in using digital media tools has developed in parallel with other evolutions in human-computer relations.

The examples of digital dance documentation we will refer to in this chapter come under the heading of *Choreographic Objects*, the title of a series of workshops organised in 2008-2009 centring on the output of four research teams working in collaboration with the well-known choreographers William Forsythe, Siobhan Davies, Wayne McGregor and Emio Greco | PC.[1] These teams were working to bring choreographic ideas and processes into newly productive exchanges with both general audiences and other specialist knowledge areas. The digital resources developed to mediate this exchange included interactive scores and installations, choreographic software agents and digital dance archives. "Created with the intention to articulate and disseminate choreographic thought" (Blades 2015: 26), these resources constituted the *choreographic objects* that were the focus of the workshops.

Seen from this perspective, the concept of *choreographic objects* can be used to frame other projects seeking to document and disseminate the unique working procedures of renowned dance artists. Some of these *choreographic objects* once published, e.g. William Forsythe's "Improvisation Technologies" or Anne Teresa de Keersmaeker's "A Choreographer's Score", have been subject to much further analysis and study. Conceived of as the beginnings of a "new form of dance literature" (Groves et al. 2007: 91), they have been valued for their potential educational benefit, as a reference for interdisciplinary research, discussed critically by performance scholars and taken as a stimulus for other artists and designers. This chapter intends to pose a new question about these *choreographic objects*. As information abstracted from the corporeal, digitised and now existing as computable data, can they still best be thought of as capturing and communicating the unique approaches of individual artists? Does the condition of being data suggest an even more fundamental change to the ways in which we think about the nature of *choreographic objects*? They have already been studied in their own right as a partial basis for a new philosophy of movement (cf. Portanova 2013; Sutil 2015). Should they be re-considered as they enter the datasphere as *digital objects*, more in line with the ideas of digital philosophers and researchers?

We will use the application, practice and function of annotation to explore the connection between *choreographic objects* and *digital objects*. There are

1 Cf. http://projects.beyondtext.ac.uk/choreographicobjects

three perspectives on annotation to pay attention to; 1) as a means of communicating principles of movement or choreographic practice which we will refer to as 'annotation for representation'; 2) as a practice of coding audiovisual media when studying human movement behaviour which we call 'coding annotation'; and 3) when the function of annotation is to assist machine-based information processing or interoperability, or 'computable annotation'. It should become clear that 'coding annotation' has particular relevance because of the practice of annotating as a way of thinking about time-based phenomena.

INTEROPERABILITY

In May 2015, Yuk Hui and Simon Worthington convened a workshop at Leuphana University Lüneburg titled *Future for the Annotation of Digital Objects* to explore "new conceptualisations and practices of annotation" of *digital objects* with a critical focus on the limits of technical annotation standards and systems developed mainly to assist machine-based information processing or interoperability on the Web (cf. Hui/Worthington 2015). Many who are not directly involved in creating or studying such annotation standards and systems will not be aware of the scope of this development. And the stakes are high when it comes to creating tools individuals can use to annotate and index text, audio and visual materials on the Web in ways that will harness the power of interoperability; that is having the capacity for linking and sharing, being tracked back to origins, stored and searchable.[2] Hui's concept of *digital objects* draws on the thinking of philosophers of technology like Gilbert Simondon and Bernard Stiegler to elaborate on a new direction of investigation that is concerned with the "relationality between the object" which has been digitised and its programmable milieu comprised of data networks (cf. Hui 2012: 390). Materials such as YouTube videos and Flickr images, are the digital objects to which Hui refers, "composed

2 Organisations involved in developing annotation tools for users include venture capital supported start-ups such as Genius (http://genius.com/web-annotator) with an initial investment of $15 million dollars in 2012, higher education coalitions supporting interoperable web annotation like Hypothes.is (https://hypothes.is/annotating-all-knowledge) and online scholarly publishing initiatives such as Scalar (http://scalar.usc.edu/scalar), funded by the Andrew W. Mellon Foundation and National Endowment for the Humanities. Technology providers have sprung up around European research projects such as Europeana, a major digital platform for cultural heritage that uses PUNDIT, a web annotation tool developed by NET7.

of data and formalised by schemes or ontologies that one can generalise as metadata" (Hui 2012: 380).

The World Wide Web Consortium (W3C), the main organisation developing open standards for ensuring "the long-term growth of the Web"[3], first began its work on annotation soon following the advent of the Semantic Web in the late 1990s. This included work on *Annotea*, a user focused project that appears to have run from 1999-2003 aiming to enhance collaboration by making it possible to attach comments to a Web document.[4] Another project was the Open Annotation Collaboration (OAC) project that ran in three phases from 2009-2013.[5] In its Guiding Principles, the OAC states that its efforts are to "allow the sharing of annotations across clients, servers, and applications. It will not, in any way, prescribe user interfaces" (OAC 2013). In other words, the OAC was set up to establish a standards framework for getting computers and programs to reliably talk to other computers and programs across the Internet, and many current projects base their systems in the OAC framework (see Footnote 2). Since 2014, it appears these two branches have merged as the World Wide Web Consortium (W3C) has a new working group dedicated to developing a specification for a decentralised and open annotation infrastructure "as a new layer of interactivity and linking on top of the Web. It will allow anyone to annotate anything anywhere" (W3C 2016).[6]

CODING, OBSERVATION AND THEORY

We turn briefly now to annotation software designed for the systematic study and annotation of audiovisual (audio-video) media for the purpose of scientific research. Specifically, we will look at multi-modal annotation tools designed to flexibly accommodate a range of various user-defined coding schemes used by researchers studying phenomena such as modes of human or animal communication, behaviour and social interaction.[7] Coding in this context does not refer to computationally interacting with a corpus of digitised material, but to classifica-

---

3 Cf. https://www.w3.org/

4 Cf. https://www.w3.org/2001/Annotea

5 Cf. http://www.openannotation.org/about.html

6 Cf. https://www.w3.org/annotation

7 Two of the more popular and widely used of these tools are ELAN and ANVIL: Cf. https://tla.mpi.nl/tools/tla-tools/elan/elan-description) and http://www.anvil-software.org

tion systems derived from conceptual taxonomical frameworks corresponding to specialised theories and approaches, e.g. from studies of distributed cognition or psycholinguistics. This means the tools are designed as well as chosen accordingly "against the background of specific theoretical assumptions" (Rohlfing et al 2006: 122). The tool's designer optimises for a limited range of these theoretical possibilities by, for example, supporting two different annotation procedures referred to by Michael Kipp, the creator of ANVIL, one of the more popular existing tools, as top-down or bottom-up coding. This is a way of expressing the different approaches the researcher who might use for coding or annotating the recording of behavior in question in ANVIL. Top down refers to higher-level concepts with bottom-up referring to the annotating of smaller units, with both procedures usually meeting in the middle in practice. For example, a study of gestures might involve the researcher coding from bottom up the "so-called gesture phases (preparation, stroke, hold, retraction) and then encode the actual gesture" (Kipp 2014: 429). But this does not say much about the depth of knowledge and methodological approaches the expert researcher brings to the study. In 2006, a widely cited workshop report comparing multimodal annotation tools made it clear that the choice for a specific software tool meant not only comparing the available programs. It also meant evaluating what the gain would be over low tech, perhaps more stable 'traditional' tools for data collection and analysis (cf. Rohlfing et al. 2006).

These software tools have emerged from the field of study they are intended to be used for and are often developed by an individual or small team for non-commercial research purposes (e.g. ANVIL is free to download and use). This is an extreme contrast with the efforts to 'annotate the web' described above, not only in terms of scale, but also technically. For example, a section on 'interoperability' in a 2014 report by Kipp still refers mainly to the possibility of importing and exporting datasets in formats readable in other software (cf. Kipp 2014). However, these tools do correspond to the development of *choreographic objects* in that they focus on the documentation and analysis or coding of time-based phenomena for the purpose of deepening understanding of a range of human activities. There are contrasts here with dance as an artistic practice, but it is not that an artistic practice does not come with a set of assumptions and methods, and it is not that process in the sciences is any more or less subjective than in the arts. But arts practice is not accustomed to nesting its assumptions in quite the same way in relation to what is valued as the outcome of its process. The particular kind of instability this gives rise to means that a more or less general coding scheme does not have the same status or value for arts practice as it might for science practice. Although a dance notation system like Laban or Benesh can be used as a kind of coding scheme, in practice these existing systems are not in general use (as compared to music notation) for a variety of reasons. However, we can annotatively subject dance to the top down and bottom up encodings of science researchers, and some collaborative inter-disciplinary work has been done in this area, e.g. a linguistics analysis of the semiotics of dance performance and a study of distributed cognition in the context of dance creation (cf. Kirsh et al. 2009; Fernandes/Jürgens 2013). In any case, what will become important for our discussion here is the process of annotation itself, the labour involved in the close study of human activity, in our case in the context of choreographic and dance practice, and the nature of the coding involved.

CHOREOGRAPHIC OBJECTS TO DIGITAL OBJECTS

The examples that follow are drawn from three projects developed by or in close collaboration with the choreographers, William Forsythe and Deborah Hay. As a reminder, there are three perspectives on annotation to pay attention to; 1) as a means of communicating principles of movement or choreographic practice [annotation for representation]; 2) an approach to coding the audiovisual media [coding annotation]; and 3) to assist machine-based information processing [computable annotation].

Motivated by a need to quickly transmit principles of improvisation he had developed with his company Ballet Frankfurt in the 1980s, William Forsythe turned to digital multi-media. Beginning development in collaboration with the Center for Art and Media Karlsruhe (ZKM) in the early 1990s as a training platform for the company, earlier versions included recordings of performance works from several angles alongside short lectures from Forsythe augmented by "graphic overlays" or video annotation (Ziegler 2007: 34). After several iterations a version was published in 1999 as a CD-ROM under the title *Improvisation Technologies: a tool for the analytical dance eye* (Forsythe 1999). The annotations are drawn directly on top of a video image of Forsythe performing demonstrations of these principles for the camera (Figure 1). The result is a collection of nearly 65 short demonstrations most using this form of annotation to show movement paths and map out "spatial relationships in and around his body" (Groves 2007: 92). This combination of movement demonstration, verbal description and annotation draws out movement ideas and makes them explicit. It also entangles the idea in a composite form of communication, which through simultaneous demarcation shows how conceptual or mental parameters can shape the force and trajectory of a movement.

Figure 1: Screenshots from Williams Forsythe's CD-ROM Improvisation Technologies

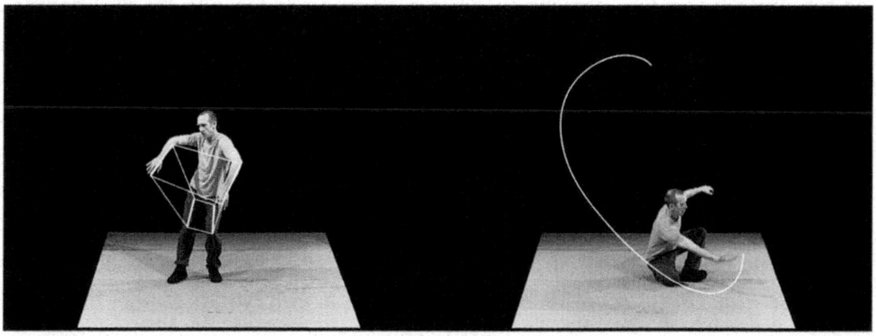

Credit: William Forsythe, Nik Haffner, Christian Ziegler, Volker Kuchelmeister, Yvonne Mohr, Astrid Sommer, ZKM/Zentrum für Kunst und Medientechnologie, Karlsruhe, Deutsches Tanzarchiv Köln/SK Stiftung Kultur.

At the time of its development, this *choreographic object* was not thought of in terms of computational data, even though some of Forsythe's compositional ideas drew on the concept of "recursive algorithms [...] fixed variations that we created through a long, painstaking process, not unlike that of computer programming" (Forsythe/Kaiser 1999: 68). The naming and organisation of the principles of improvisation themselves would have occurred in the practice, in the rehearsal studio, some time before they were transposed to the multi-media environment of the CD-ROM. For the design and development of this environment, these names would become a fixed classification or coding system that enabled cross-referencing between Forsythe's short demonstrations and video of three of his dancers using the principles. Watching one of these videos, the specific principle in use at any one time shows up on the timeline as an 'clickable' annotation. Here the background of assumptions and methods that bring the coding and annotations together into meaningful relationships correspond to a theory of movement generation associated with a single artist.

While all the audiovisual material published on the CD-ROM was digitised and programmed in Macromedia Director, as already written this particular *choreographic object* was not thought of in terms of computational data. In part this had to do with the time, the Web was in its relative infancy and it was the "multi-media era" according to Geert Lovink, Founder of The Institute of Networked Cultures. In an interview on the history of the CD-ROM in the arts, Lovink states that "the central desire of CD-ROMs was to blow up traditional forms of navigation", but the weakness of the CD-ROM was that it was "a closed environment, a data monade" (Lovink 2015). Despite the definite limitations this presents for re-imagining this particular *choreographic object* as a *digital object*, the reason for including it in our discussions here, in addition to the observations on coding and annotation above, is because of the successful precedent it set in showing how a unique set of principles of movement in dance could be effectively elucidated using computer-aided design. *Improvisation Technologies* was also the inspiration for the next example in our list.

In 2005, Forsythe embarked on another project using video annotation this time to elucidate principles of choreography with the aim of helping audiences perceive the organisational structures in a dance he had choreographed in 2000 titled *One Flat Thing, reproduced*. In collaboration with Norah Zuniga Shaw and Maria Palazzi from The Ohio University and a team of designers, animators and researchers, the project was developed over a period of four years eventually launching on-line in April 2009 with the title *Synchronous Objects for One Flat Thing, reproduced*.[8] Video annotation for representation is used extensively throughout the website, not only to draw attention to two key choreographic structuring components, the cueing and alignment systems (Figures 2 & 3), but also as a part of instructional videos. This project embraced the concept of computational data, largely through deriving calculable evidence from a close analysis, coding and annotation of the high-definition digital video shot of the dance from the front and above. In an essay titled *Dance, Data, Objects*, Shaw and Palazzi explain this process of developing the 'spatial' and 'attribute' data that was used to generate the variety of Objects that exist on their website. Much of this work was manual, either "built from the dancers' first hand accounts" of the choreographic structure, indexing their responses as attribute data into an Excel file or through the animators painstakingly selecting "pixel points on each dancer in both the top and front views of the source video" to generate the spatial data (Zuniga Shaw/Palazzi 2009). Zuniga Shaw writes, "The process of decoding OFTr was a creative dialog that dilated between insider accounts and outside observation, analytical needs and aesthetic interests" (ibid.: n. pag.).

8 Cf. http://synchronousobjects.osu.edu

Figure 2: Form Flow. Still from annotated video illustrating alignments, the way in which Forsythe designs relationships in space and time

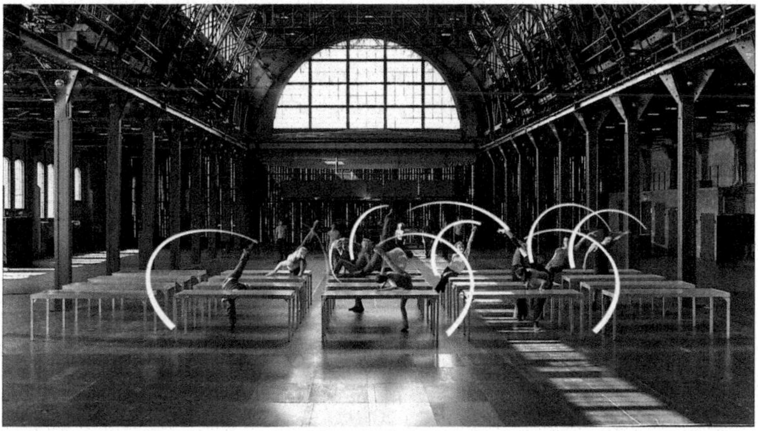

Credit: Synchronous Objects Project, The Ohio State University and The Forsythe Company.

Figure 3 Cueing System. Still from annotated video illustrating the complex system of cueing in One Flat Thing, reproduced

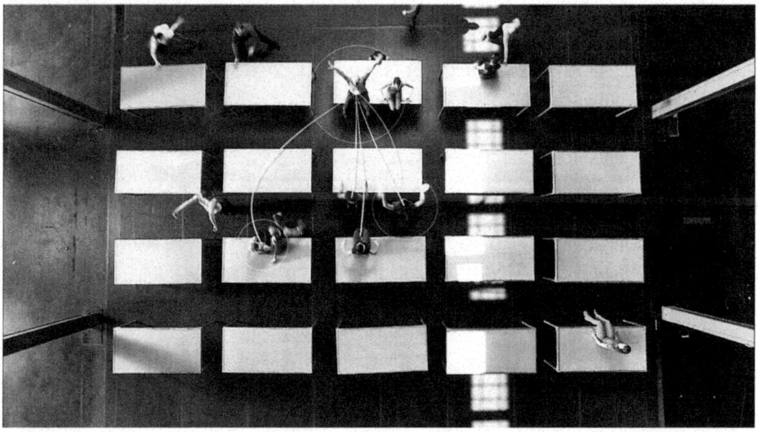

Credit: Synchronous Objects Project, The Ohio State University and The Forsythe Company.

This coding of audiovisual media involved close and extensive observation work by domain experts, dance practitioners, dance researchers and assorted animators and designers who themselves became expert observers over time. This is where the process of annotation itself, for the purposes of our discussion here, as 'coding annotation', focuses on the labour involved in the close study of human activity and how this process produces computable data. And, in the case of *Synchronous Objects*, this data when digitally re-materialised, for example as abstract animations on the website, could be said to represent different aspects of the choreography while appearing in forms that no longer look like the dance entity *One Flat Thing, reproduced.* As there are no longer dancers directly involved, this becomes choreographic thinking or movement knowledge that exists in the absence of bodies, and Forsythe, Portanova and others have both proposed different kinds of arguments in this direction, suggesting something other than a translation or symbolic representation (as with dance notation) of information is going on (cf. Forsythe 2012; Portanova 2013).

Synchronous Objects for One Flat Thing, reproduced certainly succeeds as a *choreographic object.* It has evidentially brought choreographic ideas and processes into newly productive exchanges with both general audiences and other specialist knowledge areas. And because the provenance of these ideas, the body/ not the body, has been challenged through computation the results of this project start to take on the shape of something with the potential of Hui's *digital objects.* But here is where we can apply the distinction Hui made between two processes, 1) the 'datafication of objects', which corresponds to the coding and data work done on the dance entity *One Flat Thing, reproduced*, and 2) the 'objectification of data', which refers to the corresponding computational entity, comprised of data and metadata, for which every move is 'conditioned by its technical milieu' (Hui 2012: 389). For the purposes of our discussion here and referring back to the above paragraph, this milieu is the network running between machines and other programmes, it is the Web. In this way, *Synchronous Objects* presents us with something that is not quite yet a *digital object.* But it is moving toward that possibility.

In 2010, Motion Bank a research project of The Forsythe Company was inaugurated in Frankfurt, Germany to explore further what computation could bring to the process of creating *choreographic objects.* With significant support from a variety of funders including the German Federal Cultural Foundation, the project was designed to run in its first phase for four years. The Motion Bank core team emphasized digitization as an "integral part of Motion Bank from the start" (Cramer et al. 2015) and designed recording setups to ensure that everything captured could be available to computation. All recording situations were installed and calibrated to allow for as little 'noise' as possible so software algorithms might help extract features and recognize relevant patterns in the data. This was combined with the use of an annotation tool called Piecemaker, a software that assists in scoring video recordings of dance and sharing this information with others. Piecemaker was initiated as a research project by The Forsythe Company member David Kern to support the organisation and recall of materials created by Forsythe and his performers in the rehearsal studio. Thinking back to the coding practices of scientists making close observations of human activity and using coding annotation software like ANVIL, Forsythe's rehearsal constitutes an activity for which Kern was developing a tool corresponding to 'domain expertise' in dance.

In the context of Motion Bank, this software was reprogrammed for use in the development of its on-line digital scores with selected guest choreographers and as a standalone tool for use in the studio. (Figure 4) Using this software renamed Piecemaker2 (PM2), annotation sets or markers could easily be related and provide access to multiple versions of the same event (e.g. video, audio, motion capture, scores, etc.). This enabled building connections that could generate useful representations both during and post-annotation. As with the *Synchronous Objects* project, the quantification of the dances of the Motion Bank guest artists into data involved a combination of computational and manual work. This meant often many hours of computer based video processing, for example to subtract the background of the image leaving only the silhouettes of the performers; alongside watching the same video for nearly as many hours in order to annotate and describe time based events the computer would not be able to recognize on its own.

Figure 4: Piecemaker2 (PM2) annotation software. Based on Piecemaker originally developed by David Kern, The Forsythe Company

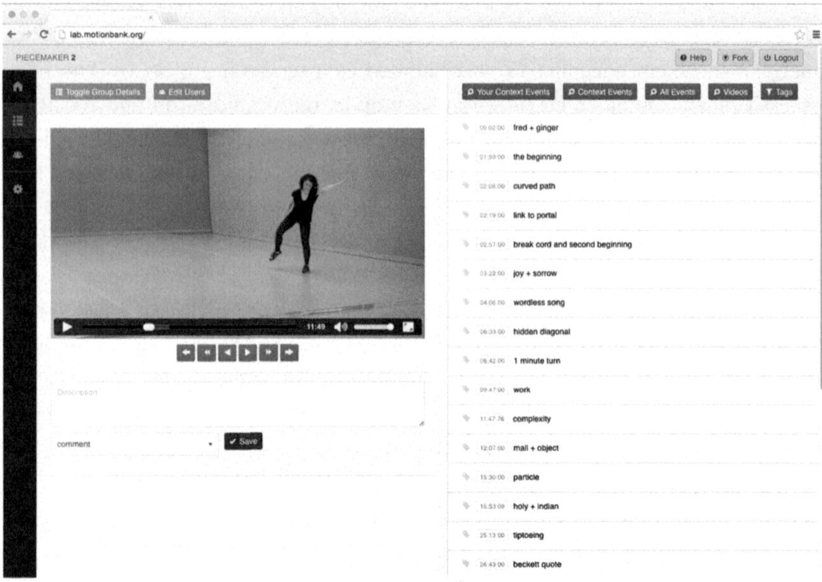

Credit: Reprogrammed by Motion Bank. Screenshot: Florian Jenett. On Video: Jeanine Durning performing her adaptation of *No Time to Fly* by Deborah Hay.

The specific example of how this coding annotation was used in (Figure 5) is drawn from the Motion Bank project with the choreographer Deborah Hay from the website *Using the Sky*[9], which is based on her existing solo *No Time to Fly* (2010). *No Time to Fly* has a written score, which the performers Jeanine Durning, Juliette Mapp and Ros Warby were each invited to adapt as an individual solo. These solo adaptations were each filmed seven times and this material provides the main recorded data for the web publication. The site also takes the score for the website's 'tempo', and the 29 sections of the score are aligned with the video recordings. One part of the website, visible in Figure 4, is based on Performer Insights. This gives the reader a chance to view a solo adaptation alongside the score and a running commentary of the performer; also functioning as 'annotation for representation'. Hay's score does not offer the performer precise movement instructions, so this commentary gives the reader insight into

9 Cf. http://scores.motionbank.org/dh

how the written score is translated into movement by the performers. Hay would refer to this as when the "body encounters language" in her work (Hay 2013).

Figure 5: Performer Insights. Using the Sky. *An online score of Deborah Hay's work* No Time to Fly

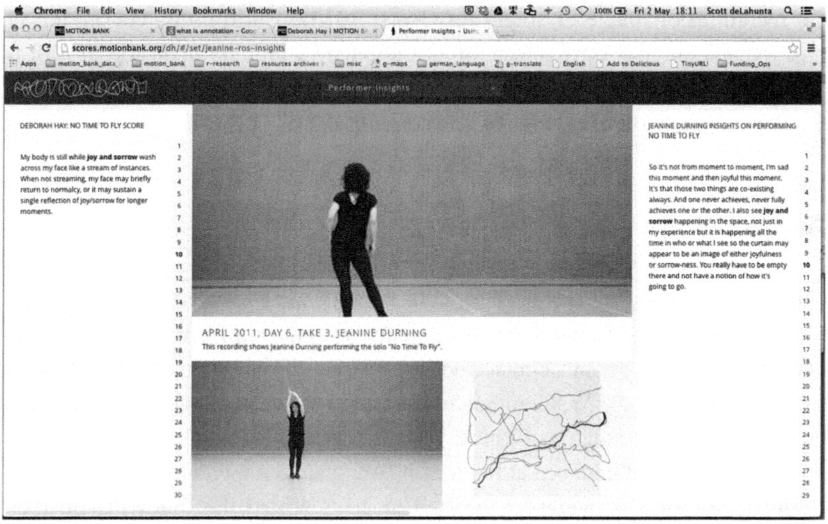

Credit: Motion Bank. On Video: Jeanine Durning performing her adaptation of *No Time to Fly* by Deborah Hay.

This description of the Performer Insights screenshot indicates the ways in which the coding [annotation] of the audiovisual material was similar to the coding [annotation] work done on *Synchronous Objects*. It involved extensive observation work by domain experts, dance practitioners, researchers coming together with the acquired dance expertise of the creative coders and computer scientists working on the project. As with *Synchronous Objects*, this coding work was essential for creating the website *Using the Sky* which aims to draw attention to and elucidate aspects of Deborah Hay's choreographic approach. In this sense, the coding annotations themselves remain "hidden to the viewer" (Blades 2015: 29); in the same way as the information in the Excel files in the archives of the *Synchronous Objects* project is hidden. It is worth mentioning that there are no annotations drawn on top of the recorded digital video because Deborah Hay's specific choreographic approach resisted such visual representations. In this sense, the published result clearly strengthens the class of things we have been describing as *choreographic objects*, as it corresponds to the idea that what is specific about Hay's approach, her choreographic ideas and processes, can be communicated via a unique *choreographic object*.

However, unlike the previous *choreographic object* projects, a cluster of new developments occurred with Motion Bank. Firstly, a new annotation tool, in ways similar to ANVIL, has emerged from the dance field. Secondly, a general set of annotation principles has been articulated that draws attention to time over the recording of image or sound (cf. Jenett 2015). Thirdly, this conception of time as the core axis of organisation has a uniquely digital dimension to it. It is part of both the data and the metadata of these objects and starts to clarify the transition from *choreographic object* to *digital object*.

ANNOTATION FINDS ITS PLACE

Our goal in writing this has been to work through some ideas about how annotation in the creation of *choreographic objects*, as emergent from the artistic practice of dance, comes into contact with the kinds of annotation efforts demonstrated not only by the W3C initiatives described above in our second paragraph, but also by projects such as Genius, Hypothes.is and PUNDIT (see Footnote 2) which were all in attendance at the fourth iAnnotate Symposium in May 2016 in Berlin.[10] iAnnotate's inaugural meeting in 2013 posted the following on their homepage: *Building a community to enable the annotation of the world's knowledge*. We can avoid this hyperbole, but we can't avoid the changes brought about by digital technologies, and how we are increasingly woven into the "media-intensive milieu comprising networks, images, sounds, and text, which we generalise as data and metadata" (Hui 2012: 380).

Hui and Worthington embed this phrase in the description of their 2015 workshop *Future for the Annotation of Digital Objects*:

> "Annotation finds its place, not only in the sense of assisting information processing and enhancing the searchability of digital objects […], but also as interaction and concretisation of relations between the users and the objects with which they interact." (Hui/Worthington 2015)

We would make a further proposal for the practice of annotation as a way of thinking that builds relations with and extends upon a background of 'domain

10 Cf. http://iannotate.org/2016/

expertise', whether that is artistic, scientific or scholarly, in time-based phenomena such as dance.

So far, we have discussed three kinds of annotation that go into the creation of *choreographic objects*: 'annotation for representation' as in drawing on top of video, 'coding annotation' or the practice of analysing audiovisual media, and 'computable annotation' to assist machine-based information processing. And we looked at the connection between our notion of *choreographic objects* and Hui's notion of *digital objects* as a way of distinguishing and investigating these modes and their various potentials more philosophically. It was our intention here to start a discussion we expect to continue as more dance documentation and digitisation projects come on-line, and we build on our choreographic coding projects to make intersections with data-driven research with various other fields.[11] One parting observation: as research becomes more "subsumed under calculation" (Hui 2012: 390) the expertise, skills and intuitions human activity researchers bring and use to recognise and code phenomena (annotation as a way of thinking) whether in dance or ethnographic work, will increasingly be fused with algorithmic procedures.

REFERENCES

Blades, Hetty (2015): "Affective Traces in Virtual Spaces: Annotation and emerging dance scores." In: Performance Research 20/6, pp. 26-34.

Cramer, Franz Anton/Jenett, Florian/deLahunta, Scott (2015): "A Conversation on Motion Bank." In: Barbara Büscher/Franz Anton Cramer (eds.), MAP (media archive performance), May 27, 2016 (http://www.perfomap.de/map6/medien-und-verfahren-des-aufzeichnens/a-conversation-on-motion-bank)

De Keersmaeker, Anne Theresa/Cvejić, Bojana (2012): A Choreographer's Score, Brussels: Mercatorfonds.

deLahunta, Scott (2013): "Publishing choreographic ideas: discourse from practice." In: Mick Wilson/Schelte van Ruiten, (eds): SHARE: Handbook for Artistic Research Education, ELIA: Amsterdam, pp. 170-177.

Fernandes, Carla/Jürgens, Stephan (2013): "Video annotation in the TKB project: linguistics meets choreography meets technology." In: International Journal of Performance Arts & Digital Media 9/1, pp. 113-132.

Forsythe, William (1999): Improvisation Technologies: A Tool for the Analytical Dance Eye, Karlsruhe: Hatje Cantz Verlag.

11 Cf. http://choreographiccoding.org

Forsythe, William (2012): "William Forsythe discusses synchronous objects as choreographic objects." In: YouTube Channel of ACCAD at Ohio State University, May 27, 2016 (https://www.youtube.com/watch?v=uQdZBOVYLdI)

Forsythe, William/Kaiser, Paul (1999): "Dance geometry." In: Performance Research: A Journal of the Performing Arts 4/2, pp. 64-71.

Groves, Rebecca/deLahunta, Scott/Zuniga Shaw/Norah (2007): "Talking About Scores: William Forsythe's vision for a new form of dance 'literature.'" In: Sabine Gehm/Pirkko Husemann/Katharina von Wilcke (eds.), Knowledge in Motion, Bielefeld: transcript, pp. 91-100.

Hay, Deborah (2013): "On Language. Introduction to Concepts. Using the Skype Motion Bank On-Line Digital Dance Scores." May 11, 2016 (http://scores.motionbank.org/dh/#/set/introduction-to-concepts)

Hui, Yuk (2012): "What is a Digital Object?" In: Metaphilosophy 43/4, pp. 380-399.

Hui, Yuk/Worthington, Simon (2015): "Workshop: Future for the Annotation of Digital Objects", Centre for Digital Cultures, Leuphana University Lüneburg, June 01, 2016 (http://hybridpublishing.org/2015/05/workshop-future-for-the-annotation-of-digital-objects-12-13-may-2015/)

Jenett, Florian (2015): "Notes on annotation." In: Performance Research 20/6, pp. 24-25.

Kipp, Michael (2014): "ANVIL: The video annotation research tool." In: Jacques Durand/Ulrike Gut/Gjert Kristoffersen (eds.), Handbook of Corpus Phonology, Oxford: Oxford University Press, pp. 420-436.

Kirsh, David/Muntanyola, Dafne/Jao, R. Joanne/Lew, Amy/Sugihara, Matt, (2009): "Choreographic Methods for Creating Novel, High Quality Dance." In: Workshop, Design and Semantics of Form and Movement, pp. 188-195.

Lovink, Geert (2015): "Q & A on the History of CD-ROMs in the Arts with Marie Lechner." In: Institute of Network Cultures Blog, May 18, 2016 (http://networkcultures.org/geert/2015/02/04/cd-roms/)

Open Annotation Collaboration (OAC) (2013): "Open Annotation Guiding Principles." May 16, 2016 (http://www.openannotation.org/documents/GuidingPrinciplesRevised.pdf)

Portanova, Stamatia (2013): Moving without a Body: Digital Philosophy and Choreographic Thoughts, Cambridge, MA: MIT.

Rohlfing, Katharina/Loehr, Daniel/Duncan, Susan/Brown, Amanda/Franklin, Amy/Kimbara, Irene et al. (2006): "Comparison of Multimodal Annotation Tools - Workshop Report." In: Online-Zeitschrift zur Verbalen Interaktion 7, pp. 99-123.

Sutil, Nicolás Salazar (2015): Motion and Representation: The Language of Human Movement, Cambridge, MA: MIT.

W3C (2016): "What are Web Annotations." In: Web Annotation Working, May 21, 2016 (https://www.w3.org/annotation/)

Ziegler, Chris (2007): "Electronic Memory Design." In: Emio Greco | PC/AHK Amsterdam (eds.), Capturing Intention – Documentation, Analysis and Notation research based on the Work of Emio Greco, Amsterdam: PC and Amsterdam School of the Arts, pp. 34-41.

Zuniga Shaw, Norah/Palazzi, Maria (2009): "The Dance, The Data, The Objects." In: Synchronous Objects for One Flat Thing, reproduced by William Forsythe, Ohio: The Ohio State University.

Affecting

Speculation about 1:0

On the productive difference of the interval

MARIE-LUISE ANGERER

In the film *Strange Days* (Bigelow 1995) a woman runs along the beach in Los Angeles while the man she meets – also running – is actually, 'in reality', sitting in a wheelchair and not only sees himself as running along the beach but above all 'has the corresponding sensation of movement'. Thanks to Squid technology, the man in the wheelchair sees and feels himself as someone running along the beach whom the young woman smiles at and waves to as she runs past. In *Strange Days*, the Squids are not just extensions of the sensory apparatus – as described by McLuhan (1964) –, but also intensifications of and even substitutes for this apparatus (instead of the person's own sensory input, those of others are 'implanted') – Squids record audiovisual data and convert them into proprioceptory data for the user: one's own sensations (and the associated visual material) are replaced by those of someone else.

Squids demonstrate and foreshadow how digital technologies enable new affective performances. *Strange Days* thus also calls upon scholars of media and performance to find a vocabulary and mode of thought that is able to reflect such affective performances and speculate about their implications. This chapter enlists affect theory and, more precisely, the notion of the 'affective interval' in order to think the productive, performative effects that the digital 'co-processing' between media technology and human body enables. To do so, the chapter first traces the genealogy of what is here called 'involuntary moments' and how they measurable and 'performable' through technological experiments. It then moves on to show how affect theory reframed these involuntary moments as 'missing half-seconds'. On this basis, the question of media technology can be posed as one of 'affective media technologies' or 'cybernetic machines' at work on even the smallest intervals. In conclusion, the chapter moves back to the 'perceiving in motion' that is non- or pre-cognitively performed in, and through the affective interval.

CONCERNING SMALL, INVOLUNTARY MOVEMENTS

No longer 'small' but not yet 'large'.
HELLER-ROAZEN 2009: 209

There is a long history of pre-forms of perception, sensation, and bodily reactions. These various 'old' subject-less movements such as in Leibniz, Spinoza, and others are re-attracting attention in theories of digital environments and performativity.

In the following significant authors un-conscious and visceral movements are presented and their thoughts discussed in view of their influence of modelling the digital (time) gaps avant la lettre. Unlike Descartes, Leibniz denied that the mind was always active, insisting instead that there were moments and stretches of time during which consciousness registers ('perception'), but without conscious perception ('apperception') of such overly small movements. According to Leibniz, consciousness as understood by Descartes and his followers always necessarily misses something, as something is always happening but not everything passes the threshold of conscious perception. Spinoza, too, understood matter, movement and mind (in the sense of immaterial being) as a sliding scale, deriving the various degrees and densities of materiality as functions of movement versus intensity. In his reading of Spinoza, Gilles Deleuze explains this by saying that each thing defines itself by its length and breadth, by its longitude and latitude. The length of a body here refers to ratios of rapidity and slowness, of rest and motion between its particles, and its width comprises the sum of its affects, all of its intensive states (cf. Deleuze 1988: 165).

Leibniz used the monad as the smallest particle that represents a microcosm of the universe. This representation takes place via perceptions. Since every monad supposedly expresses the totality of the universe, it follows that they can only ever be excerpts or gradations. This means that not everything is expressed in the same way, but on a scale of conscious to unconscious, from large to small perceptions. One often-quoted example of this is Leibniz's description of the sound of the sea, which he says we only hear because we hear each single wave, which we hear in turn only because we hear every single drop of water. But it is clear, Leibniz explains, that no ear can really hear this:

"The impressions (effects) made on our ear by the individual waves, but which we are unable to distinguish between (discern) (because they are such changes in the external world as are not accompanied by changes in our bodily organs), are a typical example of *petites perceptions.* All significant changes within our bodies are soon noticed, thus leading to contents of consciousness." (Herbertz 1980 [1905]: 45)

Leibniz distinguishes between three kinds of perceptions. Firstly, those that cause no changes to the organs, although it should be emphasized here, as Richard Herbertz writes, that they produce no "noticeable change" (ibid.: 45), but they certainly do produce changes, just ones that go unnoticed. Secondly, perceptions that occur in too large numbers, thus not capable of being registered as separate by consciousness. And thirdly, those where weaker perceptions are obscured by more powerful ones.

Whereas Leibniz still viewed his monads as being driven by a creator God, Spinoza's "impersonal uniform substance" is characterized by infinite modes that can be understood as affections. Both Spinoza and Leibniz refer to affection using terms such as force, perspective, imagination and time so as to define this substance as a oneness and a multiplicity (cf. Ott 2010). Around the same time in the 17th century, the concept of reflexes for involuntary movements of the body began to spread in the field of medicine and physiology. In this field too, then, we see an interest in such movements taking place without the mind, without conscious control or intention. Descartes is generally associated with the theory of reflexes as he defined body movements that were not controlled by the mind and which didn't touch it either. But in the middle of the last century, in his analysis of the "emergence of the concept of reflexes", George Canguilhem showed how a concept – in this case that of reflexes – may already exist, even making an appearance in terminological form, but only later, by the interaction of various forces, coming to denote a generally accepted fact. According to Canguilhem (2008), one can see that Descartes is not actually speaking about reflexes, but that he was able to choose in his discussion between heart and brain, basing his assumptions on a single movement from the inside (centre = gland) to the nerves at the outer end, but not also assuming a movement in the reverse direction, although other medical theorists before him had done so. Before Descartes's time (referring back to Galen and Jean François Fernel), a distinction was made between three spirits, the so-called "vital functions" (Canguilhem 2008: 32). A "natural spirit" (located in the liver and acting via the veins), a "vital spirit" (located in the heart and acting via the arteries) and an "animal spirit located in the brain acting via the nerves" (ibid.: 32). Descartes attempts to trace all muscle movements back to one mechanism in order to free it from any mental control. In Canguilhem's view, his theory of involuntary movement anticipates the notion of reflexes without establishing an actual reflexology. And this is because Descartes, unlike William Harvey and Thomas Willis, did not view the heart as a muscle, attributing the circulation of blood to its special warmth. As a result, Descartes remained attached to a mechanics by which animals and machines (automata) are placed alongside humankind in order to illustrate the artificial and thus natural quality of human muscle movement (cf. ibid.: 37-47). But as Canguilhem emphasizes, precisely this parallel opens up an "incomprehensible break" (between animal and human, as only the latter has a soul) which, as an "unfathomable secret" (ibid.: 72), in turn refers humankind back to God.

With the hypothesis of an animal soul, a further step was taken in the direction of reflex by Thomas Willis, following on from Descartes, bringing chemistry into play against mechanics. In Willis's theory of reflexes, the life force is associated with the force of light and, in contrast to Galen, he now assumed "the encephalic origin of all movement, without exception" (ibid.: 91). Accordingly, spontaneous or voluntary movements are controlled by the cerebral mind (cerebrum), while the natural or involuntary movements are controlled by the cerebellar mind (cerebellum) – two minds, then, one spiritual, sentient and rational, the other physical, sentient and lively. Humans and higher beasts share both minds.

Against the Zeitgeist of the late 19th century, Henri Bergson picked up this notion, writing that "there is no perception that is not prolonged into movement" (Bergson 1991: 69). Canguilhem, too, mentions this link to Bergson and remarks that he even picked up the connection between the energy of movement and that of light, a link first made by Willis, twinning the latent energy of the animal spirit with cosmic light (cf. Canguilhem 2008: 94). And later still, parallel to the cybernetic continuation of the Cartesian mechanistic view, Maurice Merleau-Ponty not only declared the primacy of movement, but also equated movement with meaning, naming it as that through which being reveals itself (cf. Kristensen/Merleau-Ponty 2012: 23-36, here 29). But this equation of movement and meaning, as Stefan Kristensen points out, means "that [there is] no ontological difference between motor function and affectivity, between the physiological and the psychological, but only gradual differences, varying modalities of meaning" (ibid.: 30).

From the mid-19th century, small movements and reflexes started to be measured, produced under experimental conditions in laboratories, captured and recorded using early forms of photography. And then, with the advent of film around the turn of the century, it became possible not only to intervene in the recording of movement (as life), but also to bring it to life as something existing in time, as a temporal sequence of images (cf. Kelty/Landecker 2002: 21-47).

These technical-media techniques (of recording and playback) convey the movement of the living as something living, presenting it as permanent delay, assomething always already deferred, although visually transparent. This is a procedure that can be mapped onto an existential life praxis that installs the delay in time (of life) as the space of the now.

Vital and temporal delays perform together the moment of the living now. Thus the most intimate moment of life is always a missed one, not yet, and already gone. This missing time will play an even more important role against the background of an encompassing cybernetic re-organization of the psychic and societal realm.

THE HISTORY OF THE AFFECTIVE INTERVAL

In the mid-1970s, students of media and communication studies in the German-speaking world heard from Hertha Sturm and her team that they had discovered the 'missing half-second'. Above all, Sturm wanted the results of her research to reach those responsible for making television, so that they could draw the necessary consequences. In her view, television needed to broadcast slower image sequences, audio and video needed to be more congruent; the text or spoken language should follow the images or vice versa, rather than supplying additional information. For as the researchers found, their test subjects (mainly children) were unable to process the excessive amount of information 'properly' and their reactions were quite simply too slow for the abundance of images. As a result, children reacted 'happily' to sad image sequences and 'unhappily' to cheerful ones. The test subject's mood was gauged by measuring pulse, heartbeat and transpiration, giving a curve of physical arousal indicating mood – or rather allowing it to be deduced – with low frequency pointing to a depressive basic mood and high frequency pointing to high spirits. Surprisingly, these findings correspond quite clearly with the cybernetic theory of affect developed by Silvan Tomkins, who also, as described above, equated lower-level activity with sad and higher-level activity with happy mood.[1] The reason for the anomalous

1 Cf. Baruch Spinoza, on whose work Deleuze based much of his concept of affect, also mentions a correspondence between a lessened ability to act and sadness, and between happiness and heightened activity. He writes: "By emotion [affect] I mean the modifications of the body, whereby the active power of the said body is increased or diminished, aided or constrained, and also the ideas such modifications." (Spinoza 1883 [1677]: 130)

moods measured, according to Sturm and her team, was the 'missing half-second' – an amount of time that passed between perception (signal, stimulus) and reaction without it being clear what occurred during this 'lost time'. When her studies on the stressed television viewer (cf. Sturm 1984: 58-65; Sturm 2000) were (posthumously) published, however, they received little attention. Such an empirical approach to viewer research was scornfully dismissed (in the German-speaking world) in favour of an ideology-critical, psychoanalytical theory of visual pleasure (cf. Angerer 1999: 74-99). With hindsight, one can say that Hertha Sturm tried at the wrong time (too early?), by the wrong means, to prove that media such as television have an emotional impact and that this is crucial to the way their verbal and visual content is perceived. What makes this emotional impact so strong, Sturm argues, is a half-second between stimulus and response that makes the (viewer's) response appear somehow 'out of synch'.

Twenty years later, however, this out of synch affect makes a comeback in Brian Massumi's cultural theory of affect, contributing to a veritable 'affective turn' within cultural studies and media theory. "The skin is faster than the word" wrote Massumi (1996a: 217-239) in the mid-1990s, paraphrasing his definition of affect as an intensity belonging to a "different order": "Intensity is embodied in purely autonomic reactions most directly manifested in the skin – at the surface of the body, at its interface with things" (ibid.: 218-219).

Besides the definition of affect proposed by Gilles Deleuze, which is based essentially on Spinoza and his life force (conatus) and which in turn forms the basis for Massumi's work, something else was also at stake here – Massumi actually referred to Hertha Sturm's "missing half-second". For him, however, it became the terrain of affect. According to Massumi, affect is a virtuality which (as a dimension of the potential) facilitates actuality: "(P)astnesses opening onto a future, but with no present to speak of. For the present is lost with the missing half-second, passing too quickly to be perceived, too quickly, actually, to have happened" (1996a: 217-239). Unlike Hertha Sturm, Massumi sees the missing half-second not as empty time, but as a space of time in which too much happens to be perceived.

In the mid-1980s, Deleuze's two books on cinema, The Movement-Image and The-Time Image, initiated a major shift within film theory whose influence extends far beyond the discipline. In Deleuze's theory, perception is the amodal, asubjective part, while memory is a movement which (following Kant) affects itself, performing a kind of self-touching. Image and movement coincide and cannot really be separated. Besides Spinoza, what Deleuze was rediscovering for film and media theory here was above all Henri Bergson's theory of image and perception, a theory that has attained new importance in the context of more recent developments in media technology (cf. Hansen 2004).

With Bergson, we have arrived in the last years of the 19th century, whose second half was positively obsessed with missing time. In *A Tenth of a Second* (2010), Jimena Canales reconstructs the history of the search for and research into this missing space of time, documenting a huge interest within the disciplines of experimental psychology, astronomy, physics and metrology. Sigmund Freud was taken with it, as was Wilhelm Wundt at his institute of psychology in Leipzig. Others like Frances Galton saw the study of the missing split-second as a continuation of craniometry on a different level: those who react slowly have a sensitive personality, those who react quickly are aggressive, more intelligent. Gradually, this interest in measuring individual reaction times, 'personal equating' or 'personal error', also began to appear in art, with noteworthy early examples including Marey's chronophotography and Muybridge's proto-cinematography. As Canales writes:

"The second half of the 19th century was marked by a burst of new research in these topics. [...] Many scientists in France and elsewhere publicised numbers for the speed of nerve transmissions not only in animals, but also in humans. [...] Various instruments came into use: Pouillet's chronoscope; Helmholtz's rotating drums; Arago's chronometers [...]; Donder's noematachometer [...], Marey's drums; [...] In the span of a few years, reaction time experiments shifted from being largely criticized by the scientific community to becoming foundational for a new discipline." (ibid.: 28)

All this began with Hermann von Helmholtz, who wrote in 1850:

"I have found that a measurable amount of time passes as the stimulus exerted by a momentary electrical current on the lumbar plexus of a frog is propagated to the place where the femoral nerve enters the calf muscle." (Schmidgen 2009: 74)

Helmholtz was a student of Johannes Müller who, in 1826, formulated the law of specific sensory energy which states that each sensory organ always reacts to stimuli in its own way, whatever their nature. The eye, for example, reacts to mechanical pressure with a sensation of light. From this, Müller concluded that objective reality cannot be recognized, and that perception is something highly subjective, based as it is on and in the body. In his *Techniques of the Observer* (1992), Jonathan Crary accords a prominent place to Müller because he defined the eye and sight as being dependent on physical stimuli, thus, as Crary emphasizes, overturning the hegemony of a neutral visual apparatus.

But what Helmholtz had discovered with his measurements was not only the disappearance of time, but also and above all the delay of energy – the energy in a muscle is not exerted completely at the moment of the stimulus, "but to a large extent only after that stimulus has already ceased" (Schmidgen 2009: 93). Between stimulation and contraction, then, time (and energy) passes – not much, but enough to be clearly identifiable. The immediacy on which previous assumptions had been based turned out to be "an interval, a period, a space of time both circumscribed and empty – an interim, *du temps perdu*" (ibid.: 93).

Now, the author of *À la recherche du temps perdu* (1922-1931 [1913-1927]), Marcel Proust, had family ties with Henri Bergson, who was married to a cousin of Proust's. Lacking confidence in language, Bergson is said to have accepted only Proust as a writer, whose search for time went hand in hand with a search for its expression in words. At the height of his career, Bergson fought a never-resolved battle with Einstein on the question of time. The philosopher of 'elan vital' never abandoned his position that time is subjective, whereas Einstein famously defined time as independent of individual perceptions.

Henri Bergson understood the world as an image in which we move, ourselves a special kind of image. "There is", he writes, "no perception which is not prolonged into movement" (Bergson 1991: 111). But precisely this moment of not-yet-movement – the interval placed by Bergson between one movement and another – is described by Gilles Deleuze as the moment of affect, and then interpreted by Massumi as the missing half-second.

AFFECTIVE MEDIA TECHNOLOGIES

Up the present, technical and living processes have developed separately. Until far into the 20th century, life and technology trod separate paths and were also kept separate in the field of theory. But media analyses such as that delivered by Donna Haraway in the early 1980s, which have been developed on since by N. Katherine Hayles, Alexander Galloway/Eugene Thacker and others, agree that media can no longer be defined as prostheses which amplify the senses, but that instead, they have attained a new immersive dimension, that they replace our senses, that they also make our senses more intense and more subjective, more intimate and more technical, that perception, memory and affect become a matter of technical modalities. With the cyborg, Haraway introduced a notion intended to render life's reliance on technology conceivable and theoretically graspable. Compared with the period of the *Cyborg Manifesto* in the mid-1980s, the ubiquity of technology has become many times greater: the net has, as Gallagher and

Thacker write, become something elementary – an invisible, all-encompassing precondition for societal, social and mental processes.

Neo-cybernetic approaches today revolve around a question already addressed by George Canguilhem in his essay *Machine and Organism*, where he advocates an understanding of technology as a universal biological phenomenon. In 1946-47, when Canguilhem was giving his lecture, he concluded by saying that for some years now, tests had been underway – at MIT under the name *bionics* – to research biological models and structures that could be used as models in technology. "Bionics is the extremely subtle art of information", writes Canguilhem, "that has taken a leaf from natural life" (1992: 45-69). Today, media are put on a level with insects, rays, instincts, stimuli and reflexes (cf. Parikka 2010), theories of imitation from the animal kingdom are transferred to the political and social crowd and swarm formations by humans. Not that comparisons between the animal and human worlds are anything particularly novel; what is new is the fact that today they are meant seriously, that the anthropological supremacy of the human is no longer capable of upholding itself in the current technical-organic overall structure.

When Canguilhem articulated his appeal immediately after World War II, warning against the reductionism of the rapidly expanding hegemony of cybernetics à la Norbert Wiener, it fell on deaf ears, not unlike Hertha Sturm's 'missing half-second'. Technology and biology, or technology as biology, was not a possible equation, for many reasons. Today, by contrast, one can observe a new liaison resulting from a linking of approaches in biology and information technology, a link established via time, life as time, and an original deferral. In this context, affect can be viewed as an interval that mediates between life and technology, or that facilitates life as technology.

These themes refer to the process philosophy of Alfred N. Whitehead, which has acquired a topical significance, especially for Brian Massumi and other media theorists, as a way of theoretically tackling sensations and perceptions without consciousness and subject. Whitehead defines physical perception as always emotional, calling it a "blind emotion" that is "received as felt elsewhere in another occasion" (Whitehead 1979: 163). This involves not an accumulation of data but always a data relationship. The perceiving subject does not pre-exist the perceived world, but emerges through and in the process of perception: "feeling is subjectively rooted in the immediacy of the present occasion, it is what the present situation feels for itself, as derived from the past and as merging into the future" (ibid.: 163).

The degree to which the philosophy of Whitehead and Deleuze influences current discussions of body, movement and affect is reflected in Erin Manning's book *Relationscapes*. Manning, who works with Brian Massumi at the Sense-Lab in Montréal and publishes a series entitled *Technologies of Lived Abstractions*[2], equates seeing with feeling, with feeling understood as movement-with:

"Affect passes directly through the body, coupling with the nervous system, making the interval felt. This feltness is often experienced as a becoming-with. This becoming-with is transformative. It is a force out of which a microperceptual body begins to emerge. This microperceptual body is he body of relation. While affect can never be separated from a body, it never takes hold on an *individual* body. Affect passes through, leaving intensive traces on a *collective* body-becoming. This body-becoming is not necessarily a human body. It is a conglomeration of forces that express a movement-with through which a relational individuation begins to make itself felt." (Manning 2009: 95)

This passage describes the entire process from perception via affect through to the moving and moved body, also making clear that it is not about individual bodies, but bodies with other bodies, and that these must not necessarily be human bodies, or at least not exclusively.

Manning, with reference to Deleuze and Whitehead, celebrates a body in movement and perpetual mutation whose reactions are controlled via intervals (ibid.: 95). Here, too, the missing half-second makes an appearance. According to Whitehead, subjectivity takes place in this zone of lost time; life "lurks in the interstices of every living cell, and in the interstices of the brain" (Whitehead 1979: 105-106).

Bergson, too, described the brain as the place where the interval resides. In contrast to the scientific wisdom of his time, he declared the brain a *tabula rasa*, a "centre" or "zone" of "indetermination" (Bergson 1991: 23, 28; Schmidgen 2008b: 107-124, here 108). The brain is defined as a gap in time, as an "interval of varying length between stimulus and reaction" (Schmidgen 2008b: 109).

A similar moment can be identified in the cybernetic debate of the mid-20th century, where the concept of reflexes is inserted as a vitalistic element of time into the gap between signal and movement of the machine/automaton. Norbert Wiener borrows Bergson's concept of "duration" and applies it to both living humans and machines:

2 Cf. https://mitpress.mit.edu/books/series/technologies-lived-abstraction

"Thus the modern automaton exists in the same kind of Bergsonian time as the living organism, and hence there is no reason in Bergson's considerations why the essential mode of functioning of the living organism should not be the same as that of the automaton of this type." (Wiener 1948: 44)

In 1951, Max Bense elaborated on this, claiming the time interval as the basis of the commensurability of machine and man in general terms. Except that, unlike humans, computer machines are capable of using (and exploiting) even the smallest interval. The interval in the human organism, empty according to Hertha Sturm or too full according to Brian Massumi, is filled by cybernetic computing machines with a speed of task fulfilment that surpasses human comprehension: "Cybernetic machines exhaust the smallest interval. An addition takes place in five millionths of a second; in five minutes, it can perform ten million additions or subtractions of ten-figure numbers." (Bense 1951: 429-446, here 440)

However, Bense explicitly associates this mechanistic-sounding operational capacity with Bergson's "duration" and sets it apart from steady, Newtonian time. And finally, as Stefan Rieger explains in his cybernetic anthropology, Bense aligns Heidegger's fundamental ontology with Norbert Wiener's cybernetics (cf. Rieger 2003: 146).

PERCEIVING IN MOTION/MOVING PERCEPTION

As well as taking a cue from Bergson's "duration", however, Norbert Wiener was also familiar with reflex theory, especially as formulated by Pavlov. In his cybernetics, he even went so far as to attribute "conditioned reflexes" (Schmidgen 2008a: XXXII) to computing machines. In his eyes, technological and biological machines were capable of "rudimentary learning" (ibid.). The fascination of these machines capable of learning and possessing conditioned reflexes extended far beyond the technical world and was also referred to by Jacques Lacan in his seminar on the ego in Freud's theory to show how far man and machine travelled a common path, diverging only at the last moment, at the point where the machine was supposed to add or subtract "itself as an element in a calculation" (Lacan 1988 [1978]: 52). Up to this point, however – in the grip of the mirror stage – the ego occupies the position of the lame man frequently seen in 15th-century visual art as a counterpart of the blind man.

> "The subjective half of the pre-mirror experience", Lacan writes, "is the paralytic who cannot move about by himself except in an uncoordinated and clumsy way. What masters him is the image of the ego, which is blind, and which carries him. […] And the paralytic, whose perspective this is, can only identify with his unity in a fascinated fashion, in the fundamental immobility whereby he finishes up corresponding to the gaze he is under, the blind gaze." (ibid.: 50)

What, then, is the relationship between this "blind gaze" and the "blind feeling" that is mentioned by Whitehead and that I have linked with affect? Very early on in his work on affect, Massumi found an example that illustrates this especially well, concerning Ronald Reagan and his experience as an actor. This experience made such a deep impression on Reagan that he chose the decisive phrase as the title for his autobiography. In the film *Kings Row* (Wood 1942), Reagan plays a tragic figure who wakes up after a car crash and stammers: "Where is the rest of me?" Returning from unconsciousness, he finds that both his legs are missing, amputated as revenge for the patient's love affair with the surgeon's daughter. So much for the plot. For his purposes, Massumi highlights another aspect, focussing not on the vengeful amputation but on the tipping point as the central moment when Reagan, the actor, stammers his line and this sentence suddenly – for a fraction of a second – becomes real. His legs are no longer there, half of his body is missing: "Where is the rest of me?" What Reagan describes here is the moment that cannot be grasped, but which, as Massumi explains, marks a space where the subject's inability to see itself in motion 'shows' itself: "He is in the space of duration of an ungraspable event" (Massumi 1996b: 18-40, here 29). Defining his approach as "the skin is faster than the word", Massumi began in the mid-1990s to elaborate a cultural theory of affect, introducing it as an intensity that belongs to a 'different order': "Intensity is embodied in purely autonomic reactions most directly manifested in the skin – at the surface of the body, at its interface with things" (Massumi 1996a: 218-239).

Coincidentally or not, the subject here is amputation of the legs, described by Reagan as a real sensation that can easily be linked to the example from *Strange Days*. While Reagan has the momentary experience of having lost his legs, the man in the film experiences himself for the duration of the film (via the Squid) as having legs and running along the beach. Whereas for Massumi, the Reagan example confirms affect's characteristic property of lacking graspable presence, in *Strange Days* this is inscribed onto the body as the experiential zone of the viewer, "at the surface of the body" – the moving images transfer a movement in action into an affective moment whose characteristic property is being not-yet-movement.

With its Squid technology, the film *Strange Days* anticipated a debate that was to begin at the end of the 20th century and focus on the status of the image in general. In *The Language of New Media* (2001) Lev Manovich put forward the theory that digital images always appear on the surface as framed pictures, while below the surface they have long since lost their frames and referential character. "[T]he image, in its traditional sense, no longer exists! And it is only by habit that we still refer to what we see on the real-time screen as 'images'" (ibid.: 100). A few years later, in his *New Philosophy for New Media,* Mark Hansen picked up this change in the nature of images, positing it as a fundamental shift with serious consequences for the viewer. Hansen's approach took the body of the viewer as the new (old) focus: "In a very material sense the body is the 'co-processor' of digital information" (Lenoir 2004: XIII-XXVI). This central task is explained by Hansen in terms of Bergson's definition of the world as an image and the body within it as a special image. According to Bergson, the body's task within the flow of perception is to filter, select, contrast and thus reduce this flow. For as Bergson remarks, the body is not a "mathematical point in space", added to which its "virtual actions are complicated by and impregnated with actual actions", leading to his unambiguous conclusion: "no perception without affection" (Bergson 1991: 60).

So when the body of the man in the wheelchair slips into the image of a man running along the beach past a smiling, waving women – or when his body affectively frames this image – this matches Bergson's description. This implies something that Merleau-Ponty called the "untouchable" (Heller-Roazen 2009: 295): a felt moment that has lost what guarantees the unity of this feeling: an ego. Or in Pierre Janet's description from the late 19th century, quoting Alexandre Herzen on the heart and cerebral activity:

> "It is psychic nothingness, the total absence of consciousness; then one begins to have a vague, unlimited, infinite feeling, a feeling of existence in general, without any delimitation of one's own individuality, without the slightest trace of any distinction between the I and the non-I." (Janet, quoted in Heller-Roazen 2009: 281)

This means that in affect, the interval is radically delayed, a gap opens up whose emptiness or over-fullness touches me where I am not. The digitally produced/induced interval performs itself.

REFERENCES

Angerer, Marie-Luise (1999): Body Options. Körper.Bilder.Medien.Spuren, Wien: Turia + Kant.

Bense, Max (1951): "Kybernetik oder die Metatechnik einer Maschine." In: Ausgewählte Schriften, Bd. 2: Philosophie der Mathematik, Naturwissenschaft und Technik, Stuttgart/Weimar: Elisabeth Walther, pp. 429-446.

Bergson, Henri (1991): Matter and Memory, New York: Zone Books.

Cameron, James (Producer)/Bigelow, Kathryn (Director) (1995): Strange Days [Motion Picture], United States: Lightstorm Entertainment

Canales, Jimena (2010): A Tenth of a Second. A History, Chicago: University of Chicago Press.

Canguilhem, Georges (1992): "Machine and organism." In: Jonathan Crary/Sanford Kwinter (eds.), Incorporations, New York: Zone Books, pp. 45-69.

Canguilhem, Georges (2008): Die Herausbildung des Reflexbegriffs im 17. und 18. Jahrhundert, München: Wilhelm Fink Verlag.

Crary, Jonathan (1992): Techniques of the Observer. On Vision and Modernity in the 19th Century, Cambridge, MA: MIT Press.

Deleuze, Gilles (1988[1970]): Spinoza, Berlin: Merve Verlag.

Hansen, Mark B. N. (2004): New Philosophy For New Media, Cambridge, MA: MIT Press.

Heller-Roazen, Daniel (2009): The Inner Touch. Archaeology of a Sensation, New York: Zone Books.

Herbertz, Richard (1980 [1905]): Die Lehre vom Unbewussten im System von Leibniz, Hildesheim/New York: Georg Olms Verlag.

Kelty, Christopher/Landecker, Hannah (2002): "Das Schauspiel der Zelle. Unsterblichkeit, Apostrophe, Apoptose." In: Marie-Luise Angerer et al. (eds.), Future Bodies. Zur Visualisierung von Körpern in Science und Fiction, Wien: Springer, pp. 21-47.

Kristensen, Stefan/Merleau-Ponty, Maurice (2012): "I. Körperschema und leibliche Subjektivität." In: Emmanuel Alloa et al. (eds.), Leiblichkeit, Tübingen: Mohr Siebeck, pp. 23-36.

Lacan, Jacques (1988 [1978]): The Seminar of Jacques Lacan: Book 2: The Ego in Freud's Theory and in the Technique of Psychoanalysis 1954-1955, Cambridge: Cambridge University Press.

Lenoir, Tim (2004): "Foreword." In: Mark B. N. Hansen (ed.), New Philosophy For New Media, Cambridge: MIT Press, pp. XIII-XXVI.

Manning, Erin (2009): Relationscapes, Movement, Art, Philosophy, Cambridge, MA: MIT Press.

Manovich, Lev (2001): The Language of New Media, Cambridge, MA: MIT Press.

Massumi, Brian (1996a): "The Autonomy of Affect." In: Paul Patton (ed.), Gilles Deleuze, A Critical Reader, New York: Blackwell, pp. 217-239.

Massumi, Brian (1996b): "The Bleed: Where Body meets Image". In: John C. Welchmann (ed.), Rethinking Borders, Minneapolis: University of Minnesota Press, pp. 18-40.

McLuhan, Marshall (1964): Understanding Media. The Extensions of Man, New York: McGraw-Hill.

Ott, Michaela (2010): Affizierung. Zu einer ästhetisch-epistemischen Figur, München: edition text + kritik.

Parikka, Jussi (2010): Insect Media. An Archaeology of Animals and Technology, Minneapolis: University of Minnesota Press.

Proust, Marcel (1922-1931 [1913-1927]): In Search of Lost Time / Remembrance of Things Past, New York: Random House.

Rieger, Stefan (2003): Kybernetische Anthropologie, Frankfurt am Main: Suhrkamp.

Schmidgen, Henning (2008a): "Fehlformen des Wissens." In: Georges Canguilhem (ed.), Die Herausbildung des Reflexbegriffs im 17. und 18. Jahrhundert, München: Wilhelm Fink Verlag, pp. VII-LVIII.

Schmidgen, Henning (2008b): "Leerstellen des Denkens. Die Entdeckung der physiologischen Zeit." In: Bernhard Dotzler/Henning Schmidgen (eds.), Parasiten und Sirenen. Zwischenräume als Orte der materiellen Wissensproduktion, Bielefeld: transcript, pp. 107-124.

Schmidgen, Henning (2009): Die Helmholtz-Kurven. Auf der Spur der verlorenen Zeit, Berlin: Merve Verlag.

Spinoza, Baruch (1883 [1677]): Ethics. Part 3. On the Origin and Nature of the Emotions, New York: Dover Publications.

Sturm, Hertha (1984): "Wahrnehmung und Fernsehen: die fehlende Halbsekunde." In: Media Perspektiven 1, Stuttgart: Intendant des Hessischen Rundfunks, pp. 58-65.

Sturm, Hertha (2000): Der gestreßte Zuschauer. Folgerungen für eine rezipientenorientierte Dramaturgie, Stuttgart: Klett-Cotta.

Wallis, Hall B. (Producer)/Wood, Sam (Director) (1942): Kings Row [Motion Picture], United States: Warner Bros..

Whitehead, Alfred North (1979): Process and Reality: An Essay in Cosmology, New York: Free Press.

Wiener, Norbert (1948): Kybernetik, Cybernetics: or Control and Communication in the Animal and the Machine, Cambridge, MA: MIT Press.

Trading

The noisy motions of instruments

The performative space of high-frequency trading

ANN-CHRISTINA LANGE

In a recent article in *London Review of Books,* Donald Mackenzie (2014a) describes the construction of fiber-optic cables and how micro wave technology is being developed at significant costs to facilitate high-speed financial trading activities. What is being built is communication lines between different financial exchanges to achieve the shortest distance and thereby transmission time, when issuing an order. The newest fiber-optic cable was finished last year and crosses the Atlantic Ocean to cut off a few milliseconds in the transmission of data from New York to London. The cables are a symptom of a fundamental digital transformation within the financial sector – one that might not best be described with reference to the notion of performativity as it has been presented from an actor-network theory/ social studies of science field.[1]

Michel Callon and Donald MacKenzie have been considered the founding fathers of this approach. They describe how models and calculative devices used by traders and financial experts to estimate the price of an instrument indeed co-produce the very price they attempt to measure. More generally this means that the theory or model do not only describe a given phenomenon in an objective fashion but in some cases helps to create it. MacKenzie empirically investigates "the incorporation of economics (a theory, model, concept, procedure, data set etc.) into the infrastructures of markets" (2006: 19). In *An Engine, Not a Camera* he studies how certain financial theories and models became authoritative and indeed shape the financial markets in quite fundamental ways. Economic models

1 Research for this paper was supported by a 'Crowd Dynamics in Financial Markets' Sapere Aude Grant from the Danish Council for Independent Research (http://info.cbs.dk/crowds).

are, according to MacKenzie, an engine that produce empirical facts, rather than a camera representing such facts.

This has been a highly important and valuable approach to make sense of financial markets and what would at first sight seem to be an obvious choice when investigating digital finance and its performative aspects. Today around 30 per cent of the total trading volume is executed by high-speed algorithms in the UK and around 60 per cent in the US (cf. Foresight Final Report 2012: 19). One would expect to find that such material devices would have a range of assumptions written into them, which would affect how the financial markets function. In fact, MacKenzie states that the deepest kind of performativity is achieved when economics (concepts, models and assumptions) are incorporated into algorithms, procedures, routines, and material devices (cf. 2006: 19). However, as I will show in this chapter, the algorithms used to process the financial orders via the high-speed cables and micro wave connections is not to be considered faithful to such concepts, models or assumptions. Especially, in the sub-field formally known as high-frequency trading (HFT), algorithms are used to execute orders faster than human perception and seem to interact in quite unpredictable ways. Based on ethnographic observations and interviews inside the field of high-frequency trading and algorithmic trading, I aim to demonstrate the more 'noisy' motions that determine the performativity of digital finance. In order to do so, I turn my focus towards the relational interaction and spatial formations that at once condition and create digital finance.

This approach poses a methodological challenge as how to study the interaction among algorithms without reference to a conscious human subject. In order to deal with this challenge, I propose to look at the topological formations at play as they have been defined by Lury et al. from a media studies perspective. The first section defines the notion of topology and explains its suitability to the field of HFT. Secondly, I describe the market microstructure and regulatory changes that gave rise to the development towards HFT. The third section investigates three features that condition the spatial relations of digital finance, namely, the exploitation of time-delay, the interaction order between algorithms and the use of special order-types (i.e. how orders are executed). The chapter ends with a brief conclusion.

NOTES ON A TOPOLOGICAL APPROACH TO HIGH-FREQUENCY TRADING

The financial technologies and infrastructures used to send orders and receive them, have been widely studied from an ANT/Callon-inspired approach of technical devices. Ethnographies have been conducted where scholars followed and described these devices, their history, and the institutions in which they are embedded (cf. Muniesa 2008; Preda 2009; Lenglet 2011). However, the rise of algorithms as an interacting agent in financial trading has implications for how to study their embeddedness. MacKenzie et al. (2012) describe trading strategies designed to identify and exploit other traders' algorithms (algo-sniffing). As a consequence, sophisticated algorithms are designed to hide their intentions from the market. The performativity thesis does not suffice to explain the spatial relations that now perform or shape the interaction that plays out between adaptive algorithms. The human traders and their infrastructure that used to be the object of ANT-oriented research and which might be said to be embedded *within* a specific spatial setting, has disappeared. MacKenzie explains himself:

> "Clearly, Latour and Callon's 'actor network theory' (e.g. Latour 2005) and Callon's actor-network economic sociology (e.g. Çalişkan and Callon 2009 and 2010) are pertinent when most market participants are algorithms. Actor-network theory is prepared to use the term 'actor' to refer to non-human entities such as algorithms. While this usage remains controversial, it would plainly be a mistake to treat trading algorithms simply as the faithful delegates of human beings. As Adrian Mackenzie notes, '[a]n algorithm selects and reinforces one ordering at the expense of others' (2006: 44), but that ordering may not be the one its human programmers intended." (MacKenzie 2014b: 3)

This means that a study of the performativity of digital finance cannot be limited to a single-sided field study – like observing the behavior inside the trading room only. The spatial setting might simply not be taken for granted. Law (1999) has developed a topological approach to space, which he defines as post-ANT arguing that objects cannot be studied without taking into account the production of the spaces in which these objects circulate. Celia and Moor (2010) developed a topological approach focusing on media-related issues. What these approaches share is the focus on spatial formations that go beyond networks and differ from what could be imagined as a place or physical (often urban) site (like the open outcry trading pit). However, what is specific about the approach developed by Lury and Moor is that it allows for what Hansen (2015: 34) refers to as an "operationality of media culture", which he further defines as "the capacity of today's media machines to generate appearances of worldly sensibilities, to directly manifest the world independently of any synthetic operation of a subject or a consciousness".

The present chapter extends and builds upon this inspiration with the aim of reapplying the concept in order to study spaces topologically different from that of the open outcry pit (i.e the space that once condition and is conditioned by the interaction between high-speed algorithms). Michael and Rosengarten (2012) identify a topological space as when points (entities or events) that are distant can also be proximal. Dispersed links might be drawn together (by contraction) as if they were in one place. Knorr Cetina and Bruegger have shown that "the screen brings that which is geographically distant and invisible near to participants, thus rendering it interactionally present [...]" (2002: 909). The performative space of digital finance is defined by external parameters (such as the physical condition of locating computer servers close to or inside the exchange to minimize transaction time and to access data faster than other market participants) which gives rise to internally generated spatial relations between different kinds of financial actors (such as high-speed algorithms trading in front of slower market participants).

As I mentioned above, and as Ignacio Farias and Anders Blok (2016: 12) also points out, investigating topological formations involves a methodological challenge: a study of the performativity of digital finance cannot be limited to one single-sided field site. In order to not only operationalize but also test the application and value of a topological approach to the study of finance, I use a combination of methods which compose a "multi-method" (Law 2004; Holmes/Marcus 2006). The methods include: qualitative interviews, observations and content analysis of documents. The data I draw upon here consist of ethnographic observations and interviews conducted inside a New York-based HFT firm near Wall Street. This data is supplemented with 50 interviews with a broad range of actors involved with HFT, including programmers, software developers, broker-dealers, exchange officials, investment bankers, and regulators (conducted in Copenhagen, London and New York since October 2013). The ethnographic work focused on the daily practices and conversations amongst HF traders, including how traders and programmers trade at their desk while monitoring preprogrammed algorithms, but the ethnographic work also followed their activities around designing and building high-frequency trading algorithms. The data offer insights into the ways in which traders reflect upon their own trading behavior and that of participants of other markets.

THE RISE OF HIGH-FREQUENCY TRADING

The transformation of the space of finance into fully automated systems started when the exchanges became electronic. Most literature dates the technological development toward fully automated trading back to the 1970s (cf. McGowan 2010; Hanson/Hall 2012). In 1971, the NASDAQ became electronic and introduced an electronic quotation system via which competing market makers could trade securities. In 1976, the New York Stock Exchange (NYSE) introduced its Designated Order Turnaround system, allowing for the electronic transmission of orders to buy and sell securities (cf. Burr 2014). This gave rise to what is called programme trading, which exploited the spread (the difference between the best offer to sell and the best bid to buy) between S&P 500 equity shares and the futures market. In the 1990s, with the introduction of Electronic Communications Networks (ECNs), this practice became widespread across different financial markets. The ECNs provided direct market access and eliminated the need for brokerage firms to facilitate trading inside the pit. In 1998, the SEC introduced the Regulation Alternative Trading Systems, which authorized ECNs. The intention was to restrict the monopoly that the NYSE and NASDAQ had gained by automating their order-matching systems. As a result, more computer systems were developed to facilitate the entry and execution of orders electronically via the use of algorithms.

However, HFT evolved more specifically as a response to both technological developments and regulatory changes. McGowan (2010), for instance, sees the rise of HFT as a direct result of the enactment of a set of US rules known as Regulation National Market System (Reg NMS). These were passed by the US Securities and Exchange Commission (SEC) in 2005 and fully enacted in 2007 in order to strengthen the US equity markets. In part, Reg NMS was a direct response to a problematization of the behavior of specialists and locals, who used to serve as market makers (meaning that if there are insufficient buyers or sellers, they maintain order flow by trading with their own capital). In 2004, however, a group of NYSE specialists were accused of not maintaining a fair market. Against this backdrop, Reg NMS aimed to secure fair competition and decrease the discretionary power of specialists (cf. Lewis 2014: 96). Among other things, this resulted in an updated rule prohibiting "trade-throughs", i.e. the execution of trades at prices outside of the national best bid and offer (NBBO). By emphasizing the need for immediate and automatic order execution at the NBBO, Reg NMS not only targeted the discretionary power of specialists; in effect, it enabled ultra-fast market participants to exploit price discrepancies (caused by a time delay) between different exchanges.

More recent factors that have buttressed the rise of HFT include the narrowing of spreads. In 2001, US stock exchanges were permitted to quote prices in decimals instead of fractions in order to increase liquidity. This move is known as decimalization, and is widely acknowledged to have affected the overall functioning of all financial markets, as it reduced the minimum tick size or spread from one-eighth of a dollar to one cent (cf. Jennings 2001; Chen/Chou/Chung 2009). This further decreased the importance of specialists on the exchanges and eventually led to a vast increase in algorithmic trading. In this new and more liquid market structure, the institutional traders were splitting up orders executed by algorithms in order to reduce their market impact and to execute trades faster and at better prices (cf. Burr 2014).

These changes all acted as catalysts for the increase of very fast, ultra-low-latency techniques, such as the use of high-speed computer programs for the execution of orders with a high level of frequency. The increased use of high-speed algorithms and the trading strategies used has led the regulators to define this as a practice with its own definition. The US Securities and Exchange Commission (SEC) defines HF traders as "professional traders acting in a proprietary capacity that engage in strategies that generate a large number of trades on a daily basis" (Securities and Exchange Commission 2010: 45). A working group under another US regulatory body, the Commodity Futures Trading Commission (CFTC), has proposed a broader definition that focuses more on the trading activity itself than on those engaged in it:

> High frequency trading is a form of automated trading that employs:
>
> (a) algorithms for decision making, order initiation, generation, routing, or execution, for each individual transaction without human direction;
>
> (b) low-latency technology that is designed to minimize response times, including proximity and colocation services;
>
> (c) high speed connections to markets for order entry; and
>
> (d) high rates of orders or quotes submitted. (CFTC 2012)

HFT is both defined as a specific organizational practice, proprietary trading and as a specific use of technological tools to execute trading strategies. The later aspect is of great importance for the present chapter- low latency technology means that algorithms are designed as rather dumb and simple entities that are supposed to read the market in real-time. In order to be fast, they can only process very limited information. This point supports the argument that the assumptions, theories and concepts written into such devices might have a limited impact on the financial markets in general.[2]

EXPLOITATION OF TIME-DELAY

The data I have collected demonstrate some common traits defining HFT strategies. One key factor is that HF traders are able to exploit the price differences between exchanges. One HF trader explained that "we profit from correlation and hedge ourselves. We exploit securities that move in sync due to them being tightly hedged". This means that the traders issue orders and when that order is "filled" – if it bought what it was asked – some of the traders' other algorithms would react to the price information. Similarly, a programmer from a research firm specializing in HFT stated that "what [HF traders] do is to empirically measure the correlation between securities. Virtually every pair of securities in the market has a positive correlation".

So, in most cases HF traders speculate on the correlation between different financial products, which means that if the price of one stock moves up or down it is very likely that another stock will do the same. It might be that they are traded with the same index and have the same probability of following the price moves of the whole index or that they are dependent upon the same factor, such as oil prices or political initiatives etc. HF traders speculate on being faster than the price move between two highly correlated financial instruments. In the words of a CEO of a small HFT firm in New Jersey:

> "People are in the business of propagating that price impact to other securities [...] So what we are doing, basically, is transferring the price impact of one security to a large set of other securities. That's where liquidity comes from, we're sourcing liquidity from other securities and transferring them to a specific future contract and then we're taking the price impact from that future and spreading it to other securities."

What the CEO characterizes as spreading is exactly this idea about profiting from the time delay between different exchanges. This may materialize in various ways. The algorithms used by HFT firms can be divided into three basic types.

---

2 For a more detailed description of the transition from the open outcry trading pit to high-frequency trading see Borch et al. (2015) and Borch and Lange (2016).

The first type is called a spreader. It buys one instrument and sells another with as little internal latency as possible. For instance, the algorithm buys shares traded at the NYSE and futures traded at the Security Futures Exchange in Chicago (OCX). There is a 13-millisecond delay in the transmission of data from New York City to Chicago. This delay creates arbitrage opportunities of exploiting the price discrepancies between Shares traded at the NYSE and futures traded at the OCX. When the price of a share on the NYSE and its corresponding futures contract at OCX are out of sync, the algorithm would buy the less expensive one and sell it on the more expensive market.

The second type of algorithm is a scalper. This type of algorithm earns minimum incremental profits in a single instrument by buying and selling that same instrument many times a day across different trading venues.

This type of strategy is described by a trader who designs his algorithms to exploit slower market actors:

"What you do [in one HFT strategy] is making markets. So you are offering and bidding competitively on one exchange. That way when someone pays the spread, when someone buys the offer or sells the bid, they are first to know because they got filled. If they are part of that sell or buy, they find out immediately and that gives them the time-jump to go on to the next exchange and if they sold they can buy on that exchange and make profit on the difference."

So, here, HF traders act upon a specific price move and at the same time participate in the resulting price move. They do so by constantly issuing and cancelling orders to be in front of the price move that they aim to profit from (cf. Lange 2016). Another trader, also acting CEO of a major HFT firm in Chicago, described a similar strategy:

"The fact that I am participating on the market gives me time to speed-jump because the information was a fill and that preempts market data significantly [...] and when you receive that fill, that's what triggers your hedge orders essentially, to these other exchanges."

As one trader explained:

"We take advantage of the noisy motions on instruments where you'll have price fluctuations that are not linked to any meaningful information, and in that case you know you can profit from that noise". This involves reading the depth of the order book (that display the bid- and ask-prices) and taking advantage of the probability that "there's a large resting size at a certain level."

The third type of algorithm is a market maker which seeks to quote bids and offers in the same instrument and makes the market buy and sell according to certain basic rules to control the risk in the same way that a scalper seeks to take advantage of noise in a single instrument. This type is explained to be a rather passive strategy since the algorithms are in fact doing nothing but waiting for the order to come in and act upon that information. In this case the HF trader does not act as a buyer or seller but acts more like a middle man that makes the buyer and seller meet.

INTERACTING ALGORITHMS

However, the story of HFT is more complicated than the exploitation of time differences between exchanges. As I explained previously, order execution works as messaging to the market and algorithms are designed to detect and counteract other order executions – so for example, if the algorithm puts in an order it would immediately react to the information that it gives to the market. However, if the market moves up, it waits instead of automatically executing a buy order not to get "spooked". Similarly, larger investors with what the traders defined as "real money" (i.e. institutional investors, banks and pension funds) have developed randomization tools to hide their buy or sell intentions from the market and thereby prevent being read/predicted by HFTs. Normally they slice the order size in a way so only one-third of the order size would be revealed to the market every other second. This type of executing is done with the use of what is called an iceberg order (cf. Lenglet 2011; Lange 2016).

As a consequence, sophisticated tools are built by HF traders to detect such market moves initiated by larger investors in order to act upon or counteract expected price moves. A programmer explained his activity as "seeing if there are other people obscuring the signal, i.e. the edge that you are trying to capture, and part of that is doing constant market recognos [i.e. pattern recognition]". Another trader offered a specific example of this kind of market recognos, the purpose of which is to detect the rhythms in buying and selling interests that the rest of the market is not aware of or does not know about:

"The shop that I started trading at, first thing they did – you know, I came from an automation background – was that they introduced me to markets and they immediately said, 'we know that banks are using iceberg orders', you know, hidden size, and they wanted to be able to detect the hidden size, because they are market makers and hidden size changes the typology of the market in ways that they can't readily identify. So the first thing I did when I entered this business was to build an iceberg detector. And that is very much that kind of recognos where you're looking for patterns that indicate other high-frequency or micro-structure activity and base decisions on that."

What this means is that algorithms are designed to detect patterns of other algorithms with the purpose of trading in front of them. Thus a hierarchy exists between different 'species' of trading algorithms – between the slower and the faster ones. Iceberg orders are a device that is both conditioned and conditions how financial interaction plays out in space and time.

THE INFLUENCE OF ORDER-TYPES

The last aspect that characterizes the transformation of the performance of financial space is the use of special order types. How traders send a message to the market (execute orders) is determined by which order types they use. The different order types are offered by the exchanges. Up and until the implementation of rule mentioned above, the Reg NMS only limit orders and existing market orders. A market order is an order that the trader uses to buy or sell an asset immediately at the best available and current price. A market order is set to execute a trade immediately with no time restrictions or the price range within which the order can be executed. The risk is that the bid and ask prices are a lot higher or lower than the current price at which the order is executed because of the time delay. A limit order on the other hand is an order used by the trader to buy or sell a set number of financial instruments at a specified price range. This means that if the price range for the specific asset (the difference between the bid and ask price is too big) the order will not be executed – it will be cancelled (rejected). If it is executed within the price range the order "got filled". Limit orders are also used to limit the length of time an order can be outstanding before being cancelled.

One aspect of the Reg MNS was that every order had to go to the exchange offering the best price. This effected a proliferation of more or less advanced order types (execution commands) reaching far beyond basic market and limit orders. More than 200 different order types now exist. Exchanges imitate and invent new and different order types in order to differentiate themselves and to serve and attract HF traders to trade at their exchange. HF traders are considered as the liquidity-providers and makes sure that the exchange always have someone to be on the other side of a given bid or offer (which means that the trade will be executed at their venue and they will earn the transaction fee).

Direct Edge's "hide-not-slide" order type is a good example. The basic principle at US stock exchanges is that the trader who places the order first at the best current price is the one being allowed to execute his trade first. But in some cases the rule is difficult to maintain for instance in a situation where no seller is there to fill the buy order. To avoid this situation the order should be routed to the next exchange with a matching sell order. However, traders can place an order to be executed only at one specific exchange, so in the case of no matching sell order, the offered price will slide to a lower level until it gets filled. The hide-not-slide order type offer traders to issue a trade that is not displayed in the order book so that the price will not slide, but it will wait until a matching sell order comes in and only then will it be displayed. This means that the hidden order has a time advantage over other traders as that order will be executed before new incoming orders. HFTs can actually jump the queue. Apart from such special order types, rebates are offered to HF traders by most exchanges – a reduction in the fees they would normally have to pay per order executed – a feature the HF traders are highly dependent upon as they execute a high level of orders every second.

What is established here looks like a rather complex feedback structure where high-speed trading algorithms condition a specific market microstructure, without which it cannot exist. The trading algorithms that have been presented here in fact condition and shape the social structures in which they are also embedded.

CONCLUSION

The models and theories that lay the ground for the performativity thesis presented by Callon and MacKenzie were designed with the purpose of representing, predicting or even forecasting the movements of the market. High-speed algorithms on the other hand, are pre-programmed to read price moves directly as they appear in the order book. Based on a dynamic interaction with other financial actors, high-speed algorithms work by issuing an order to see how other actors (human traders and other algorithms) react to that order and is pre-programmed to issue another quote based on that information. This means that financial devices are not performative in the sense described by Mackenzie and Callon, as they do not work to increase its 'predictive fit' (cf. Stark 2011).

Instead complex spatial relations are constituted where each financial actor (HFT-algorithms, execution algorithms, the exchanges matching engine etc.) exploit the inefficiencies of other species and in the process, creates new inefficiencies, again exploited by yet another kind of actor. A financial algorithm is not simply an automated rule but a device that is both conditioned and conditions, which exploits inefficiencies and at the same time, creates the interdependence of the different kinds of algorithms. It is from this background that the performative space of HFT is probably best understood as a topological one composed by interacting agents. Thus the feedback relation between interactive algorithms does not only apply to structurally correlated instruments but also to the interactional algorithmic responses between the exchanges' matching algorithms (and order types), institutional investors' and broker-dealers' executing algorithms and other HFT algorithms.

What makes topology a distinctive approach to the study of social dynamics vis-à-vis other approaches to the study of finance is that it provides tools for the understanding of the financial markets that reach beyond the study of its actor-networks or agent-based interaction within the trading room. What is offered in this chapter is a presentation of how the rise and function of algorithmic trading strategies and execution technologies contribute to the making and reshaping of financial markets. Algorithms both act within and outside the market; they are both ahead of the price move they aim to profit from while also creating it. Such deformation comes with and enacts a particular spatialization of finance, in which distances and temporalities are continuously redrawn or folded into each other, complicating notions of inside and outside, distance and proximity. The elementary component of physics and non-linear algebra might inspire the analysis of how dispersed actors create an economic pattern opposed to an Euclidean geometry, to which the prevailing economic system aspires (Deleuze/Guattari 1980; Delanda 2002).

REFERENCES

Borch, Christian/Hansen, Kristian Bondo/Lange, Ann-Christina (2015): "Markets, bodies, and rhythms: A rhythmanalysis of financial markets from open outcry trading to high-frequency trading." In: Environment and Planning D: Society and Space 33/6, pp. 1080–97.

Borch, Christian/Lange, Ann-Christina (2016): "High-frequency trader subjectivity: emotional attachment and discipline in an era of algorithms." In: Socio-Economic Review, forthcoming.

Burr, Andrew C. (2014): "Cancelling the Order: How High Frequency Traders are Disrupting the Derivatives Market, and What the Regulators Can Do to Stop Them." December 1, 2014 (http://works.bepress.com/andrew_burr/1)

Callon, Michel (ed.) (1998): Laws of the Markets, Oxford/Malden, MA: Wiley-Blackwell.

Chen, Wei-Peng/Chou, Robin K./Chung, Huimin (2009): "Decimalization and the ETFs and futures pricing efficiency." In: Journal of Futures Markets 29/2, pp. 157-179.

Delanda, Manuel (2002): Intensive Science and Virtual Philosophy, London/New York: Continuum.

Deleuze, Guattari/Guattari, Felix (2003[1980]): A Thousand Plateaus: Capitalism and Schizophrenia (B. Massumi, trans.) London: Continuum.

Foresight (2012): "The Future of Computer Trading in Financial Markets (2012), Final Project Report." In: The Government Office for Science, May 2, 2016 (https://www.gov.uk/government/uploads/system/uploads/attachment_data/file/289431/12-1086-future-of-computer-trading-in-financial-markets-report.pdf)

Hansen, Mark B. N. (2015): "Topology of sensibility." In: Ulrik Ekman/Jay David Bolter/Lily Diaz/Morten Sondergaard/Maria Engberg (eds.), Ubiquitous Computing, Complexity and Culture, London: Routledge, pp. 33-48.

Hanson, Thomas A./Hall, Joshua R. (2012): "Statistical arbitrage trading strategies and high frequency trading." October 30, 2014 (http://dx.doi.org/10.2139/ssrn.2147012)

Holmes, Douglas/Marcus, George (2006): "Cultures of expertise and the management of globalization: Toward the re-functioning of ethnography." In: Aihwa Ong/Stephen J. Collier (eds.), Global Assemblages: Technologies, Politics, and Ethics as Anthropological Problems, Oxford: Blackwell Publishers Ltd, pp. 235-253.

Jennings, Robert (2001): "Getting 'pennied': The effect of decimalization on traders' willingness to lean on the limit order book at the New York Stock Exchange." In: NYSE Working Paper 2001–01.

Knorr Cetina, Karin/Bruegger, Urs (2002): "Traders' engagement with markets – A postsocial relationship." In: Theory, Culture & Society 19/5-6, pp. 161-185.

Lange, Ann-Christina (2016): "Crowding of adaptive strategies: Swarm theory and high-frequency trading." Forthcoming.

Law, John (1999): "After ANT: Complexity, naming and topology." In: The Sociological Review 47/S1, pp. 1–14.

Law, John (2004): After Method: Mess in Social Science Research, London: Routledge.

Lenglet, Marc (2011): "Conflicting codes and codings: How algorithmic trading is reshaping financial regulation." In: Theory, Culture & Society 28/6, pp. 44–66.

Lewis, Michael (2014): Flash Boys: Cracking the Money Code, London: Allen Lane.

Lury, Celia/Moor, Liz (2010): "Brand valuation and topological culture." In: Melissa Aronczyk/Devon Powers (eds.), Blowing Up the Brand, New York: Peter Lang, pp. 29-52.

MacKenzie, Donald (2006): An Engine, Not a Camera, How Financial Models Shape Markets, Cambridge, MA: MIT Press.

MacKenzie, Donald (2014a): "Be grateful for drizzle." In: London Review of Books 36/17, pp. 27-30.

MacKenzie, Donald (2014b): "Sociology of algorithms: High-frequency trading and the shaping of markets." Forthcoming.

MacKenzie, Donald/Beunza, Daniel/Millo, Yuval/Pardo-Guerra, Juan (2012): "Drilling through the Allegheny Mountains: Liquidity, materiality and high-frequency trading." In: Journal of Cultural Economy 5/3, pp. 279–96.

McGowan, Michael J. (2010): "The rise of computerized high frequency trading: Use and controversy." In: Duke Law & Technology Review 16, pp. 1–24.

Michael, Mike/Rosengarten, Marsha (2012): "HIV, globalization and topology: Of prepositions and propositions." In: Theory, Culture and Society 29/4-5, pp. 93-115.

Preda, Alex (2009): Framing Finance, Chicago: The University of Chicago Press.

Stark, David (2011): The Sense of Dissonance: Accounts of Worth in Economic Life, Princeton, NJ: Princeton University Press.

Encrypting

Performing encryption

SUSAN KOZEL

A political, performative and affective landscape is revealed in this chapter as a way of approaching the topic of performing the digital: from the macro of the upheaval caused by Edward Snowden's revelations of mass data surveillance to the micro of a phenomenological account of a crisis following an artistic performance using mobile media. "Performing Encryption" is a response to working as a dancer and philosopher with mobile networked digital media that can be read as a part of a larger narrative of transitioning from one state to another. The state of viewing the fine interweaving of mobile technologies in our lives as a positive expression of social choreographies gives way to a state where it is impossible to regard the potential for surveillance and capture of daily activities as anything but provocative, troubling or even threatening. The risk is not just the "capture all" aspects of dataveillance, but of increasing control over gestural and affective exchanges in urban life. In saying networked technologies, I point not just to mobile phones but also to the Cloud and the Internet-of-Things which, in combination, are potentially devastating from the perspective of embodied agency. This narrative of questioning and transition is typical of others arising at the beginning of a century, let alone a millennium. It is no longer possible to avoid asking what we have created. And how we can respond to the technological and cultural conditions of our world.

Throughout these reflections performance is defined as emergent bodily practices, in the context of mobile networked media. The linking of performativity with emergence emphasises the generative potential of performance – an ontological dimension of bringing something into being that was not there previously. Performance is a play between the escape and re-containment of movement or expression, the transformation of something that was previously virtual into being.[1] Emphasising the emergent qualities of performance can seem wonderfully liberating and creative, but the reality is relational: we perform with digital media, at the same time as acts of watching and regulation are performed upon us by systems and by people. New expressive and relational ways of performing with and through the digital may emerge from the use of mobile media but simultaneously new forms of surveillance arrive. The Deleuzian term "luminosity" has been taken up by Angela McRobbie (2009) to replace surveillance, describing contemporary performances of gender within a wide range of technologies (from fertility manipulation to social media). She identifies how the "theatrical effect" of luminosity acts like "a moving spotlight", softening, dramatising and disguising "the regulative dynamics" of media and politics (McRobbie 2009: 54). Significantly, when one is in the luminous glow of such a moving spotlight, one sees and sees oneself as one is seen.[2] Mapping this term further into digital cultures luminosity resonates on many levels: from moving images or data suspended in digitally illuminated screens to the act of shedding light on what may have been obscured in shadow, it lends paradoxical qualities of both magic and pervasive watching to performance. Performances of encryption will be explained throughout this chapter, but for now it is possible to say that they are emergent counter practices for manipulating the degrees of luminosity, playing with focus and legibility, brightness and obscurity. Not confined to theatrical or dance practices, these are performances within digital cultures which intend to ambiguate or obfuscate bodily data that might otherwise be clearly transmitted by our devices.

THREE WHISPERS

Three whispers begin this chapter, three phenomena within digital cultures. Faithful to the affective qualities of the verb 'to whisper,' they circulate inner states or personal stories. These whispers radiate states of immanence and intimacy into political and social spheres.

---

1 For an extended discussion of performance defined in terms of emergence, see Kozel 2012.

2 This "seeing-seen" can be understood as a basic reflective loop or chiasm of phenomenology (Kozel 2007).

1. Whisper App (2012-2014)

The Whisper app surged in popularity and then exploded dramatically. An application running on mobile phones, it attached itself to the Twitter phenomenon by offering something its much bigger counterpart lacked: anonymity. It's app store entry loudly promised "If you have ever had something too intimate to share on traditional networks, simply share it on Whisper!"[3] Perhaps the shout should have been a clue to tensions between the poetics and politics of the app. Whisper asserted that the short messages, "sent by millions of people around the world and viewed by billions of people each month", were anonymous and private (Ball 2014). It was as if the opening of a protected space, a bubble for sharing but not owning intimate thoughts, met a need within users of social media.[4] People's postings were personal, poetic, funny and at times tormented; these were thoughts and "confessions" that would normally be self-censored prior to posting on social media platforms (cf. Lewis/Rushe 2014a). Intensely felt, translated into words, released into the cloud, then circulating separately from the bodies that generated them: Whisper messages might seem like perfect examples of autonomous wisps of affect, more autonomous than tweets because of their supposed anonymity. Did these affective states really circulate freely from the people who generated them? Sadly no, the affects and their bodies were soon reunited.

Two stages of deception enacted by Whisper were reported by journalists writing for *The Guardian*. The first was that despite claims to anonymity, the messages and their metadata (such as date, time, GPS coordinates, language) were recorded and stored indefinitely by the service provider. The metadata held by Whisper revealed geolocation within a "fuzzed" zone of approximately 500 hundred metres which, when stored over time, tells a lot about the person using the app. Whisper also circumvented users who disabled their geolocation services by extracting their approximate location information from IP data (cf. Lewis/Rushe 2014a). The second level of deception should not come as a surprise, but it did because many social media users continue to separate the social applications they live with on a daily basis from the corporate ownership of these apps. Whisper adopted a standard Silicon Valley business model for digital start ups which is to "collect and package user data in the pursuit of more venture capital funding, with an eye to a multibillion-dollar exit" (Ball 2014). Soon after learning that their privacy abuses would be published, Whisper quietly changed its privacy terms of services to say that location can fairly easily be determined

3 Cf. https://whisper.sh/

4 Other confessional apps include Secret and Yik Yak.

and they might reveal this to others based on the law, safety, technical reasons and research studies and corporate transactions (cf. Lewis/Rushe 2014b).[5]

A performance perspective on the Whisper phenomenon reveals a clash between expression and monetisation: a growing desire to translate inner states ('secrets') into images and texts, and to circulate these via mobile networked devices, collides with the political reality of apps and platforms provided by multinational corporations that value the mass accumulation of such information.[6] On a discrete level, post by post, such expressions may seem like intimate ephemera but once affective expression meets big data there can be massive implications for bodily, affective and social freedom. Jaron Lanier, in his book *Who Owns the Future*? (2014) asks us why we are surprised. What did we expect when multinational corporations offered us services for free? (Gmail, Google, facebook, Twitter, Whisper, etc).

> "The NSA forced its way into those private computers in secret, but why did anyone think that near unanimous consumer support of a titanic surveillance industry would not eventually morph into a surveillance state?" (Lanier 2014: xiii)

2. The Whisper(s) Wearables Project (2002)

The second whisper involves a little time travel. Just back to 2002, but the shifts in political and corporate practices relating to user generated digital media in the decade between these whispers was seismic, leaving embodied expression compressed and vulnerable. The *Whisper(s)* garments were embedded with biometric sensors and haptic outputs to facilitate the exchange of non-verbal communication.[7] In 2003, at an installation open to public participation, one participant expressed a concern that she did not want to have her heartbeat recorded because she feared what might be done with the data.[8] At first I did not understand what she meant – "done" with the data? Then she explained: "if it reveals that I have a

---

5 There is some disagreement over exactly when the revised terms were drafted, prior to or after Rushe and Lewis threatened to publish. Whisper insists it was drafted a few months prior. See: http://whisper.sh/privacy

6 SnapChat is another example of an app acting as a conduit for extraordinary amounts of intimate bodily communication, particularly amongst teenagers. See: http://www.snapchat.com

7 See: http://whisper.iat.sfu.ca

8 This was mentioned briefly in *Closer* in a chapter devoted to discussing wearables and the *Whisper(s)* research project (Kozel 2007: 304).

health defect and you record it, it might it end up in the hands of an insurance company and I might be denied coverage." This seemed to me to be a fabric woven of quite a few "what ifs?": if we recorded it (we did not); if the data was legible and intelligible (it was not); if it was stored (it was streamed live and never archived); if the storage was in the Cloud (we had no link to any Cloud); and if the data could be accessed by someone else (how could it?). I calmed her by assuring that we did not store data, and even if we did it would be meaningless because we poeticised it, transposed the bio data into visuals or haptic output, we amplified and remapped, in effect, we distorted and obscured the truthful biodata.

3. The Whisperers, Interactive Installation (2013)

The third whisper acts to ground the performance of intimate communication unequivocally within a social and political context. An installation called *The Whisperers* created by designer Christopher Koelsch (based on historian Orlando Figes book by the same name) delves into the devastating impact of wide scale surveillance in Stalinist Russia. While some of this was electronic, a large swathe of the snooping was done by people watching, listening to, and recording the actions and words of others. Often family members informed on each other, and neighbours could not be trusted. Koelsch designed and built a structure, roughly 4mX4m, resembling a mid 20th century Soviet tenement building with exposed pipes, windows, and vents. Set in a gallery space, when a visitor whispered into any part of the structure they received information about those who dwelled inside. The visitor could not enter into the private space of the imaginary inhabitants of the building but was able to speak and listen. Sensors and electronic recordings of sounds were used to animate the installation, giving the sense that "walls can have ears, the vents in your floor can have eyes, and the pipes in your bathroom are dark tunnels snaking through an atmosphere of conspiracy".[9] Viewing this installation from the perspective of performing encryption, attention shifts from those who listen to those who know they are being surveilled. What did they do? They whispered, played the radio, ran the tap, avoided having conversations near doors or windows, or refrained from talking at all. Linguistic, gestural and affective expression became subtle plays of ambi-

9 See: http://christopherkoelsch.com/whisperers.html

guity and distortion, with the dismaying predominance of somatic[10] and performative practices of self-censorship.

What can we extract from these three disparate but similarly named materialisations of digital culture? From the *Whisper* app it is possible to read a large-scale breach of trust and the need to protect ourselves without completely censoring our digitally mediated expression. From *whisper(s)* the wearables project, we see how the poeticising of bio-data to obscure actual physiological information is a play of ambiguity: this was a first glimpse of what I am now calling performing encryption. And from *The Whisperers* we see a picture of a society forced to rely almost exclusively on analogue, physical, verbal and somatic performances of encryption. This last whisper is the cautionary tale: the desperate repression that can result from pervasive systemic surveillance. Together these three cultural events act as a prologue to this chapter, grounding the dilemma of how performers and researchers into performativity can preserve digital expression while maintaining affective privacy. In more politically straightforward terms, the dilemma is how to facilitate a cultural shift away from passive acceptance of dataveillance (data surveillance) in order to reclaim agency over our bodies and digital traces. This is ontological because it goes beyond ways of acting or thinking, it relates to new materialisations that may take the form of human actions, political constructs or technological configurations. This is the terrain for performing encryption.

A POLITICAL ONTOLOGY

This is not a manifesto or a call to action – at least not yet. It is too simple to identify a difficult political situation and point to solutions from the world of performance. It is important first to deepen and, in fact, to trouble the task a little further by revealing one of the most worrying and at the same time hopeful dimensions: how bodies performing with mobile media (assemblages of technologies and flesh) are both complicit in politically suspect digital practices and able to produce counter-practices. This can be understood if we look to the political ontology of dance proposed by Andre Lepecki in *Exhausting Dance* (2006), and

10 Somatic in this instance refers to internal bodily reactions, not to formalised systems of somatic therapies. A somatic level of knowledge and reaction is deeply embedded in the body, it is frequently pre-reflective and pre-conscious, and makes itself known in a range of ways that are difficult to clarify in words or standard medical mesurements (cf. Kozel 2013).

then transpose his argument into performances, both artistic and social, with digital networked devices.

Lepecki constructs a two-layered argument by describing how dance is not only related to politics but can be ontologically and politically embedded in the formation of repressive political events. In terms that are relevant to performing encryption, he witnesses rearrangements and refigurations of dance in relation to politics. "[R]earrangements of the very notion of dance" refer not only to "the position of dance in relation to politics, but of the ontological and political role of movement in the formation of those disturbing events" (Lepecki 2006: 16). Experimental self-critique in dance can act as a performative critique of wider political regimes, in particular the dancer's "participation in the general economy of mobility that informs, supports and reproduces the ideological formations of late capitalist modernity" (ibid.). Mobility in Lepecki's argument refers to an interpretation of modernism as based on kinetic motion to the exclusion of stillness. I expand his argument from theatrical stage dance to a wider set of participatory and performative practices, but also render it more specific by transposing it into a set of digital cultural practices: mobile networked media and the unavoidable dark side of surveillance that underpins their use for artistic or personal expression. No longer dealing with the late capitalist modernity of Lepecki's argument, we are squarely in what can be called neoliberal "surveillance capitalism" (Zuboff 2015: 75). The implication is that choreographic or performative experimentation with mobile media does not just document, critique or analyse the ideological and economic formation of the times, but also participates in its construction. The result is an unavoidable loss of innocence but also a potential upsurge in political agency.

This shift in agency, still emerging, is contingent upon transformed attitudes toward performative experiments with technology, and toward mobility in general. I have called this a shift from "closer to closure", referring to my own stance in *Closer: Performance, Technologies, Phenomenology* (2007) which was much more optimistic regarding the potentials for corporeal expression and transformation when bodies became "close" to technologies.[11] This is not to say that the premise of this book was apolitical or naive, but that the performative experiments in the 1990s and early 2000s upon which the philosophical discussion was based were enacted in a far more utopian sense of the digital world. The affective cloud in which we lived at that time was still coloured by the feeling that digital connectivity was inherently democratic and inclusive. The minia-

11 The shift from closer to closure is the premise my forthcoming book, *Social Choreographies* (expected 2017).

turisation and wearability of technologies were, in particular, seen to be both fascinating and liberating, impacting not just communication or entertainment, but mobile modes of being. This is reflected in sociologist John Urry's writing from that period in which he recasts the social sciences by developing the new mobilities paradigm. There are unavoidable performative or choreographic qualities to his description of the convergence between mobile technologies and physical travel:

"Physical changes appear to be 'de-materializing' connections, as people, machines, images, information, power, money, ideas and dangers are 'on the move', making and remaking connections at often rapid speed around the world." (Urry 2007: 5-6)

The rapid play between materialization and de-materialisation, communication and connection, provided by mobile technologies in his writing is mostly "a positive category" with the exception of his critiques of hypermobility (ibid.: 7).

Other notable instances of transformed attitudes towards digital cultures include Sherry Turkle, who describes her own turning point in her book *Alone Together* (2011) and Jaron Lanier who refers to his own reversal of position, from being a of web pioneer to saying he was, in effect, mistaken and it has turned out quite differently from the heady utopian ideals of the 1970s (cf. Lanier 2014: xiv-xv). In an adjacent but related field, Angela McRobbie's presents a "self-critique" to her earlier stance that feminist subversive strategies could exist within neoliberal consumer culture. With a strong emphasis on media production in the form of micro-publishing, she asks "Just how oppositional were these seemingly subversive practices?" (McRobbie 2009: 2-3). These shifts reveal not just political transformations but are imbued with ontological dimensions captured by Lanier's characterization of the time in which we now live as a moment where "humanity is deciding *how to be* as our technological abilities increase" (Lanier 2014: xviii; emphasis added). *How to be* is a fundamentally ontological category because it pertains to being, *how to perform* is the dynamic mode within such an ontological state. The political ontology shaped by performative practices with networked technologies spans the thin membrane between artistic performance and the mobile choreographies of daily life, and will gain a greater degree of urgency with the expansion of the Internet-of-Things (IoT), promising 25 billion connected devices by the year 2020 (or more, depending on which authoritative prediction you choose to read). Ontologies are not fixed, of necessity they transform. The rest of this chapter is devoted to charting such a transformation.

AFFEXITY: PASSAGES & TUNNELS

The artistic research that generated the ideas in this chapter is *AffeXity*, part of a larger research project addressing contemporary archiving practices called Living Archives.[12] A collaboration initiated by screen dance artist Jeannette Ginslov and myself in 2010, *AffeXity* began with a convergence of three questions: one political, one technological and one from dance. The dance question we set ourselves was whether it is possible to improvise (with bodies and cameras) by attending to affective sensibility rather than emotional states or formal patterns. The technological question was whether Augmented Reality (AR) browsers running on devices such as mobile phones and iPads could support the visual, affective, kinaesthetic and participatory qualities we desired. The political question was how to respond to the warning that we ignore affective manipulations in our cities "at our peril".[13] A beta version of a performance/installation, *AffeXity: Passages & Tunnels,* premiered in 2013 at the Re:New Festival in Copenhagen.[14]

We used the AR browser Aurasma because it was at least free and very user friendly if not open source, and it used visual triggers to download media.[15] The visual images (acting as QR codes) were frames from the video material, thus creating a play across stillness and motion because the video was suspended in the display of the device as a transparent layer through which the static trigger image could be viewed. These trigger images of various sizes and shapes were attached to the damp brick outside walls of the Nikolaj Kunsthal, formerly a church built in the 19th century but now a Contemporary Art Center in Copenhagen. When visitors held mobile devices up to the images, archival video imagery was downloaded onto their devices. This produced a multi-layered choreography across the still images, the video and the multiple devices of the group of people standing together. Added to this archival choreography was the presence of dancer Wubkje Kuindersma, performing live in the space between the still imag-

12 Held at Malmö University, funded by the Swedish Research Council. See:http://livingarchives.mah.se

13 The citation comes from Amin/Thrift (2002). It can be read in combination with their assertion that urban life offers "performative improvisations which are unforeseen and unforeseeable" (ibid.: 4).

14 Artists/designers: Susan Kozel, Jeannette Ginslov, Daniel Spikol, Jacek Smolicki, Camilla Ryd. See: http://livingarchives.mah.se/affexity-passages-and-tunnels

15 In 2015 Aurasma was purchased by Hewlitt Packard. See: https://www.aurasma.com

es, the devices and the people. Some of the archival imagery was of her improvising in Copenhagen two years previously.[16]

WHAT HAPPENED NEXT? (A PHENOMENOLOGICAL INTERLUDE)

Several events transpired immediately following this performance.

1. I realized on a somatic level that surveillance is the dark side of archiving
2. The implications of Edward Snowden's revelations continued to reverberate though political and personal realms.
3. I burnt out.

Juxtaposed with the unexpected success of *AffeXity: Passages & Tunnels* was the unease I felt with our entire research programme. No longer just channeling affect into artistic content for the project and opening access to archival material, I was forced to recognize the wider affective cloud permeating the entire project. In short, mobile technologies felt like a beacon to inner states, making them vulnerable to detection, tracking, recording and analysis. By whom? I couldn't say with any specificity, but the power dynamics were impossible to ignore and as a long time feminist (concerned with agency) and phenomenologist (concerned with corporeal experience) I found myself unwilling to peel away the last layers of unintelligibility, of protection, existing between inner bodily states and total transparency in the face of the ever expanding and complexifying network of connected devices and sensors. Slavoj Žižek (2013) explains the relocation of power behind the transparency of functionality:

> "Here are two telltale words: abstraction and control. To manage a cloud there needs to be a monitoring system that controls its functioning, and this system is by definition hidden from users. The more the small item (smartphone) I hold in my hand is personalised, easy to use, "transparent" in its functioning, the more the entire setup has to rely on the work

16 The description of *AffeXity: Passages & Tunnels* in this chapter is condensed to support this argument, but documentation exists on the Living Archvies website and the following scholarly articles discuss it from various perspectives: on affect and the devising process (Kozel 2012), on affect, phenomenology and somatics (Kozel 2013) on archives and participatory performance (Kozel/Spikol/Smolicki 2014).

being done elsewhere, in a vast circuit of machines that co-ordinate the user's experience. The more our experience is non-alienated, spontaneous, transparent, the more it is regulated by the invisible network controlled by state agencies and large private companies that follow their secret agendas." (Žižek 2013)

In terms of "rearrangements" of the ontological status of dance, I shifted squarely to the position where the political and ontological complicity of our artistic work had to be acknowledged. So I stopped. And I fell ill, suffering from the typical condition of the media-saturated, multi-tasking, always-connected life. I burnt out. And I dropped my mobile devices as if they had burnt my fingers.

ENTER ENCRYPTION

> The Snowden leaks made people all over the world feel violated. We don't know who has read our most tender emails. It feels bad, and if we ever get used to that feeling, that would feel even worse.
>
> LANIER 2014: XIII

Here Lanier captures the beginnings of an affective approach to the politics of digital surveillance: it feels bad. Affect is more than feeling, but can begin with feeling, with an attention to body states. Then it ripples outwards to an exchange of forces and intensities between bodies of all sorts (organic and inorganic). Some affect theory points towards transcending physical corporeality, but much philosophical writing on affect is helpful to cultivate a sense of materiality that can reveal the ever more subtle and complex ways bodies exist and recombine in relation to technologies.[17] That technological systems are in themselves performing bodies is no longer a fantastical metaphor. In Edward Snowden's famous video statement from June of 2013, produced by filmmaker Laura Poitras, he revealed the extent of the data-snooping impacting every digitally networked being on the planet and invoked a physical metaphor for the US National Security Agency: "the NSA targets the communications of everyone, it ingests them by default, collects them in its system, filters them, analyses them, stores them"

17 I do not have the space to expand upon affect here but have discussed it at length in Kozel (2012; 2013).

(Snowden 2013). The NSA is described as a body: digesting, remembering, somatic. The metaphor for the system is bodily, the data captured is of actions and attitudes. Both system and data are bodily performances. Yet, it is no longer enough to state in a general way that performativity exists practically and metaphorically across bodies and systems. Speaking with greater precision: the performativity of capture is mirrored by a performativity of encryption.

The call to encrypt echoes widely, I map it and transpose it into the discourses and practices of digital performance. When Snowden addressed the SXSW conference in 2014, appearing by videoconference through seven proxies, with heavily lagged visuals and audio he urged everyone to use encryption software: "Our networks have been designed with surveillance in mind" (Snowden 2014a). His many videoconferenced presentations have become his own telematic performances of "From Russia with Love", calmly clarifying the extent of the mess we are in. In this one he explained the threat of predetermination, reminding us that the NSA would "figure out uses for the data down the road". From a performance perspective this is future performance, not performance as a repetition of the past or revelation of the present, but the performance of predetermination. It is a sinister rehearsal of the future because we participate unknowingly.

The political dimensions of encryption are by no means stable: neither rights nor practices are enshrined. The latest versions of Apple and Google's mobile operating systems are now encrypted by default, while other popular messaging services, such as WhatsApp and Snapchat, also use encryption. This has prompted calls for action both for and against strong encryption from activists and government officials.[18] Glenn Greenwald, the journalist and lawyer Snowden contacted to release his story, urges everyone to encrypt. Indeed he almost missed out on connecting with Snowden entirely because it took him so long to install encryption software (cf. Greenwald 2014). Tim Berners-Lee, famously the founder/developer of the protocols that established the internet, asked Snowden at SXSW what he would do to design a new security system. An open question that invited either a technological or socio-political response, Snowden's answer was "accountability" – about people not technology. He pointed to the soft side, the fleshy side: disruptive actions such as encryption and whistle-blowing. Meanwhile, British PM David Cameron and his government, notorious for attacking personal data privacy, demanded in the wake of the 2015 shootings in Paris at Charlie Hebdo and the Jewish Deli: "In our country, do we want to allow

18 Since writing the first draft of this chapter, the Apple-FBI legal procedures have dominated news in the first part of 2016, with the FBI demanding that Apple provide 'backdoors' or ways to hack into encrypted communication on iPhones.

a means of communication between people which we cannot read?" (Ball 2015). His words assume that communication is already readable and read, that encryption and ambiguity are not practiced in any materially significant way. Yet Snowden pointed out in his testimony to the EU on data security that the primary challenge of mass surveillance is not merely how you collect the communications but how you interpret, understand and analyse them (cf. Snowden 2014b). There is much noise in the system.

AFFECT TO AMBIGUITY TO ENCRYPTION

If there is much noise in the system, then what happens if we deliberately and, with full awareness of our political ontology, perform this noise? Returning once again to performance practices, I extract a stage of the *AffeXity: Passages & Tunnels* artistic process that was key to understanding the crucial link between affect and ambiguity. This moves us a little closer to understanding how encryption might be performed.

As choreographers know, the use of archival dance material is as constrained by copyright as any archival project in cultural heritage – perhaps even more so because of the many layers of attribution (costumes, music, dance, choreography, makeup, lighting, scenography). In conversation with Martin Larsen and Uffe Borgwart of the Royal Danish Theatre in Copenhagen we considered what material we could safely use. One of the archiving principles in the Living Archives project is that archives don't have to be traces from the distant past. With pervasive, some might say chronic, documentation through social media a performance perspective opens up the possibility of including what we call "the archive of 10minutes ago." Borgwart, responding to this, suggested that we video rehearsals for a new piece being choreographed at that moment. He obtained the permission of Corpus, the young experimental ballet of the Royal Danish Theatre, and the consent of dancer Oliver Starpov to video his solo. This became the basis of 'The Oliver Series'. Borgwart did the original shoot of Oliver's lyrical and very beautiful solo, performed to Satie-like music. He sent the raw video to Ginslov who produced a series of three edits which she called "Corpus Solo 01", "Corpus Solo 02" and "Corpus Kelp Arms".[19]

19 Oliver's material can be found between minutes 2.31-2.57 in the documentation of *AffeXity: Passages & Tunnels.* Note the extended arms inviting the adjective "kelp" referring to rippling seaweed. See: http://livingarchives.mah.se/2013/10/affexity-passages-tunnels-re-new-2013

The transformation of affect, movement and sound that occurred through these edits was striking. The affective choreographic and editing vocabulary Ginslov had been developing for two years manifested itself through the qualities of distortion and ambiguity to such an extent that the original dropped away and was replaced by iterations with substantially different affective tones. The point is not to raise the sticky question of the relation between archives and interpretation, far more significant from the perspective of this argument was the performance of ambiguity through media manipulation. Ambiguity and affect were revealed to be intimately entwined, and one way they played out was through distortion. The Oliver series helped me to understand, through artistic practice, the philosophical point that *affect is already a play of ambiguity* because it exists in liminal states. Affect is ambiguous because it is in a perpetual and dynamic state of exchange or transition, it is impossible to pin affect down to one person or one definable emotional state: it is an "inventory of shimmers, of nuances, of states, of changes […] of the borderline nature of human existence" (Barthes 2005: 77). The ambiguity of affect is due to its dynamic qualities but also due to an innate obscurity: an "opacity in transparency" (ibid.: 100). If we add to the qualities of shimmering and opacity the awareness that the ontological condition of affecting and being affected is not passive, it is possible to say that ambiguity can be performed.

The step from the performance of affect through ambiguity to the performance of encryption was a simple one to make. Recalling the context of political surveillance captured by Koelsch's installation based on Figes' book *The Whisperers*, specific contemporary examples can ground what may seem like an abstract aesthetic argument. In an interview with journalist Carole Cadwalladr, Laura Poitras makes explicit the parallels with contemporary digital surveillance, when each person's Google search terms are a psychogram of their thoughts. "I'm so careful about that", says Poitras, and she provides a small glimpse of her own practices: "I use different computers for different uses." And throughout Berlin, the city where Poitras now lives in order to obtain a modicum of personal privacy, "there are people working on ways to fight the technology with technology; who've devised the crypto equivalent of what, in the former German Democratic Republic, was done by turning on the radio or running the tap." (Cadwalladr 2014: 8).

Saying that affect is already a play of ambiguity means that it is imprecise, unintelligible or differently intelligible. This sense of creative or expressive unintelligibility, one might even say meaningful unintelligibility like running a tap of water to obscure one's words, is a thread linking affect and ambiguity to encryption.

PERFORMING NOISE

Earlier I referred to the three whispers as a prologue, but this entire chapter can be seen as a prologue for a much wider research programme. This becomes clearer as I expand a working definition of encryption. Encryption is a set of practices that render confidential communication unintelligible, or intelligible only to those with whom we desire to communicate (Piper/Murphy 2002). Thus far, this is quite a standard definition but here it becomes more refined for performance and affective exchanges: *encryption is not a wall, it is a re-patterning, or a distortion, of a flow*. There is a reason for using the expression performing encryption rather than performing cryptography: cryptography refers quite broadly to the history and science of keeping information or communication secret, while encryption is a stage within this process. A plaintext (readable message) is encrypted by means of an encryption algorithm (also called a key) into incomprehensible ciphertext, it is then decrypted by the designated recipient. Classic encryption systems were symmetrical, meaning the sender and the receiver had to know each other and use the same key, but the contemporary encryption that underpins all confidential internet transactions (such as banking) is asymmetrical, meaning the sender and receiver do not need to know each other (cf. Piper/Murphy 2002: 4-8). Currently, the performance research being developed alongside further versions of *AffeXity* is a workshop series called *Performing Encryption* which aims to expand the poetic implications of asymmetric encryption systems at the same time as trying to bridge the gulf between computational encryption processes and physical performance. Even the fairly open mode of a participatory performance felt too sealed to explore encryption. An exploration and development of the philosophical foundations, the politics and the performativity requires workshops conducted in a way that merges performance and interaction design methodologies. We have begun by trying to break open what is essentially the black-box process of digital encryption, and to address the psychological and technological hurdles to encryption.[20] Of course this description in itself sounds cryptic, not just because of the early stages of the research but due to the very nature of the topic.

Matthew Fuller and Andrew Goffey, authors of *Evil Media* (2012) would say that this venture is entirely pointless because of the sophistication of dataveillance algorithms and forensic computing technologies (cf. Fuller/Goffey 2012: 31). Feeble, body-based attempts to obfuscate, loop, ambiguate or slide across

---

20 For a description of the workshop and an argument that closely follows the one in this chapter see Kozel (2016).

registers are futile in the face of big data capture, storage over time and data-mining. No doubt this is true, and yet Snowdon reminds us:

> "Hey, we can spy on everybody in the world, all at once, it will be great we will know everything. [...] But the reality is when the NSA did it they found out it didn't work. [...] The stored mass of all metadata [...] two independent white house investigations revealed it has no value at all. It is never helpful." (Snowden 2014a)

So there is a fissure. A crack. In terms of affect this is enough. It may be a crack in the soil, or a ripple of dissonance in cultural discourse. It is a shimmer. A small opening for performing otherwise.

REFERENCES

Amin, Ash/Thrift, Nigel (2002): Re-imagining Cities, Cambridge: Polity.

Ball, James (2014): "Think you can Whisper privately? Think again." In: The Guardian, March 2, 2016(http://www.theguardian.com/commentisfree/2014/oct/17/whisper-private-secret-sharing-app-anonymity)

Ball, James (2015): "Secret US cybersecurity report: encryption vital to protect private data." In: The Guardian, March 2, 2016(http://www.theguardian.com/us-news/2015/jan/15/-sp-secret-us-cybersecurity-report-encryption-protect-data-cameron-paris-attacks)

Barthes, Roland (2005): The Neutral (R. Krauss/D. Hollier, trans.), New York: Columbia University Press.

Cadwalladr, Carole (2014): "Berlin's digital exiles: where tech activists go to escapte the NSA." In: The Guardian, February 15, 2016 (http://www.theguardian.com/world/2014/nov/09/berlins-digital-exiles-tech-activists-escape-nsa)

Figes, Orlando (2008): The Whisperers: Private Life in Stalin's Russia, London: Penguin.

Fuller, Matthew/Goffey, Andrew (2012): Evil Media, Cambridge, MA: The MIT Press.

Greenwald, Glenn (2014): No Place to Hide: Edward Snowden, the NSA and the Surveillance State, London: Hamish Hamilton.

Kozel, Susan (2007): Closer: Performance, Technologies, Phenomenology, Cambridge, MA: MIT Press.

Kozel, Susan (2012): "AffeXity: Performing affect using augmented reality." In: Fibreculture Journal Issue 21, February 15, 2016(http://twentyone.fibrecul

turejournal.org/fcj-150-affexity-performing-affect-with-augmented-reality/# sthash.p4FDqFIx.dpbs)

Kozel, Susan (2013): "Somatic materialism or is it possible to do a phenomenology of affect?" In: Site Journal of Art, Philosophy and Culture, Issue 33, pp. 153-167.

Kozel, Susan (2016): "From Openness to Encryption." March 2, 2016 (https://medium.com/the-politics-practices-and-poetics-of-openness/from-openness-to-encryption-a57e49917a88#.cc4jrbeq2)

Kozel, Susan/Spikol, Daniel/Smolicki, Jacek (2014): "Affective and Rhythmic Engagement with Archival Material: Experiments with Augmented Reality." In: NODEM Proceedings, Warsaw.

Lanier, Jaron (2014): Who Owns the Future? London: Penguin.

Lepecki, André (2006): Exhausting Dance: Performance and the Politics of Movement, London: Routledge.

Lewis, Paul/Rushe, Dominic (2014a): "Revealed: how Whisper app tracks 'anonymous' users." In: The Guardian, February 2, 2016(http://www.theguardian.com/world/2014/oct/16/-sp-revealed-whisper-app-tracking-users)

Lewis, Paul/Rushe, Dominic (2014b): "Whisper app rewrites terms of service and privacy policy." In: The Guardian, February 2, 2016(http://www.theguardian.com/world/2014/oct/16/-sp-whisper-privacy-policy-terms-of-service)

McRobbie, Angela (2009): The Aftermath of Feminism: Gender, Culture and Social Change, London: Sage.

Piper, Fred/Murphy, Sean (2002): Cryptography: A Very Short Introduction, Oxford: Oxford University Press.

Snowden, Edward (2013): Video statement on NSA surveillance, filmed and edited by Laura Poitras, March 2, 2016(http://www.theguardian.com/world/2013/jun/09/edward-snowden-nsa-whistleblower-surveillance)

Snowden, Edward (2014a): Teleconference presentation, SXSW Conference 10.04.2014, March 2, 2016(http://www.theguardian.com/world/2014/mar/10/edward-snowden-nsa-sxsw-live-stream)

Snowden, Edward (2014b): Testimony to the EU Parliamentary Committee on Surveillance 04.08.2014, February 15, 2016 (https://www.youtube.com/watch?v=3f8Lunf1a2w)

Turkle, Sherry (2011): Alone Together: Why we expect more from technology and less from each other, New York: Basic Books.

Žižek, Slavoj (2013): "Edward Snowden, Chelsea Manning and Julian Assange: our new heroes." In: The Guardian, February 15, 2016 (http://www.theguardian.com/commentisfree/2013/sep/03/snowden-manning-assange-new-heroes)

Zuboff, Shoshana (2015): "Big other: surveillance capitalism and the prospects of an information civilization." In: Journal of Information Technology 30, pp. 75-89.

Protesting

Mobile phone signals and protest crowds

Performing an unstable post-media constellation

OLIVER LEISTERT

> Only crowds have acted, only crowds have changed things.
> PIT SCHULTZ

THE CAPTURE OF AFFECT AND HIGH FREQUENCY MODULATION

Twenty years after Pit Schultz' praise of the exclusive agency of the crowd,[1] the relation between the individual and the crowd has become a matter of digital processing. New levels of affective production, captured by new levels of continuous over-coding of the resulting affective intensities into regimes of equivalence and control, become the trajectories of our media-technological environment under the aegis of contemporary capitalism. Today, sociality amongst local peers passes through data silos on the other side of the planet. Never before have topologies of sociality been put under such a geo-spatial spreading.

Prior to this spread routing, sociality undergoes multiple and rigid formatting procedures to fit into digitally viable regimes of expression. Contemporary subjects, who are constantly mediating their modes and modalities of expression with the corporate social media platforms' interfaces and their mobile devices,

1 "Techno: Psycho-Social Tumult" published in the archives of the 2nd *next five minutes* website, from 1996. See: http://www.tacticalmediafiles.net/n5m2/media/texts/schultz.htm

are amassing and stratifying this dispersed and dissected socius as if it were a collective search for a new metastability.

This reciprocal processing and production of affective signals between subjects and machines indicates a new formation of techno-regimes of expressions that tap into previously uncharted sources for soft social engineering and control. Likewise the multi-faceted and complex dependencies that ultimately rest on such algorithmic processing of social relations are also important. One such dependency is the availability of individually-modulated electromagnetic signals. The Universal Mobile Telecommunications System (UMTS), the 3rd generation mobile cellular system based on GSM, operates in Europe somewhere in the range of 1900 MHz (uplink) and 2100 MHz (downlink). It is via such frequency modulations that contemporary subjects turn into *physically isolated* and anonymous, but *bodily connected* and personalized subjects.

This split, where affective modulation takes place independently of physical co-presence, addressing the person by frequency modulation while enforcing the subjects' physical isolation, effects the becoming of crowds today. Following Spinoza, affects support or diminish the agency of bodies. Affect modulates a body's ability to relate and its spectrum of relationalities. The becoming of crowds used to rely on affective relations between physically co-present bodies; yet in the paradigm of digital connectivity, affect seems to have abandoned the necessity of physically-bodily co-presence.

Its translatability into computable vectors of individual control, deterritorialized by pulsed modulations of high frequencies, asks for a new investigation into the problem of the crowd. What is the effect of multiple physical-bodily co-presences in combination with individualizing mobile media circuits of affect? How can a highly individualizing media technology be turned into a crowd (war) machine? This text is my first exploration of such complex mobile media assemblages, whose functionalities install both harsh limits and new paths for collective enunciations as presented by the problem of the crowd.

My aim is to investigate if and how, 'post-media', a concept that Félix Guattari coined somewhere in the late 1970s after his Radio Alice pirate radio experiences, is applicable to the emergence of crowds in the age of ubiquitous mobile data. Guattari was rather optimistic in regard to new media constellations after or in parallel with the era of centralized mass media. In his intense search for devices that would help the individuated subject of enunciation to become a collective assemblage of enunciation with others, he regarded emerging media technologies, such as the Minitel in France, as at least promising candidates for "a site of desire driven by dissensus yet composing a collective diagram of commonalities" (Genosko 2013: 15). Post-media for Guattari, then incorporates the possibilities for "innovative forms of dialogue and collective interactivity" that finally would lead to "[t]he multiplication to infinity of 'existential operators', permitting access to mutant creative universes" (Guattari 2009: 299). Post-media assemblages, in other words, can provide means for existential reconfigurations opening new universes of references for the affected subjects via dissensual collective problematizations.

Working with the notion of post-media today means to transpose and rework it into the contemporary media-technological situation. It is obvious that the precalculated pseudo-individual 'choices' that corporate social media or other sophisticated platforms offer, have nothing in common with Guattari's post-media concept. The search for post-media devices for the production of collective assemblages of enunciation certainly has not become easier since ubiquitous mobile data connectivity and corporate data silos have inscribed themselves into the very core of contemporary post-fordist subjectivities, as instigators of a governmental soft-imperative of participation (cf. Wiedemann 2011; Bröckling et al. 2011).

But as I will show, a new perspective, a decentering of perspectives, becomes possible once different components of the mobile phone infrastructure are taken into account, such as the frequency modulation components, and conceptually understood as possible post-media devices. While this certainly seems to be an odd change of view of mobile phones and their infrastructures, it nonetheless follows the idea that an escape, a *line of flight,* in Guattari's terminology, from the perpetual over-coding of desire by the capitalist production of subjectivity, involves a destabilization of the dominant signifying regimes that capture affect for algorithmic modulations.

THE TRANSFORMATION OF PROTEST CROWDS INTO MEDIA ASSEMBLAGES: PROTEST CULTURES BETWEEN CONJUNCTION AND CONNECTION

Much has already been written about the new protest cultures that are saturated with digital and mobile communication technologies and how these are changing the very nature of activism and protests (cf. Dencik/Leistert 2015; Milan 2015; Renzi 2015; specifically for mobile phones and protest cf. Leistert 2013). New temporalities, modes and models of protest and its (non-)organizational structures have emerged, intensifying the crisis of the old institutional models and producing tensions with those of established large social movements. This culture of *new* new media activism has embraced networked mobile digital devices without hesitation. It has integrated all kinds of digital tools into its workshop arsenal and employs the vast corporate database empires it relies on as scattered, voluminous containers, to be filled with all kinds of jabber, desires and aspirations. In addition, this new mobile media protest culture frequently occupies central urban plazas, thereby temporarily overthrowing the order of consumerism and installing a new public.

This around-the-clock, week-long presence of thousands of protesters on the occupied squares show and emblematize their societal situation of joblessness or precariousness and their yearning for a new collectivity. Nonetheless, such enduring presences of large crowds in urban centers, not long ago an exceptional situation for most European cities, soon lost their evening TV news-value and were degraded into just another snapshot of young people without jobs.

This recurrent attraction of central squares for these new protest cultures indicates that at their dissensual core, they are very much imbued by a rather traditional political imaginary, which materializes through its traditional concept of hierarchic territories: to seek out the central squares as incubators of (non-/anti-) politics echoes a modern idea of power as locatable and centralized. This locational expression of modernity manifested itself at many recent and enduring protests in Europe and North America.

Such a choice of territorialization stands in odd contrast to a second emblem of the new protest cultures: the negation of representation, or at least a tremendous doubt, and often refusal of the installed representational or authoritarian regimes along with their configuration of discourses.

It is interesting to look at these two elements combined – the magnetism of central urban squares and the denial of the classical modern model of representation – because together they mirror the current and devastating conditions of habitat and the miserable and demeaning quality of political discourse for the population: while it has become altogether impossible for most younger individuals to live in centrally-located (shared) flats, the hegemonic discourse distributed permanently through all media channels has nothing to offer but the old zombie tales of happiness through consumption and thus continues to poison and alienate language, perception and empathy. In short, it cuts the young people off from pragmatic experiments of collective enunciations.

In this sense, the agglomeration of bodies – sitting, singing, lying, sleeping, moving and slacking on central urban places, while they shuffle data around the globe with wiping digit gestures – echoes a desire to escape the confinements of solitary apartments and mini-flats in the urban outskirts, and become re-affected by the proximity and intensity of a public multiplicity. At the same time, the dominant signifying regimes that adhere to the capitalist mode of semiotization –

naturalizing capitalism's hold over life – have lost their addressees. One could say that the newly-built territory (square) is primarily constituted by an inversion of quality and quantity: the production of a new space, made of and for proximate bodies and affective resonance, overcomes the scarcity of inhabitable room, imposed by capitalist gentrification and displacement, while a language that is able to resonate with the emerging collectivity of bodies, that invites new experimental modes of expression, such as collective polymodal uttering, begins to be pragmatically invented within the duration of the protest.

BODILY CONJUNCTION VERSUS BODILY CONNECTION

Guattari relates the emergence of the body to the possibility of a process of singularization:

"When the body emerges as such [...] it's because we find ourselves at a certain crossroads of articulation between, on the one hand, assemblages that are potentially productive of a singular possible and, on the other hand, social assemblages, collective facilities that expect a certain normalizing adaptation." (Guattari/Rolnik 2008: 409-410)

The emergence and endurance of unordered bodies thus correlates with an oscillation, a shift from ordered, structured and normalized signifying semiologies to a-signifying semiotics. 'A-signifying semiotics' is the most radical element of Guattari's reconception of semiotics (cf. 2013), since it "works flush with the real" and has "direct purchase on the continuum of material flows in the purport'" (Bosteels 2001: 899). Because they (re-)open the possibility of new diagramatic pathways for an encoding and decoding of the material flux, they are strategic elements for the machinic production of new universes of reference and their articulation within collective assemblages of enunciation. During such processes, individuated subjects delocalize and deprivatize, while at the same time, deterritorialize into new machinic conjunctions which construct new modes of sensibility and relation to the other through problematic interactions and changes in perception, expression (e.g. polyvocality, gestures) and affect.

The important operator at work in such a cycle of transformation is *conjunctive*. Conjunctions of abstract machines and material fluxes free and singularize the production of desire from the tyranny of the signifiers, from the rule of the law, from "national, familial, personal, racial, humanist, and transcendent values" (Genosko 2002: 170).

While a conjunction provides lines of flight from the representational regimes of signification and self-identification through new diagrammatic pathways, a different operator is at work in contemporary media-technological environments by default - *connectivity* along with its governmentally linked companion *participation.* This powerful duo has brought the subjectivities of self-governance to an unforeseen level of productivity and established a frame of reference. Functionally integrating networked devices in the subjectivities' milieu, that continually produce, monitor and replay a quasi unalterable feed of pseudo-individual intensities (affects) and their modulations, connectivity has become the main modal operator of self-identification and capitalism's production of subjectivity. Invested with captures of affect through current media-technologies, connectivity organizes a discrete continuum of redundancies with small deviations that calibrate such subjectivity according to the empty networked world time of flat infinity, while it strategically mobilizes its creativity and self-control for capitalist modes of exploitation (cf. Lazzarato 2014).

By constantly producing affective intensities, delivered from a physically-absent social network, connectivity effectively *splits the physical and bodily universes of individuals.* Connectivity, as continued and productive sociality, dislocates the individual from its physicality, which now turns into a reservoir of tensions rather than a foundation. The new milieu of body and dislocated, algorithmically-processed, but connected sociality subdues the physical proximities of the body as an impossible, incompatible alterity. The body becomes quasi absent from its physical locality and proximities as its affection is organized by packets of data that are wireless, hidden and ephemeral. The physicality of the body and its conjunctive capacity is hereby depreciated and degraded. This split of the body, as I call it, is a pragmatic solution on the conceptual level for the description of a body that is situated locally in the physical sense, but claimed socially through affect modulation by a mobile device. Tensions occur because the body has to negotiate two distinct temporalities and two distinct kinds of durations, one as a body within its local milieu, and one as a body within its networked milieu.

FROM FREQUENCY MODULATION TO DISSENSUAL POST-MEDIA ASSEMBLAGES

This unprecedented roll-out of technologies of affective capture and modulation rests on a combination of cellular and wired networking infrastructure that manages the populations' connectivity – its sensing and probing. In Europe today, wireless communication infrastructures cover most of the urban and suburban terrain, effectively becoming environmental to city dwellers, and sinking into the collective unconscious.

But ubiquitous mobile data connectivity for the masses had to be engineered and designed under complex and demanding conditions of frequency scarcity and heavy competition. The 1st and 2nd generation mobile telephony standards offered far too slow and not enough mobile data connectivity for the deterritorializing forces of neoliberalism's restructuring of capital accumulation. The 3rd generation of mobile telephony standards, such as UMTS, flushed open the gates to total connectivity for the individualized mass and thus supported and brought new powers to the fully pseudo-individuated production of contemporary subjectivity, a kind of mass template individualization.

The engineering task to provide data rates which would allow for an affect modulation of as many bodies as simultaneously present within the range of the cell, was solved via a micro-fragmentation of the signal on the level of two orders: time division and code division. By combining these channel access methods into the Time Division Code Division Multiple Access (TD-CDMA) method, essentially two things happen: within increments of 5 MHz (spread spectrum, code division) a radio frame with a duration of 10 milliseconds is divided into 15 time slots (time division, 1500 per second) (cf. Forkel/Jin 2002).

Code division offers temporarily predetermined slices of frequency to each receiving body: an operation of allocation by division. It basically allocates pockets for temporary use within the frequencies of UMTS. Time division further folds and discriminates the signal, allowing multiple passageways for affective transportation within bursts of 10 milliseconds divided by 15 slots.

A UMTS connection therefore oscillates within the range of 5 MHz and modulates time down to steady units of 10 milliseconds, offering 15 slots. This is one of the ontological foundations for the affective mobilization of the individually discriminated population. Bursts of 10 milliseconds divided by 15 within a range of 5 MHz are its material-energetic layer and thus its 'onto-pacer'.

This hyper-nervous electromagnetic signal pulsating far beyond human capacities to register, has become the carrier system for large parts of today's sociality. Whatever other layers or protocols it modulates with, it does so within an extraordinarily fast and jumpy time-frame. In addition, all of this perfectly synchronized and coordinated time and code shifting is happening at a frequency rate around 1900 MHz and 2100 MHz.

Such electromagnetic manipulations, where "[s]ignal is energetic and its force and matter persist outside our attempts to encode and decode it" (Munster 2014: 154) effectively provide "the nexus between a-signifying and signifying flows in contemporary regimes governed by real time media", as Anna Munster (ibid.: 158) suggests, following Maurizio Lazzarato's philosophy of the video signal (cf. Lazzarato 2002). Indeed, the signaletic qualities of wireless transmissions offer a bridge between different regimes of a-signifying and signifying processes.

"The difference between a signal, a hormonal signal for example, and a linguistic sign, lies in the fact that the former produces no signification, engenders no stable system of redundancy that would make it possible for anyone to see it as identical to any representation." (Guattari 1984: 167)

Accordingly, Munster proposes to focus on transmateriality as "matter in movement, matter as relations of forces, matter as an energetics" (2014: 158) to understand the technological modulation of time as an unbecoming of time (cf. ibid.: 160) while it entails possibilities for modulations that are "aesthetico-political and offer new possibilities for the signaletic" (ibid.: 160). Referring to Gilbert Simondon, Munster sketches transmateriality as "a metastable process that ontogenetically precedes a given material individuation. It denotes the potential to become some individuated material as a result of differentiation transforming this potentiality in the direction of a structuration" (ibid.: 159). And further: "Transmaterial relations, then, are both the metastable, virtual ones of pure difference and the processual actualising ones of a singular materiality assembling" (ibid.: 159).

Taking up this proposal and applying it to the electromagnetic UMTS mobile phone signals that permeate protest crowds, the full spectrum of de- and reterritorializing processes which control the becoming of crowds and their disintegration into individualized subjects, becomes perceivable, because the subject "in contact with desiring machines in a-signifying semiotics oscillates between reterritorializations on signification and deterritorializations into new machinic conjunctions" (Genosko 2002: 171).

In other words: by situating signaletic energies as ontological relation from which processes of individuation (Simondon) or machinic conjunctions (Guattari) actualize, the problem of significational semiotic regimes presents itself only as a *particular phasing* of the material-energetic modulations, calling into question what other phasings the modulation virtually entails and what is needed to bring them into actualization. Situating signifying semiotical processes as particular phasings of a larger repertoire of a-signifying and signifying regimes, whereby each establishes circuits between the actual possibilities, the actual real, the virtual possibilities and the virtual real (depending on the degrees of machinic integration) shows how the becoming of crowds as an a-signifying deterritorialization process *and* processes of capture and control provided by signifying semiotic registers of messaging, *together* belong to a dissensual post-media assemblage. As a precarious and unstable multiplicity of actual and virtual functions, the tensions within such an assemblage are becoming apparent only after actualization, or rephasing.

Inseparable from these couplings and decouplings within post-media assemblages of protest crowds and mobile phones, are affective pathways of bodily resonances, to which I turn now.

AFFECT AS HETEROGENESIS *AND* SOCIAL SERIALIZATION

So far, I have only vaguely indicated the concept of affect used here. In order to connect the becoming of crowds with the ultra-fast modulated material energetic layers of mobile data connectivity, the concept of affect needs some clarification.

From Spinoza (2002) to Gilles Deleuze (1990), from William James (1884) to Brian Massumi (2002), affect is characterized as an intensity relating to bodily activities in movement that register in pre-individual strata, whereas emotion is delegated to the reflexivity of individualized subjects. Advocates of the affective turn, such as Patricia Clough, tend to install affect as the base of all sociality: "sociality is a matter of affective transmissions across bodies in a machinic assemblage with technology and technical arrangements" (2010: 225).

This resonates with Guattari, for whom "[a]ffect is thus essentially a pre-personal category, installed 'before' the circumscription of identities, and manifested by unlocatable transferences, unlocatable with regard to their origin as well as with regard to their destination" (1996: 158). The power of this category resides in its "process of existential appropriation through the continual creation of heterogeneous durations of being" (ibid.: 159) and thus "is an instance of the engendering of the complex, a processuality in the throes of birth, a place for mutational becomings", arising "from intensive and intentional categories, which correspond to an existential self-positioning" (ibid.: 160). Clough suggests that the "temporality of affect is to be understood in terms of thresholds, bifurcation, and emergence" (Clough 2009: 50), invoking rhetorics from complexity theory, another link to Guattari's conceptual language.

But Guattari, who developed his concepts and theories vis-à-vis his clinical and political activities, distinguishes affects according to their onto-relationality: sensory affects may effect feelings of being, whereas problematic affects effect active ways of being (cf. Guattari 1996: 167). In addition, "affect is not a massively elementary energy but the deterritorialized matter of enunciation" (ibid.: 174). By subsuming affect into his modes of enunciation, Guattari can provide a scheme of affect functors that operates "just as well in the sense of an individuation as of a social serialization" (ibid.: 174). He proposes the concept of the ritornello as mediator of affect, working as

> "[...] reiterative discursive sequences that are closed in upon themselves and whose function is an extrinsic catalyzing of existential affects. Ritornellos can find substance in rhythmic and plastic forms, in prosodic segments, in facial traits, in the emblems of recognition, in leitmotifs, signatures, proper names or their invocational between equivalents." (ibid.: 162)

As the list of substantiations shows, for Guattari, affect as pure intensity, a common phrase used by protagonists of the affective turn, would be beyond the scope of his pragmatism. Affect needs mediation (or it remains "proto-enunciation" (ibid.: 166) and depending on the kind of mediation it may effect radically different enunciations. Ritornellos mediate affects: problematic affects adhere to content ritornellos (relating enunciation and the form of the content), whereas sensory affects adhere to ritornellos of expression (relating enunciation and the form of the expression).[2] Guattari thus manages to deploy a pragmatic rather than speculative use of the problem of affect. I will return to this pragmatics at the end when I try to show how crowd becomings and mobile phone signals can be described as alterations within different fields of enunciations. But to get there, the problem of the crowd needs to be addressed.

THE PRECARIOUS ONTOGENESIS OF THE CROWD AND ITS ACCOUNTS

By turning to the problem of the crowd, the first step is to conceptualize crowds as situated, historically and locally specific and ontologically unstable. Thus, the works of Le Bon (2001), Canetti (1981), or Tarde (1903), which come to mind first, have little to offer in terms of an analysis of contemporary crowds (cf. Kølvraa 2015). To regain insights from their accounts, one would first have to disassemble, deconstruct and subtract the many layers of bourgeois resentments against the imagined destabilizing forces of crowds they are impregnated with.

2 Indeed, Guattaris deployment of affect is much more complex than it can be sketched here (cf. Guattari 1996).

Becoming crowd, the machinic singularization as conjunctions of bodies that develop their own temporalities, durations, rhythms and so forth, relate to these classic descriptions of crowds (whether openly pejorative as with Le Bon, esoteric as with Tarde, or agonizing as with Canetti) much like early ethnographic descriptions to their other (the primitive). It is the same cosmological and ontological disjunction between researcher and researched.

Much the same applies to contemporary descriptions of crowds in social psychology. Of course, "[t]he energy of the crowd invests it with a transformatory potential" (Reicher 2001: 213). But to model a crowd by proposing that "crowd members seek to construe a contextual identity by reference to and within the limits set by the superordinate categorical identity" (ibid.: 195) only shows the continuing modernist fixation on identity in this discourse, which necessarily leads to the fatal misconception of crowds as made up by crowd members that are occupied with identity formation. Quite the contrary, the crowd is naturally indiscriminate. Bodies of a crowd, as seen from the outside, constitute it, but they are undergoing an ontogenetic process of becoming, that precisely subtracts identity and self-reference from them.

Christian Borch investigates the precarious state of the crowd within sociology and seeks "to trace the evolution of sociological crowd semantics" (ibid.: 4). He argues that a problematization of crowds is "essentially a problematization of modern society and its social and political set-up" (ibid.: 15). Thus, he investigates, amongst other themes, how the problem of the crowd has been instrumental in designating disciplinary boundaries between sociology and psychology, or as a means "to define proper approaches, methodologies, conceptual frameworks, etc. within sociology" (ibid.: 300). The crowd thus served as a medium and mirror for the constitution and development of sociology. I would add that, given the crowd's dynamics and ontological finitude, it has a tendency to escape all Western modes of thought that ground themselves in stasis and being, and thus the crowd consequently must remain at the margins of analysis.

In more general terms, which suffice for the portrait presented here, it is enough to understand that if bodies are socially and culturally produced, and if media-technologies play a key part in their formation, crowds, too, are subjected to socially and culturally-specific historical structuration.

In addition, as the ontogenetic principle of a crowd's becoming is relational, they offer varying vectors for capture, colonization and serialization, provided by their historical milieus. Fascism, to name just one example, learned to serialize crowds into disciplined masses of bodies without triggering their refragmentation into individuals.

The capture of the war machine by the state, in many ways resembles this process on a larger scale (cf. Deleuze/Guattari 1987: 351-422).

The becoming crowd unfolds on a spatial plane, which it tries to colonize (square) as milieu. It relies on affective modulations with and within its environment through a multitude of perceptive pathways. Crowds resonate within their environmental conditions which are never under the control of the crowd, forcing the crowd to continually reinvent their becoming according to environmental factors. For example, darkness at night affects a crowd in its becoming, because it diminishes the visual as the primary affective gate to the body, while it increases affective capacities of spatial hearing. A crowd in open daylight is exposed to the individualizing visual senses that infer a separate tendency from their continuous rendering of discrete objects. If, on the other hand, it is spatial hearing that leads the orientation, a continuous multiplicity of sounds and echoes enforces a process of singularization.

The problem of the visual for crowds is common knowledge and led to the invention of strategic devices to mitigate it. Amongst such devices are the Black Bloc's monochromatism which weakens identificational trajectories. This is not only a strategy to decrease identification by police. It serves the becoming crowd fundamentally by weakening capacities to visually discriminate altogether.

Many more such devices have been invented, ranging from strategic applications of sound and music, to the emergence of bodily movements freed from individualized pacing. Alterations in the body's chemical composition show that a crowd's becoming takes place even on the molecular level of neurotransmitters such as serotonin and dopamine.

Since temporal and rhythmic alterations are amongst the most powerful relational affective registers for crowds, the most common means to bring about the death of a crowd is to withdraw its access to the temporal or to movement in general. Within an instant, a crowd falls apart if it is submitted to a standstill from outside, as crowd control police knows very well. But it would be wrong to infer from this a shortcoming or weakness of the crowd.

Crowds, as opposed to individuals, assume their finite nature and thus increase the value of their becoming (cf. Guattari/Rolnik 2008: 430). Their capacity to disintegrate under hostile environmental conditions is their necessary condition to become again, but of course differently, since each becoming is singular.

Unstable and precarious processes of crowd becoming hint towards the ethics of crowds, one that the individual occupied by capitalist subjectivity lacks, since death is barred within the void of self-referential identities. By producing temporalities that are intrinsically linked to its becoming and occupying bodily conjunct territories as milieus, the deadly passage towards transcendental references is blocked. The crowd has established "devices that can articulate living processes" (ibid.: 216) from within, including its own universe of reference.

THE PHASE-SHIFTING VECTORS OF MOBILE PHONES: A SCENARIO

As I have outlined, current protest cultures have embraced the governmental assemblages of connectivity and participation, manifested in a split of bodily presence: digital networking organizes and modulates bodily affect from a distance while the physical-bodily presence depends on its surrounding and proximate milieu. As such, mobile phone use is the antidote of crowds: it addresses the individual and thus reinvokes it each time it interferes with the development of dispersed, but resonating bodily temporalities and movements, and finally, with collective assemblages of enunciation. In the context of crowds, mobile phones are first of all a disruptive vector, interfering with the powers and on the level of individualizing affects and semiotic regimes of subjugation.

But it would be wrong to understand this as a necessarily total rupture. Three considerations have to be taken into account here: in contrast to a forced standstill, as executed by the police, such an interference is soft and it retains a degree of openness towards a-signifying processes. Second, critical data that ultimately may prolong the becoming of crowd can inform it through messaging channels. And third, the signifying phase of mobile devices is only one of many phases that such high-frequency modulation constantly emits into the environment. The a-signifying matter-energy modulation itself needs to be accounted for in this context as a nexus of machinic assemblages. To illustrate all three considerations, what follows is an example of a very common situation for protest crowds, from where each consideration becomes clear.

In this scenario, all of a sudden a mass sending of text messages to the crowd begins, that provides logistical information. This sending has to actualize the relay of individual "nodes", and in this very moment, the affective distributions of the crowd are reorganizing themselves. They organize according to a split of the body into a bodily-message-receiving milieu and physical-bodily remnant of proximity on which the relational ontogenesis of the crowd continues to depend. But before the reading of the message finalizes the individual's actualization, it is the phone that articulates its presence through vibrations or sounds. So, first, the crowd vibrates and rings within a small time-frame that, transposed onto the spatial dimensions of the crowd, jumps from here to there within the occupied space. The signalling is distributed within the spatial plane of the crowd and actualizes the individuals non-synchronously, because each phone receives the message slightly de-phased in relation to any other. The interfering vector does not attack the crowd at once, but only segments or dispersed, physically unordered blocks, patches. The becoming of crowd thus continues as such, but it has to endure local conflicts between the two affective orderings of connection and conjunction that are signalled through ring tones or vibration. But there is more to this signalling phase: in the course of locally jumping signalling within the crowd, the redundancy of the message is expressed. This in itself informs the becoming of the crowd, since the signal can be ignored by large blocks of the crowd without any loss of information.

Second, how much bodily split is effectuated by the phone's intervention? Effectively, not much consciousness is needed for building a path between a device and the eyes, rather non-conscious bodily gestures, such as setting up the device for use. Thus, plenty of local phone–body machinic assemblages emerge within the crowd.

The next bit of the signalling path is complicated for the crowd: the message has to be read, which means a completely different register, one of semiotic signification, is invoked. Such an invocation and its outcome highly depends on the message received. In the context of this scenario, the message contains traffic information, relating to activities by the police who are installing a capturing blockade ahead of the crowd. This is a message of ultra affective intensity in such a situation and since its value is intrinsically linked to the physical-bodily other of the split body, it translates from connection to conjunction within instance. The invocation of the semiotic registers can resonate intensively with the a-signifying machinic singularization of the crowd. Or, put otherwise, the crowd's information by the message, in Simondon's sense, actualizes its individuation, and without further hesitation, the crowd knows in which direction to proceed (cf. Simondon 2007). Once a critical saturation of this affection within the crowd has been reached, this mutual, common knowledge can not be separated from action anymore, it invokes a new ontogenetical structuration of the crowd. The crowd has been altered in that this information is now redirecting the crowd. The message received was in its fullest sense a proceed signal, not a stop signal.

Finally, the signalling path of matter-energy modulation in high frequencies not only provides this particular phasing of semiotic signification, but is comprised of bursts of milliseconds jumping within a code-controlled oscillation range. This means that each mobile device's signal path is de-phased in relation to the path of every other mobile device addressed by the cell. The matter-energy modulation at one moment thus may contain hundreds, if not thousands, of phase shifts and time bursts that ontologically integrate into the assemblage of crowd and phones, as expressed by a de-phased and locally unordered ringing and vibrating. The infra-allocation of one phase for each individual signal corresponds to the inference caused by each signal within the crowd. And the signal stream in its totality that emanates from the cell tower, turns into a multiplicity of redundancies. This stream depends on the powers of at least 3rd generation mobile networking technologies, as I have explained above. By solving the addressability of crowds with multiple time-shifting bursts, *connectivity regains conjunctive qualities*. This is most certainly news to the telecom providers.

CONCLUSION: MOBILES AND CROWDS AS POST-MEDIA ASSEMBLAGES

If "post-media emphasize the modular and open process of the production of subjectivity at the heart of each media-inflected process" (Brunner/Nigro/Raunig 2013: 13), it is important to consider the whole spectrum that is at work in such a process. If semiotic signification is separated from the flux of other semiotics, as so forcefully and repeatedly criticized by Guattari (cf. Guattari 2013), machinic becoming oscillates towards re-serialization. I have shown that only if the complete multi-phased material-energetic modulation of UMTS is made explicit *and* its operative functors within the assemblage of crowds and mobile devices as a redundancy of locally shifting signalling paths shown, it is only then that an individualizing media technology such as mobile devices, may itself transform into a tool to prolong the alterity of the crowd, supporting conjunctions.

For Guattari "the shift from mass into post-media would not be sequential and definitive but coexistent, contestatory, and messy" (Genosko 2013: 15). Yet, there is more to it, if we want to use the notion of post-media: this contribution situates this shift along the axis of individualizing media technologies and shows how co-existent the problem of post-media remains in a post-mass media assemblage. But if media here relates to "the production of a completely different middle", one that "take[s] part in the production of sociality and become in a new sense *social* media" (Raunig 2012: n. pag.), it is because the bodily split enforced by mobile data connectivity becomes transformed into conjunctive multiple bodily processes. Such a performative agency adheres to the transformative powers of becoming crowd while successfully integrating the powers of mobile data connectivity. This coupling of two predominantly distinct ontological spheres exhibits a performativity that spans from the high frequency modulation of digital signals to the indiscriminable multiple bodies of the crowd. To show the performativity of this post-media assemblage with its two modal operators, connection and conjunction, it was necessary to interrogate the media technology in operation, down to its material-energetic layer. Each media technology operates under specific time modulations (cf. Ernst 2013) and each wireless media technology provides specific modes of frequency distribution which have critical effects on machinic becomings and singularizations, such as the problem of the crowd.

In addition, a more comprehensive account of effecting vectors safeguards the analysis from a blunt speculative thrust. Such a speculative programmatic, as provided by Nigel Thrift (2008), or partly by Clough, which indeed helps to map the conceptual landscape of affect studies, often has an open flank towards, if not mysticism, then at least analytical opacity. Or, to put it otherwise: the "what it effects" question, which was necessary to establish affect as a promising and challenging theoretical horizon and tool, needs to be supplemented with the question of "how it effects"– just like semiotic signification must be extended towards a-signifying semiotics to sense its potentials.

REFERENCES

Borch, Christian (2012): The Politics of Crowds: An Alternative History of Sociology, Cambridge: Cambridge University Press.

Bosteels, Bruno (2001): "From text to territory: Felix Guattari's cartographies of the unconscious." In: Gary Genosko (ed.), Deleuze and Guattari: Critical Assessments vol. 2, London: Taylor & Francis, pp. 881-910.

Bröckling, Ulrich/Krasmann, Susanne/Lemke, Thomas (eds.) (2011): Governmentality: Current Issues and Future Challenges, London: Routledge.

Brunner, Christoph/Nigro, Roberto/Raunig, Gerald (2013): "Post-media actiism, social ecology and eco-art." In: Third Text 27/1, pp. 10-16.

Canetti, Elias (1981[1960]): Crowds and Power, New York: Continuum.

Clough, Patricia T. (2009): "The new empiricism: Affect and sociological method." In: European Journal of Social Theory 12/1, pp. 43-61.

Clough, Patricia T. (2010): "Afterword: The future of affect atudies." In: Body & Society 16/1, pp. 222-230.

Deleuze, Gilles (1990): Expressionism In Philosophy. Spinoza, New York: Zone Books.

Deleuze, Gilles/Guattari, Félix (1987[1980]): A Thousand Plateaus: Capitalism and Schizophrenia (B. Massumi, trans.), Minneapolis: University of Minnesota Press.

Dencik, Lina/Leistert, Oliver (eds.) (2015): Critical Perspectives on Social Media and Protest: Between Control and Emancipation, New York: Rowman & Littlefield.

De Tarde, Gabriel (1903): The Laws of Imitation, New York: H. Holt.

Ernst, Wolfgang (2013): Chronopoetik: Zeitweisen und Zeitgaben Technischer Medien, Berlin: Kadmos.

Forkel, Ingo/Xin, Jin (2002): "Performance comparison between UTRA-TDD high chip rate and low chip rate operation." In: The 13th IEEE International Symposium on Personal, Indoor and Mobile Radio Communications 5, pp. 2102-2106.

Genosko, Gary (2002): Félix Guattari: An Aberrant Introduction, London/New York: Continuum.

Genosko, Gary (2013): "The promise of post-media." In: Clemens Apprich/Josephine Berry Slater/Anthony Iles (eds.), Provocative Alloys: A Post-Media Anthology, London: Mute Publishing Limited, pp. 14-25.

Guattari, Félix (1984): Molecular Revolution: Psychiatry and Politics, Harmondsworth: Penguin.

Guattari, Félix (1996): The Guattari Reader. Edited by Gary Genosko, Oxford: Blackwell Publishers.

Guattari, Félix (2009): Soft Subversions: Texts and Interviews 1977-1985, Los Angeles: Semiotext(e).

Guattari, Félix (2013): Schizoanalytic Cartographies, London: Bloomsbury Publishing.

Guattari, Félix/Rolnik, Suely (2008): Molecular Revolution in Brazil, Los Angeles: Semiotext(e).

James, William (1884): "What is an emotion?" In: Mind 9/34, pp. 188-205.

Kølvraa, Christoffer (2015): "Affect, provocation, and far right rhetoric." In: Britta Timm Knudsen/Carsten Stage (eds.), Affective Methodologies, Basingstoke: Palgrave Macmillan, pp. 222-235.

Lazzarato, Maurizio (2002): Videophilosophie, Berlin: b-books.

Lazzarato, Maurizio (2014): Signs and Machines: Capitalism and the Production of Subjectivity, Los Angeles: Semiotext(e).

Le Bon, Gustave (2001[1895]): The Crowd: A Study of the Popular Mind, Mineola, NY: Dover Publications.

Leistert, Oliver (2013): From Protest to Surveillance: The Political Rationality of Mobile Media. Modalities of Neoliberalism, Frankfurt am Main/New York: Peter Lang.

Massumi, Brian (2002): Parables for the Virtual, Durham: Duke University Press.

Milan, Stefania (2015): "When algorithms shape collective action: Social media and the dynamics of cloud protesting." In: Social Media+Society 1/2, pp. 1-10.

Munster, Anna (2014): "Transmateriality. Toward an energetics of signal in contemporary mediatic assemblages." In: Cultural Studies Review 20/1, pp. 150-167.

Raunig, Gerald (2012): "n-1. Making multiplicity. A philosophical manifesto." In: Transversal Texts, March 5, 2016 (http://transversal.at/transversal/1011/raunig2/en)

Reicher, Stephen (2001): "The psychology of crowd dynamics." In: Michael A. Hogg/R. Scott Tindale (eds.), Group Processes. Blackwell Handbook of Social Psychology, Malden, MA: Blackwell Publishers, pp. 182-208.

Renzi, Alessandra (2015): "Info-capitalism and resistance: How information shapes social movements." In: Interface: A Journal for and about Social Movements 7/2, pp. 98-119.

Simondon, Gilbert (2007): L'individuation psychique et collective: à la lumière des notions de forme, information, potentiel et métastabilité, Paris: Aubier.

Spinoza, Benedictus de (2002): Complete Works, Indianapolis: Hackett Pub.

Thrift, Nigel (2008): Non-Representational Theory: Space, Politics, Affect, London: Routledge.

Wiedemann, Carolin (2011): "Facebook: Das Assessment-Center Der Alltäglichen Lebensführung." In: Oliver Leistert/Theo Röhle (eds.), Generation Facebook, Bielefeld: transcript, pp. 161-81.

Mapping

Mapping invisibility

Surveillance art and the potential of performative cartography

SIGRID MERX

A man guides us through Amsterdam. We follow him. He stops at every traffic light, carefully waiting for it to turn green, even if there is no traffic to be seen. During our four-hour walk, he tells us about his life in Africa and why he decided to leave his country to try to build a life in Europe. We ask him questions. He replies. After a while we stand in front of the public library. The man says he loves the library. The calm atmosphere of people reading and studying. The knowledge that is piled up in there. The fact that there is free internet. And that it is one of the few places in the city where it is quiet, no one bothers you and you can take a short nap. The man explains how entering this public building without a library card has become increasingly difficult. A card you can only obtain with a Dutch passport or other identity papers. Documents he doesn't possess.

The group is carrying a recording device documenting the conversation and a mobile phone with a mapping application that traces our walk in real-time. Somewhere else in a cultural venue in the city centre, people look at a projection screen that shows a map of the city centre of Amsterdam. A blue line crawls through the streets. That's us. The longer we stand still at a certain location, such as the library, the more the line thickens, transforming into a dot. Other lines trace other groups that are simultaneously walking through the city with their guides, jointly creating a collective map. When our tour ends, our conversation is made available online as an audio download. People can only 'unlock' the story on their mobile phone by physically standing on the exact starting point of the walk and following the exact same route. Deviating from the route results in the voices fading out. In order to engage with the story, the audience is required to literally and carefully retrace the steps of the undocumented person and his or her movements.

Figure 1: Screenshot Map from 'Mapping Invisibility'

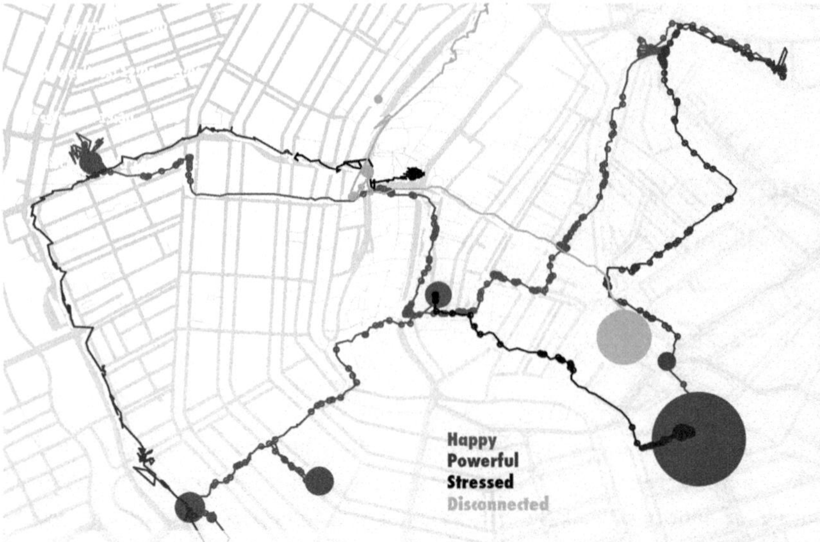

© Naomi Bueno de Mesquita

I have been participating in 'Mapping Invisibility', a workshop on performative digital mapping designed by spatial designer Naomi Bueno de Mesquita (TRADERS)[1] in collaboration with Platform-Scenography.[2] The workshop is part of *Out of State*, a four-day cultural program with performances and public debates about the practical consequences of Dutch immigration policies for immigrants. Based on my experience as a participant, this short text aims to reflect on the potential of such a performative cartography to produce a space for civic engagement. To do so, I will pay particular attention to practices of walking as acts of both social engagement and co-producing the city, and I will position the workshop within the framework of surveillance art. The framework of surveillance art helps to point out the critical and subversive nature of the project and

1 TRADERS (short for 'Training Art and Design Researchers in Participation for Public Space') researches the ways in which art and design researchers can 'trade' or exchange with multiple participants and disciplines in public space projects and – at the same time – trains them in doing so. Naomi Bueno de Mesquita is one of TRADERS' PhD researchers.

2 Platform Scenography, based in Rotterdam in the Netherlands, is an analogue and digital network by and for scenographers dedicated to scenographic thinking and working (cf. http://www.platform-scenography.nl/).

how digital surveillance technologies can be used to create alternative regimes of visibility and participation.

WALKING AS A WAY OF PRODUCING THE CITY

The act of walking the city lies at the heart of the project 'Mapping Invisibility'. Walking functions both as method and content, both in terms of the workshop where participants walk the city collectively with a guide, and in terms of the audio tour where the participant walks the city individually.

For most participants, walking the city is usually a matter of logistics (getting from A to B) and/or consumerism (shopping, culture, dining, tourism etc.) For the guides, however, the largest part of their day consists of walking around the city out of necessity. The so-called 'bed, bath, bread policy' ensures that undocumented immigrants are entitled to a place to sleep during the night, where they can wash up in the morning and have a meal in the evening. During the day they are required to leave the shelter and to live on the streets, regardless of the weather. Since working is not an option for these people, they don't have money to buy anything, and since standing still is potentially dangerous because it might identify them as 'illegal' immigrants, they are forced to pretty much just walk around all day.

According to Michel de Certeau, to walk is to compose a path. What makes up the city is the collection of an innumerable amount of these intersecting paths (Certeau 1984: 97). The city space, Certeau suggests, is "actuated by the ensemble of movements deployed within it" (ibid.: 117). Through their spatial practices, the undocumented citizens participate as much in the production of the city as their documented counterparts. The idea that urban space is socially produced in and through our collective movements – an idea that has been theorized in most detail by Henri Lefebvre (1991, 1996) – has a distinct emancipatory potential. It suggests that the production of space is not limited to planners, bureaucrats and administrators, but takes place in the everyday activities of inhabitants and users. This is not to say, however, that our movements in the city are free and spontaneous. They are characterized by repetition and dictated by state and market-modelled patterns of behaving and being.

Lavrinec (2013: 25) describes this repetition of movement by urban citizens as the performance of a "routine choreography". It might seem that the undocumented somehow escapes these urban routines, wandering all day through the city, not working, not consuming, just being there, creating their own alternative paths. However, not following the predesignated paths, not performing the dominant choreography and not adopting to the rhythms of capitalist society is of course not a radical choice, but the ultimate and inevitable consequence of not being recognized and acknowledged as a citizen and therefore as a co-producer of the city. In a way, the urban trajectories performed by the undocumented are as much a form of routine choreography as are those of the other citizens. Most of them, as becomes clear in the conversations during the walk, have developed a set of routes and routines that they repeatedly use depending on their personal needs and desires. For example, if they want to be able to sit down for a while without calling attention to themselves they go to Central Station and mingle with the people who are waiting for a train. Or, as already indicated in the introduction, if they need free Wi-Fi or take a nap, they can try to get into the public library and find themselves a reading booth. If they need God, they can go to a church. Their day ends by returning to their shelter. They wake up the next morning and continue with their daily routine. In this respect they are, to use a term by Certeau, 'blind walkers', strolling along predetermined paths without self-control and agency.

Figure 2: Workshop Mapping Invisibility

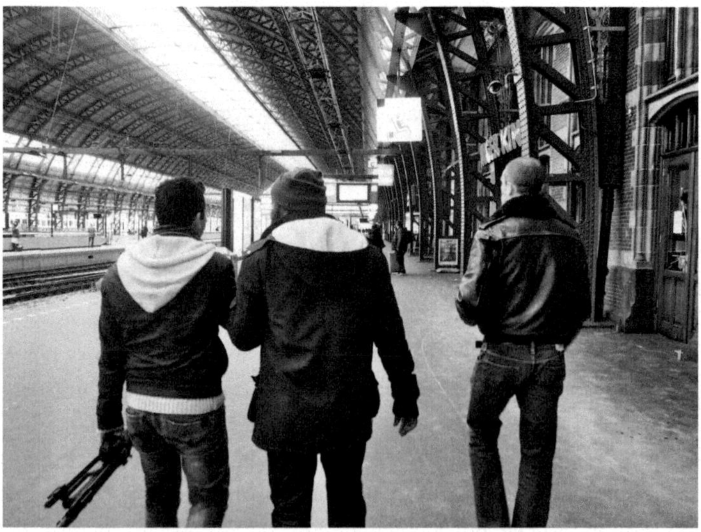

© Naomi Bueno de Mesquita

Opposed to the figure of the blind walker we often find the 'flâneur', the urban stroller that counters the monotonous routines of everyday life in a capitalist society. The Situationists believed the 'flâneur' to be critical and subversive in the sense that he wandered around without a specific aim or plan, adopting to another rhythm, allowing him to perceive and experience the city in a 'new' way (Sadler 1999). We could consider the walk in this project as an urban drift in the tradition of the Situationists; an unplanned urban journey that allows one to perceive and experience the city in a new way and according to an alternative logic and to make a connection between urban settings and bodily-emotional experiences of the city (Lavrinec 2013: 56). For the undocumented guide, not only is the city revealed as a social space, a place where you can encounter people instead of hiding from them, but also as a public space in which you have the right to appear and to act. Walking others through the city becomes a political act. The participant of the workshop or the audio tour is invited to an alternative city tour with an unlikely guide and is thus confronted with a parallel and often unknown reality of exclusion, invisibility and oppression, and with an other that inhabits and lives this reality on a day to day basis. Co-performing these trajectories through the city thus disrupts the daily routines of both undocumented guides and documented participants; and it opens up a space of encounter between them.

SURVEILLANCE ART

Using strategies and technologies of digital mapping, tracing and tracking the project aimed at bringing undocumented and documented citizens together by making the everyday practice of walking in the city as an undocumented citizen visible and perceptible. Considering the particular use of surveillance tools and strategies, I propose to understand this project as an example of so-called 'surveillance art'.

According to performance scholar Elise Morrison, surveillance art can be considered a particular genre of political activism and performance in which (digital) surveillance technologies, such as CCTV cameras and GPS devices, are used and appropriated to create "an array of technologically savvy, politically conscious and aesthetically innovative alternatives to the current structures of power and participation within surveillance society" (Morrison 2015: 126-127).

Within the broad field of surveillance art and performance, Morrison (2015) distinguishes three ways in which surveillance art can interrupt and counter our contemporary surveillance society. First, through physical intervention in habitual patterns of movement and usership as conditioned by state, military and corporate design of surveillance interfaces. Secondly, through the appropriation of surveillance technologies for subversive ends. Thirdly, through critically highlighting blind spots in surveillance society.

Morrison's examples of surveillance art range from performances like *Tracking Transcience* in which Hasan Elahi, having been spied on by the FBI on a regular basis, develops a website that updates his whereabouts every hour of the day on a world map; the *Surveillance Camera Players*, who develop plays for CCTV cameras; the *Transborder Immigrant Tool*, a tweaked cell phone that is redesigned to function as a GPS mobile device that helps Mexican immigrants safely cross the border; the *iSee software* developed by the activist-engineer collective, *Institute for Applied Autonomy,* that allows users to interactively map 'the path of least surveillance' through cities around the world.

As Morrison stresses, surveillance not only entails a top-down process of discipline. In our everyday lives, using credit cards, webcams, tagging our pictures on Facebook, navigating through a city with our smartphones, we constantly participate as citizens in the surveillance society (Morrison 2013). In this respect, surveillance is by design participatory. However, in surveillance art and performance, "participation becomes a tactic of political critique and subversive action" (ibid.: 7). This is certainly the case in *State of Shelter* where surveillance technology is appropriated to allow for alternative models of participation, agency and subjecthood.

In any other context, following an undocumented immigrant through the streets of Amsterdam, checking and mapping his whereabouts, documenting his life story and exposing it to others, could be considered a rather problematic and even unethical act of control and surveillance. Moreover, it is quite paradoxical to make visible the urban trajectories of people who have no legal right to be there, considering that much of their daily life and fate is about being invisible, staying off the grid and under the radar. Nonetheless, it is precisely this fact that motivated these immigrants to participate in the event. They are all part of *We Are Here,*[3] a group of refugees in Amsterdam who are not entitled to housing, not permitted to work and as a result, are forced to live on the streets. Not wanting to hide any longer and claiming a place in society, they decided to actively start making visible the inhumane conditions they have to deal with. Participating in this workshop has been just one of many ways the group has called attention to their situation. In doing so, they both critique and subvert the structures of power that keep them from participating in society and forces them to live off the grid. The project is political in the Rancièrean sense, in that it entails a redistribution of the senses, of what is visible and sayable, and produces an alternative politics of vision (Rancière 2004). It restages bodies that have been disem-

3 See http://wijzijnhier.org/ (accessed July 23, 2016)

powered and made invisible through government policies. In a very literal sense, as we will see later, it puts people back on the map.

With respect to the people guided through the city by the undocumented both during the workshop and the audio tour, the participants were invited to navigate through public space in an alternative way, experiencing the city – if only for some hours – through the eyes and stories of their guides. Stopping for each traffic light, even without any traffic around, does make sense when your guide tells you that being caught while crossing the street with a red light might lead to his arrest and eviction from the country. Perceiving the public library predominantly as a great place to take a nap is perfectly understandable when you learn that the shelters are crowded and full of noise. According to Morrison, surveillance art and performance can "expose audiences to their own habits of watching and being watched" (2015: 127). Participating in this walk revealed different understandings and possible meanings of public space, of being and acting in public space, of alternative subjectivities in public space and also of the participants' own presence and behavior in public space. Such temporary aligning with the movements of the undocumented also highlights in an embodied way the tension between hiding and making public – a daily recurrent theme for the undocumented.

PERFORMATIVE MAPPING

A particularly interesting aspect of the workshop, is how the map for this subversive city tour was created through collaboration. Not only were the different trajectories of different groups mapped in real time on one digital map, but the legend of the map had been generated prior to the walk by the participants (not the guides) and decided upon collectively. The map's legend consisted of emotions, which the participants thought the undocumented might experience while walking through the city, such as despair or fear. Every hour, the guide would respond to a particular emotion by bringing his group to places and locations he personally associated with this emotion. While walking, the group had the chance to evaluate their preconceived ideas in direct dialogue with the undocumented. Each emotion would be marked by a color on the map, making visible the specific trajectory connected with that emotion. Moreover, every time the guide decided to stop at a certain location, the line on the map would turn into a dot, growing bigger depending on how long one would stay at that particular location, revealing the importance of the location in relation to the emotion. The workshop therefore also experimented with the genre of emotional maps, which chart human feelings onto a cartographical landscape (Perkins 2009). The maps that were produced not only depicted the actual trajectories of walking but charged them with affective and subjective meaning. This is what Katherine Harmon (2003) refers to as 'personal geographies'. Such personal geographies reveal how a map is never an objective representation of reality, but always implies a particular perspective. Normally this perspective is obscured, allowing us to use the map without any further questioning. However, by bringing the subjectivity of the map to the foreground, we are invited to look beyond its functionality and ask ourselves what these trajectories actually mean. What narratives do they perform? For example, what is this huge blue dot, connected to the emotion 'hopeful', that appears on all the maps on the exact same spot? It turns out to be 'Het Wereldhuis', a centre for information, counselling, education and culture for undocumented migrants and one of the few places in Amsterdam where the undocumented can go to find advice, comfort, food and most importantly fellow migrants. Through the strategy of real-time digital visualization, then, the map invites reflection, understanding and engagement.

In order to understand how the workshop not only subverts dominant structures of participation but also produces a particular space of engagement, it might be helpful, then, to not only position the project within the context of surveillance art, but to also approach the work from the perspective of cartography and in particular as an example of performative and collaborative mapping. (Verhoeff 2012) Performative mapping is part of the so-called 'performative turn' in cartography in the late 20th century, which shifted the attention from maps as representations to the process of mapping. Not only are maps understood as a product of co-creative relationships between maps and users, they are also considered to have agency. Maps can 'do' things and produce certain effects. According to James Corner, mapping produces a particular understanding and experience of the world that is being mapped. As Corner argues, mapping is never neutral or without consequences, but instead a creative act "first disclosing and then staging the conditions for the emergence of new realities" (1999: 216). This quote also points to the performative and creative potential of maps to constitute and produce (new) worlds. Corner foregrounds the notion of imagination in relation to mapping: "Its agency lies in neither reconstruction nor imposition but rather in uncovering realities previously unseen or unimagined, even across seemingly exhausted grounds. Thus mapping *unfolds* potential" (ibid.: 213; orig. emphasis).

Returning to the workshop, we see how the conditions are indeed staged to facilitate a different understanding of the city and to reveal the harsh reality of 'illegal' immigrants. In this particular case, it is precisely the act of *collaborative* mapping that allows for the emergence of a new perspective. It is only through an encounter between undocumented and documented that this shift in perspective can occur. The space for this encounter is produced in and through the process of collaborative mapping.

In digital cultures, networked technology-led interactive mapping is facilitating new forms of collaborative mapping. According to media scholar Nanna Verhoeff (2012: 13), one of the most striking characteristics of screen-based interfaces is "the possibility for people in transit to co-create the map of the spatial arrangement in which they are operating". With increasing interactive qualities, mapping has allowed users to also become producers.

It is precisely this emancipatory potential that explains why collaborative mapping as a strategy is so appealing to activists and socially engaged artists and designers. Co-producing its maps entails co-producing the city. It allows for reclaiming the city. In the case of the undocumented, this project is not only about being a subject that can actually be put on a map, but more importantly about being part of the map, being in a position to co-create the map and being acknowledged as a co-producer of the city and therefore as a citizen.

Even if this agency only can exist within the temporary framework of the workshop and people are forced back into invisibility, the marks they have left on the city while mapping it remain and are there to stay. Or as Corner (1999: 225) puts it: "The map 'gathers' and 'shows' things presently (and always) invisible, things which may appear incongruous or untimely but which may also harbour enormous potential for the unfolding of alternative events".

I would like to suggest that this potential is located in the downloadable audio tour. Through this app, the stories of the undocumented will be forever linked to the locations where they were shared; stored metadata can be retrieved whenever someone takes the time and makes the effort to revive them by activating the app and retracing the steps of the people who went before them. Because of this element of geotagging, something has been added to the city. It is charged with the potential of new encounters, ready to unfold in other instances, hopefully leading to other, more humane futures. In this respect the project functions as an open and lasting invitation, and as a call to engage.

CONCLUSION

Surveillance technology, such as GPS and other mapping devices, is a tool for (self)control and oppression. As I hope to have demonstrated, however, the mapping performances it supports can also encourage emancipation and individual and collaborative agency. In the case of 'Mapping Invisibility', the act of trying to understand through mapping helped to make visible – and to engage with – the undocumented and their performances in a world that is constantly being mapped, and where they are normally forced to remain invisible. Here, cartography became performative, in that the map was not a mere digital representation, but something that was produced in a co-creative relationship between the map and its different users. Through producing different modes of encounter and interaction between documented and undocumented that would normally not meet each other in public space, the project opened up an understanding of performative cartography as enabling, or perhaps provoking, a space for civic engagement.

REFERENCES

Certeau, Michel de (1984): Practices of Everyday Life, Berkeley: University of California Press.

Corner, James (1999): "The agency of mapping: speculation, critique and invention." In: Denis Cosgrove (ed.), Mappings, Chicago: Chicago University Press, pp. 213-252.

Harmon, Katharine (2003): You Are Here. Personal Geographies and Other Maps of the Imagination, New York: Princeton Architectural Press.

Lavrinec, Jakaterina (2011): "From a 'blind walker' to an 'urban curator': initiating 'emotionally moving situations' in public spaces." In: Limes: Borderland Studies 4/1, pp.54-63.

Lavrinec, Jakaterina (2013): "Urban scenography: emotional and bodily experience." In: Limes: Borderland Studies 6/1, pp. 21-31.

Lefebvre, Henri (1991[1974]): The Production of Space (D. Nicholson-Smith, trans.), Oxford: Blackwell.

Lefebvre, Henri (1996[1968]): "Right to the City." In: Eleonore Kofman/Elizabeth Lebas (eds.), Henri Lefebvre: Writings on Cities. Oxford: Blackwell, pp. 63-184.

Morrison, Elise (2013): "User - unfriendly. Surveillance art as participatory performance." In: Theater 43.3, pp. 5-23.

Morrison, Elise (2015): "Surveillance society needs performance theory and arts practice." In: International Journal of Performance Arts and Digital Media 11/2, pp.125-130.

Perkins, Chris (2009): "Performative and embodied mapping." In: Nigel Thrift/Rob Kitchin (eds.), Encyclopaedia of Human Geography, London: Elsevier, pp.126-132.

Rancière, Jacques (2004): The Politics of Aesthetics: The Distribution of the Sensible, London: Continuum.

Sadler, Simon (1999): The Situationist City, Cambridge, MA: MIT Press.

Verhoeff, Nana (2012): Mobile Screens. The Visual Regime of Navigation, Amsterdam: Amsterdam University Press.

Tagging

The big urban game, re-play and full city tags

Art game conceptions in activism and performance

MARGARETE JAHRMANN

The practice of technological tagging of locations in contemporary urban spaces can be seen in relation to the concept of the 'Re-Play' of urban space and urban life using performance practices. The performance of technological play with mobile technologies in everyday life serves as the starting point for a new interpretation of modern cities as a positive utopia. Re-Play is introduced in this paper as an idea of staging knowledge. In my approach to performance, I consider play a method to identify topographies of cultural or historic interest in urban spaces and to frame potential inter-action on such sites. Play consequently enables the extraction of new stories and new knowledge concerning narratives of the urban. The idea of Re-Play draws on the Situationist principle developed in the 1960s (Constant 1972), of a playful and open society living in a 'New Babylon' that offers zones of play and relaxation as a basis for creativity and a self-determined life – in relation to and through the constructivist use of technologies.

Contemporary activist play and performative urban games have to deal with a specific precondition: the electronic, electromagnetic and logic topography of the modern city, which is marked through 'tags'. Tagging can be understood in two ways, first as an expression of an urban sub-culture of graffiti arts and secondly as a technological term to indicate a virtual-reality marker in physical space. My own work as an artist deals with technologies of ubiquitous topographies in the city – in relation to the individual – in order to raise questions around the cultural implications of tagging technologies.

The ambiguity of the term 'tagging' best expresses the general parallels between practices of performing data and performing the city. The increasing use of smart phones and the technological possibilities of navigation in urban space that they present, and electronic and visual urban markers – commonly called 'tags' – have become a leitmotif of urban life.

Building on the investigation of technological evidence and its theoretical analysis, the practice of using such technologies to track individuals demonstrates new requirements for political agency through play in electronically networked cities. Games and play dealing with these technologies can be explained theoretically by the concepts of perceived, conceived and lived space – or the 'spatial trialectics' – developed by Henri Lefebvre (1991).

THE TRIALECTICS OF URBAN SPACE, AGENCY AND TECHNO-PLAY

The bourgeoisie and the capitalist system thus experience great difficulty in mastering what is at once their product and the tool of their mastery, namely space. They find themselves unable to reduce practice (the practice sensory realm, the body, socio-spatial practice) to their abstract space, and hence new, spatial, contradictions arise and make themselves felt (Lefebvre 1991: 63).

Lefebvre's theory of 'trialectics' of common social spaces can inform contemporary urban play performances in the city. In technologically enhanced kinds of play in urban spaces, topographies can be simultaneously perceived, conceived and lived. As a consequence of the technological information exchanged through contemporary mobile devices, and the personal use of the devices in relation to geographical traces stored via the networks, city spaces are understood by players as a cultural history of changes. In contemporary cities, Lefebvre's seminal theory about sociality in urban environments is radicalized through the technological condition of ubiquitous computing devices – like mobile phones and tablets. To the same degree as their use has become an everyday reality, they affect the experience of a space gradually perceived through a constant stream of information, they alter conceived space through the images and texts uploaded to particular sites, and they reconfigure lived urbanity experienced through the communication aspects offered by devices as an everyday practice of a playful use of technology.

The question of privacy has become pressing with the continual use of these technologies. A critical view of these practices in modern life must inform and shape the conditions of urban games and performances. Only through the critical potential of arts performances can the technologically lived city be addressed as a space where we express ourselves as self-determined citizens. The ability to build new worlds can be enabled by a slightly modified use of technologies.

With a gentle twist, introduced through playful arts experiments, current devices can become a platform for meaningful physical intervention – in contrast to the perceived urban space being experienced as a predefined space. Technologically defined spaces familiar from online mapping systems such as Google Maps can be experienced as a tool of control by industry, yet this control of personal movement can be re-interpreted as a conceived, deliberated, technically re-written and overwritten space of critical consciousness.

BIG DATA IN THE CITY: AN INVISIBLE PERFORMANCE PLAYGROUND

The necessity for a political awareness about the role of electronic topographies in relation to Big Data and its role in economies, surveillance, and espionage is seminal for our contemporary societies of techno-fetishism. Accordingly, the use of mobile devices in urban gaming can be identified as everyday performance practice that enhances the critical use of technologies in a subliminal way. Virtual and physical tags are increasingly used in a way that was not necessarily foreseen by industry. Geographical caching games tend to make visible the combination of storage of individual data about activities, movement patterns, geographical location and network traces, all of which is invisible with ordinary use of the devices. Through their game mechanic, new hybrid urban games support – intentionally or not – the inherent surveillance capabilities of mobile devices and demonstrate how the industry exploits players.

For example, the commercial urban game, *Ingress. The Game* (2014), builds on user image uploads, texts, and on the human ability to identify sites of relevance in geographical space. It constantly collects all available navigation data and exploits the conceived space as well as the space that is generated by a sites' narratives, which are generated in *Ingress* by the players. After a closer look into its game mechanics, it becomes evident that the long-term aim for its release was a consolidation of the Google Maps system as a high-quality content database of lived urban spaces. The game's aim, evidently, is to collect the performance data of players for the increasing development of quality content for sites on Google Maps. In this sense, the game builds on unpaid user work to generate geographical data. This demonstrates an exploitation of user labor based on the joy of play in the mapping geographical data to a perceived space in the city. *Ingress* unfolds as a hybrid game melding technology and reality in urban space. But an analysis of the macro mechanics of the game makes clear that it not only includes the storage of data traces with the purpose of generating a publicly accessible, collectively built map but also tries to achieve a deeper monetization of play performance through user surveillance. Tourist apps hold the promise of being data mines, especially if the content is user centered and combined with playful narrations, as it is in the case of data generated through Ingress. The micro mechanics of the game focuses on public sights like monuments and sculptures. In the game narrative, such objects of art become play objects, they are defined as star-gates to another reality, because the game reality is only made accessible by the technological definition of such sights as 'natural markers' read through a mobile phone camera in urban space. The functionality and viability of such natural-marker technologies depend on the density and size of the related marker databases, consisting of images of the marker objects. At the end of the day, the technology can only function with the help of smart phones and human labor. In this case, the urban performance of players targets the generation of a new unpaid mapping of cities, which can be used later by Google as an alternative city guide mapped by user movements.

As a side effect of conditioning users to constant use of a device in-game, the game play establishes the use of electronic tablets as a user interface for city walks. This effect stems from an advantageous main feature of computer games, which historically was to establish the use of certain, often user-unfriendly, interfaces. Evidence for this dates back to early graphic computers from the 1960s like the Programmed Data Processor-1 *(PDP-1),* up to the use of laser guns for Spacewar games and the modern use of the mouse and touchscreen in personal computer gaming (Pias 2002).

Thirdly, the *Ingress Online* news channel psychologically motivates a community of worldwide players to upload their video data. This takes advantage of practices established by social networks such as Facebook or video channels like YouTube. The Ingress news channel uses elements of a social network, elements of real-time news channels and, not least, of featuring the new tags at urban sites uploaded by players.

In the example of *Ingress. The Game*, Google targets the establishment of user habits to get them to accept a monopoly of mapping. A side effect of the game is establishing social acceptance of user tracking as an everyday practice and forces users to playfully absorb a parallel view of the world we live in on a smart phone or tablet while moving through the real world. The players act as unpaid agents for Google, exercising play within the city as a playground and becoming notorious tagging masters for commercial purposes.

Summing up the 'Ingress experience', it can be said that contemporary play and performative urban games have to deal with a shared precondition: the electronic, electromagnetic and logical topography of the modern city. Everyday life and urban games involve technological sensations and fictions. On closer inspection, they also inherently contain the possibility to raise public awareness about the political dimensions of ubiquitous computing technologies. Being part of a preconceived intervention through electronic artifacts enables players to discover the invisible network and surveillance dimension of common objects in urban space. Urban games can support the uncovering of the mystery of the tools in everyday life. The following art piece description opens the black box of our mobile devices in a very distinct way.

WARDIVE: A DATA TRANSPARENCY STREET PERFORMANCE

The urban game *wardive 1.o* created for iPhone & iPod touch was rejected from Apple's *iTunes Store*. The official explanation for the ban by Apple, sent to the artist developers, was that the app should not publicly display names of user's personal hotspots, which the game intentionally does, during a physical city walk. The obvious reason for a 'too dangerous' classification can be identified in the app's potential of showing data insecurity and data transparency to casual gamers.

Figure 1: wardive, Augmented Reality Screen

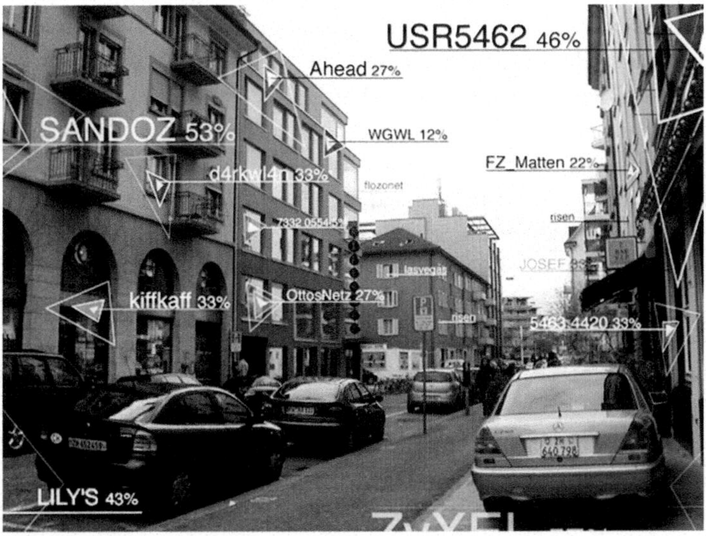

Urban game by andor.ch

According to the artists' description, *wardive* is an adaptive game with locative levels. It converts WLANwaves into game objects and levels, displays the names of the hotspots in the players' immediate area and turns them into enemies in an urban battlefield scenario. As a consequence, the individual perceived space of electronic access points – and its linkage to individual information – influences the behaviour of players in a city. The walking routes chosen by players are selected according to the expected density of individual WLAN access points. The play experience makes no difference to the technical functionality of such individual access points in urban space, but by indicating them dynamically, the app makes a big difference in how the reality of the electromagnetic topography of the city is brought to the consciousness of the individual player on the street, how it is reflected, and how the individual mobile device in the player's hand is used. The interface instructs the player to 'walk through e-toxic streets', to defeat hotspots and WLANs as private property. This game rules the extent to which invisible urban data is present in a technical sense, and which information is given about the accessibility of individual data streams.

Essentially, *wardive* is informed by strategies of a historic electronic subculture, called 'wardiving'. Hacker activists have been players in urban space for years. They perceived the invisible city of the 'electrosphere' as their environment by scanning it technologically and analysing its value systematically. They were trying to find and indicate insecure electronic access points in the city. Using a 'throw-back' practice of tagging a house in the city with chalk, they opened the hermetic space of limited access and privacy. In a world of data streams that are like new streets of a city, insecure access points mean easier surveillance, and can be indicated by an app instead of chalk on the walls. Tagging symbols in general were inspired by chalk tags used by beggars to mark houses in the 19th century. Learning from practices of rejected groups of society in digital performance practice implies a number of associations. Firstly, it expresses solidarity. Secondly, it compares the data poor and data rich to social hierarchies of earlier times. Thirdly, it builds a bridge between the city-dwelling tramp and urban hacker as independent figures in society.

The game also exemplifies the massive accumulation of data as value: each time you play, *wardive* captures different data and creates a new level. This can be translated into the fact that collecting data about access points and users generates a merit. In that sense, *metro wardive* is not only an adaptive game with locative levels. It also changes according to its real-life location as much as it does according to its virtual data world and mutates the player into a *wardive* activist and critical data performer – who experiences the urban space as his or her perceived, conceived and, most importantly, lived space.

Comparably, a related work entitled 'sniff_jazzbox' creates an audible city.[1] It converts the 'electronic ether' waves into sound waves. Technically, the mobile app captures the WLANs in the immediate area and produces a stream of WLAN names. This stream of words might be understood as a subconscious expression of the existing communication networks. The game renders private data visible, translates it and makes it audible as a melody of yearning for contact and exchange. In relation to the number and names of access points the game generates an individual soundtrack of the city that indicates different layers of data. Such a multi-layered concept can be perceived as urban performance, which each player enacts in a hybrid state of physical walking through the city and drifting through an audible data world.

Figure 2: Augmented Reality Screen

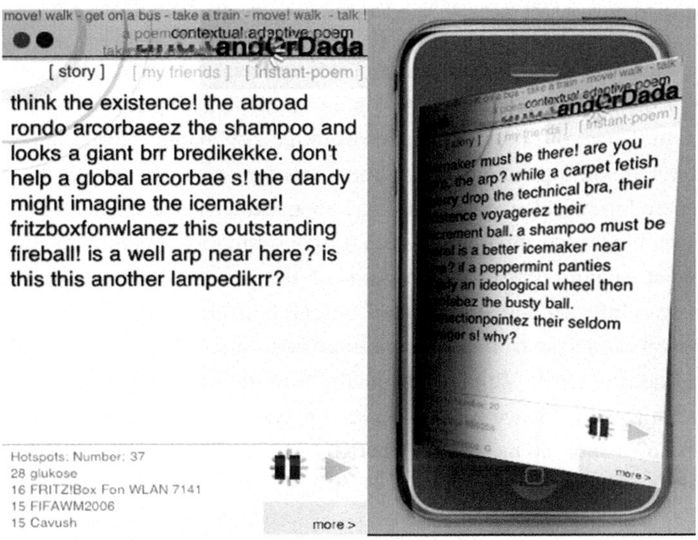

Urban game by andor.ch

The third work of this urban game series associated with the 'and/or group' is of particular interest for theater and performance. The piece *andorDada* is a road poem.[2] The player, also known as the/a performer, strolls through town while the game renders a poem according to the location. It reads, writes out and interprets

1 Cf. http://www.and-or.ch/sniff_jazzbox_audible_city

2 Cf. http://www.and-or.ch/andordada

the subconscious social structure of a town. The result is an endless poem in an emerging digital performance art genre: I would call it 'adaptive locative Dada'.

Such urban games experiment with the concept of agency through the functioning of a technological system, or in other words, the game mechanics. The power of game mechanics is critically questioned in plays more oriented towards theater performance, such as by *machina eX*[3] or *Invisible Playground*. The latter define their games as play in public spaces in order to explore a gray area between game design and participatory art:

> "By referencing playful traditions like video games and sports, we connect to something known and remix it to something new and one-of-a-kind. Our games are post-digital. They use technology, but know of the power of bodies in shared spaces and at a specific site. By creating games that make stories and histories of places playable, we aspire to contribute to the development of play as a cultural technique and an art." (Invisible Playground n.d.)

The contemporary experimental Urban Gaming scene, introduced by Katie Salen (2003) in the Big Urban Game,[4] builds on the deliberating power of game mechanics. In the act of urban performances in the city, hidden stories are revealed and activated, and potentialities for transformation are explored. Each situation is considered to reveal something unique about urban space, yet with connection points to a bigger narrative. I see such a play setting as a method of immersive research: it requires the full immersion of the researcher in a play situation, which is carefully accompanied by self-observation and context observation. The research gets so close to 'the subject researched' that it can then be brought into a critical debate, which stems conceptually from the art movement of *Situationism*. Urban game evidence links to *Situationism* as a source of inspiration for the digital performances in the city in general.

3 Cf. http://machinaex.de

4 The Big Urban Game was commissioned by the Design Institute of the University of Minnesota as a part of its Twin Cities Design Celebration with the goal of encouraging the residents of Minneapolis and St. Paul a way to see their surroundings in a whole new way, and to think about the design of urban space.

SITUATIONISM, REPLAYED

The tactical questioning of everyday-life technologies by game mechanics was already expressed in earlier forms of urban games and play, in the Situationist art of the 20th century. In the 1950s, the Situationists understood performance and play as a means of reordering social and economic relations and to evaluate new systems of thought (Debord 1958). Through the means of urban intervention, a political and social utopia was outlined in which new technologies and arts were considered as the main vehicles of the creation of society. Guy Debord (1958) expressed a general interest in play as political practice in his essay, *A Situationist Definition of Play,* in the magazine *L'Internationale situationniste.* Here, play was introduced as a method and vehicle to radically reclaim urban spaces, to appropriate hegemonic power and to overcome social restrictions of love and life in contemporary societies through 'ludic' time and space. This kind of free play time was supposed to be achieved through technology. Further Situationist writing described the city of the future as a site of total interaction enhanced through mechanisation, in which the need to work is replaced with forms of creative play.

Figure 3: New Babylon

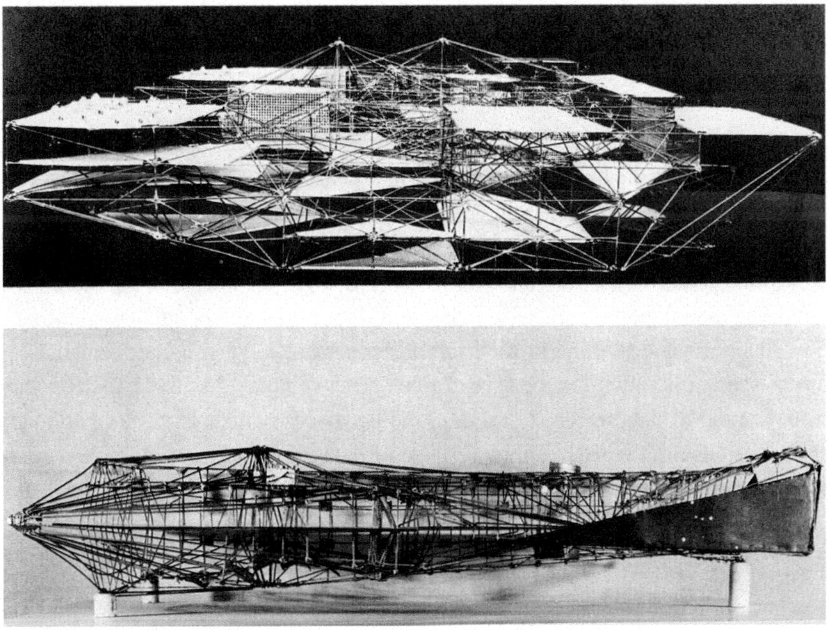

© Constant Nieuwenhuys, 1958

The idea of a technologically informed city was originally introduced by the Dutch artist and architect Constant Nieuwenhuys (1959). He suggested a technological utopia as playfully experienced, perceived and lived spaces. In regard to the role of technology and mechanization, he also spoke about an emerging new society, the playful Ludic Society. This form of life is based on creativity as a process of public play, enabled by the technology of a machine-like city: a moveable and toy-like gamified city, wherein mechanization would liberate the individual from the domination of time and labor. His fictional model was based on an idea of social design triggered and enhanced by intelligent architecture, where mechanisation offers a positive chance to overcome capitalist demands of work. Social interaction, artistic performance and technology were considered to be the main vehicles for creating an open society. Contemporary activist play systems and performance-based urban games about the electronic, electromagnetic cities seem to increasingly appropriate these ideas of a Ludic Society, based on performances in real space, paired with the subversive use of technological objects of everyday life.

In the magazine *Potlatch* (1959), Constant positioned another related idea of a mechanically liberated *homo ludens* in the new Ludic Society:

> "The opposite of utilitarian society is Ludic Society, where the human being, freed by automation from productive work, is at least in a position to develop his creativity. […] He learns by playing. […] Such play is possible due to the integral technical control of all those elements, which thus become a conscious creation of the environment." (Constant 1959: 6)

Today the role of the homo ludens is key in order to develop practices of creative resistance against the hegemonic control of communication technologies. Unfortunately, the new homo ludens of Big Data society is not liberated by play, but controlled and forced into individual self-exploitation and unpaid labor, disguised as casual gaming. The following section introduces dystopian evidence of how technological framing of the everyday has shaped everyday performance in urban space into such exploitative forms. The examples discussed include the visualization of data traces we leave in public spaces, which serves as a counter strategy to dealing with the omnipresence of data as a marker of individual consumer behavior and/or misbehavior.

URBAN MARKS THAT MAKE A DIFFERENCE

Meta information for digital data is usually called a tag. To tag means to mark a place with an individual sign. Tagging is also used for images on Flickr and other social networks. It can also be understood in the sense of a technological marker suitable for Alternate Reality apps, calling up data and layering it over the image of reality, which is reminiscent of the original meaning of tag used in street cultures. On murals, tags are usually linked to an artist's 'street name' and are an attempt to reclaim an urban site through a personal marker. Such artworks indicate the potential of a particular, often devastated urban location, as public space in order to animate urban life. Nowadays, in networked cultures, the connection of physical commodities to electronic networks is increasingly made possible by ubiquitous computing devices.

Figure 4: RFID world tag, 2006, used in the Plymouth RFID Performance

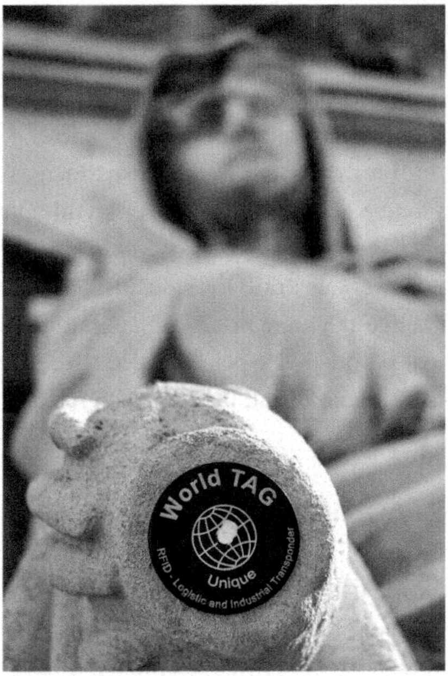

© Mike Lang, UK

In 2006, the Fraunhofer Institute had already defined Radio Frequency Identification (RFID) tags, which are currently used in many mobile phones under the name 'Near Field Communications (NFC)'. It is one of the most influential hybrid technologies to connect materiality and immaterial databases. The technology was developed to make the location and history of goods electronically detectable. It functions based on an electric induction principle: a radio wave is sent to a transponder, which consumes the energy of the initial radio wave and sends data back to the sender/receiver unit. When public awareness of this technology first emerged, artist and activist Rob van Kranenburg (2008) crticically investigated the digital tagging and tracking of objects. He saw such technologies as enhanced states of public surveillance. The sensual dimensions were the subjects of his inquiry. The worlds of electronically tagged things change the role of the subject/object dualism, highlighting the way electronically marked things influence and shape society.

In modern, RFID-equipped stores, customers are under permanent suspicion. Control of the subject by ubiquitous traceability is established by the networking ability of this technology. Furthermore, the possibilities of drawing conclusions from patterns of movements of both objects and people give another meaning to the idea of 'leaving a mark'. The aim to produce a smart supply chain that thinks, responds and adapts has today become a tool of public control. The alternate realities accessed through these markers usually claim a virtual space for commercial reasons. However, urban games of activists and artists have appeared as a counter-reaction to this trend of digitally supported surveillance in urban space – a subculture of art activism dealing with the subversive use of such technologies as a tool for urban performances is increasingly visible. Only critical practice and discourse achieved through a playful approach to technologies can alter the given conditions of technological objects in public spaces. Through this observation, we can draw the conclusion that only creative play with technologies can change the commercial object into a public object, which redirects suspicions. Most promisingly, performance with electronic toys on the street critically questions technology and power structures.

CRITICAL URBAN TAGGING GAMES

A decade ago I introduced, in reference to Constant's ideas of a deliberating technological space, the label of Ludic Society.[5] We designed street games that paved the way for a potential everyday-life subversion of electronic tags and geographical positioning systems. The LS games embraced play, technologies, discourse, and live urban plays. With the help of modified interfaces and stage per-

5 Cf. http://www.ludic-society.net

formances we tried to educate audiences, as expressed in public workshops we held in relation to each street game.

Figure 5: Plymouth Road Runner Superbird, car used in the Plymouth RFID Performance

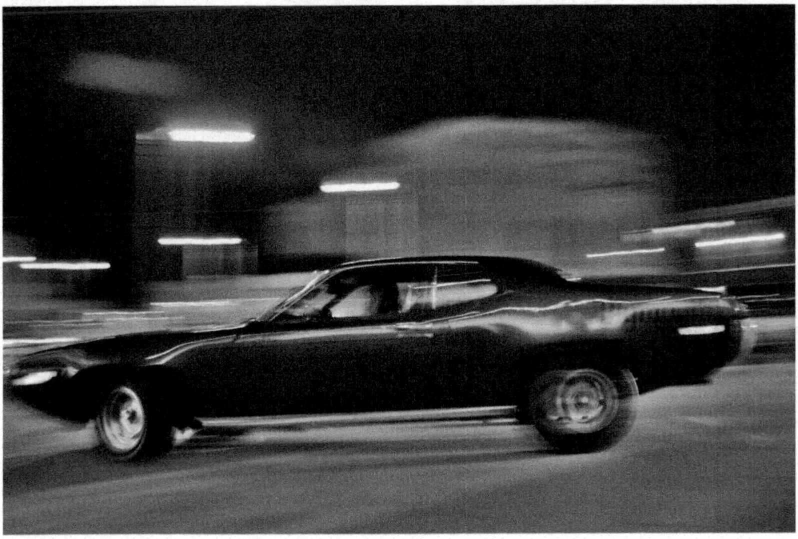

© Mike Lang, UK

The urban game *RFID Judgement Day for 1st Life Game Figures* performed in Plymouth in 2007 consisted of electronic tagging and an implant session. As 'spectacle' in the sense of Situationism, we used a 1970 Plymouth Road Runner Superbird, a sports car, to perform reverse gear races as a game opener on the common English roundabouts. On the original games website, I describe the concept as follows:

This *Tagged City Play* for *Real Players in Real Cities* uses a Plymouth [car] for the Plymouth Play. A local shop serves as a pit stop/workshop location: Being Tagged! Tagging! To tag the city, real world objects, subjectively chosen things, are tagged with working but useless RFID-Tags, so called ZeroNull Tags. To achieve that, Real Players get a flexible tool-kit suitcase, containing spray cans, stencils and stickers, which are part of each Real Player's inventory. Each Real Player is personally tagged by a RFID implant, to generate an individual street art graph, displayed over a satellite online map. The goal is to find and overwrite tags with zero information. A specially designed toy gadget sniffs and alters the state of RFID-Tags, the refreshing electronic little tree. Tagging The

City is played in the real cities with RFID over-clocked Plymouth cars, equipped with self-designed and etched electronic *Wunderbaeumchens.*

Figure 6: Human Tagging Performance, 2006, Plymouth Art Centre, UK

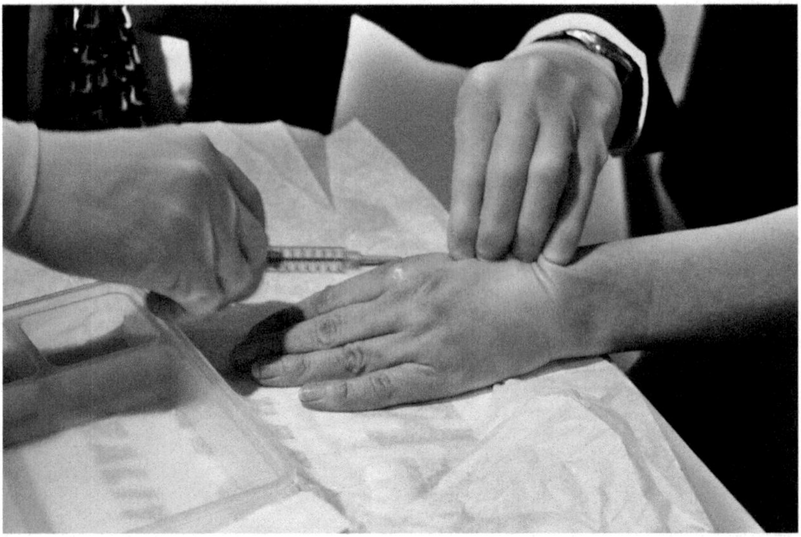

© Mike Lang, UK

A RFID implant session was also performed publicly, as a spectacle. While watching this provocative act of public harm, the audience could perceive the concept of a change of status of the individual by technology being applied to the body in a very direct way. Through their tags, which emitted waves, the players were turned into electronic objects. In the course of the urban game, the players experienced the absurdity of being tagged; of being put on the same level as a semi-synthetic object.[6] In that sense, the game created public awareness of

6 Ludic workshop, Wednesday 21-24 March 2007, Plymouth Art Centre, UK. Workshop topics were tag teams, game play development, last man standing, tool kit box, being tagged, tagging cities. Workshop exercises: Tag and de-valuate objects, reprogramme tags and toy gadgets, adding the value Zero. Tag the city with stencil graffiti to achieve a Full City Tag (=the complete city is systematically tagged). Fully subjectively and collectively, every player can pass judgement by tagging objects, buildings, vehicles, persons and is judged by wearing a RFID Tag under the skin. Second: scan tags with the *Wunderbäumchens* and change the Internet of things into the value Zero. Third: take souvenir photographs of Plymouth tags and the Plymouth. The Real

hybrid technologies as invaders of privacy; even of the most intimate space of the body. While watching this provocative act of public harm, the audience could perceive the concept of a change of status of the individual by technology, which is applied to the body in a very direct way. It created public awareness of hybrid technologies as invaders of privacy; even of the most intimate space of the body. Accordingly, we gave performance lectures explaining that anonymity no longer exists if the individual is marked under the skin and becomes a permanent emitter of electromagnetic waves. In the map of the piece, each player's number is rendered in an individual graph online. This movement pattern is displayed on an individual map for every player as a layer over Google Maps. All player uploads were layered, and when automatically cycled through, the result was a movie of player movements. The film was shown in the Plymouth Arts Gallery as an online-generated 'performance-map movie'.

Figure 7: we sell play no games! RFID workshop in the Plymouth shopping center, UK

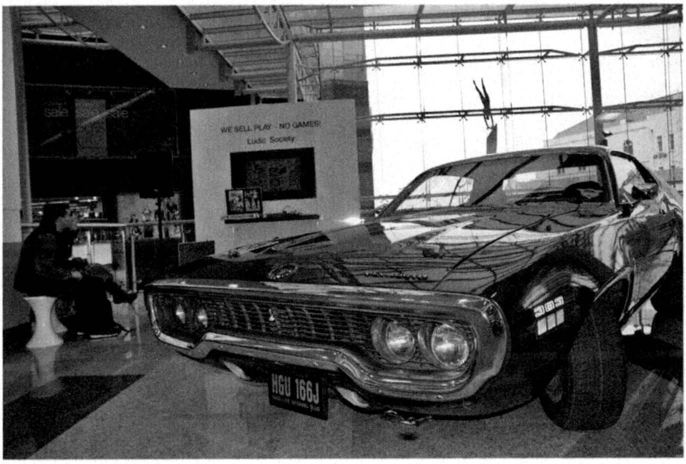

© Mike Lang, UK

Play extends the game zone into a situated locative play in a real city. Come and judge with your tag! See: http://www2.kurator.org/wiki/main/read/workshops

Figure 8: Plymouth Play, 2007. Online Interface of map of RFID implants

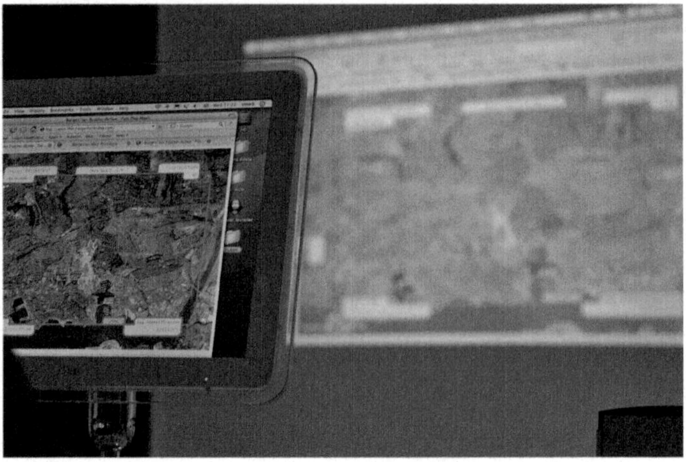

© Mike Lang, UK

With the help of combinatory interfaces of serious information, storytelling and, most importantly, play, a seed of doubt is sewn in the enjoyment of technological everyday-life tools. Such critical urban game concepts can be best developed through the observation of players in commercial urban games and the inversion of their introduced logics and game mechanics.

Reviewed from the perspective of agency potentials in play with technologies, the theoretical framework of trialectics can be applied to an analysis of performance works in urban space, which are consequently produced as a reaction to a social history of technological changes. According to this logic, the urban tagging games in this paper are categorized into three distinct types of performance play. They are perceived as applications of concepts of data performance in a perceived agency. This means that the model of agency is demonstrated by the urban game, in order to make agency perceivable to the public. Referring to Lefebvre's concept, conceived conceptual performance made out of urban data appears as conceived agency. The construction of a situation in an urban space – the performance, so to say – is the basis for the conceived space. In the course of the performance and based on the experience from the performance in raising awareness about the wealth of data collected about the individual player, a new form of agency is opened up, one which combines play and activism in one. Lived interventions of principles are finally fully experienced by the players of urban games – a category of lived agency as a strategy against Big Data surveillance through performative digital play.

REFERENCES

Debord, Guy (1958): "Contribution to a Situationist definition of play. Internationale Situationniste #1." (R. Keehan, trans.), In: situationist international online, September, 23, 2015 (http://www.cddc.vt.edu/sionline/si/play.html)

Invisible Playground (n.d.): "How we make games". October 15, 2015 (http://www.invisibleplayground.com/en/category/games)

Kranenburg, Rob van (2008): The Internet of Things. A Critique of Ambient Technology and the All-Seeing Network of RFID. Amsterdam: Institute of Network Cultures.

Lefebvre, Henri (1991[1974]): The Production of Space (D. Nicholson-Smith, trans.), Oxford: Blackwell.

Muñoz-Cremers, Omar (2007): "Playing the arcades project with the ludic society." Report by Omar Muñoz-Cremers about The Evening of Ludic Society, DEAF07, March 9, 2016 (http://v2.nl/archive/articles/playing-the-arcades-project-with-the-ludic-society)

Nieuwenhuys, Constant (1958): Utopia New Babylon, September 12, 2015 (http://intern.strabrecht.nl/sectie/ckv/10/Architectuur/Babylon/CKV-f0011.htm)

Nieuwenhuys, Constant (1974): New Babylon. A Nomadic Town, September 12, 2015 (http://www.notbored.org/new-babylon.html)

Pias, Claus (2002): Computer Spiel Welten. Berlin: Diaphanes.

Sutton-Smith, Brian (1997): The Ambiguity of Play, Cambridge: Harvard University Press.

Games

"andorDada" (http://www.and-or.ch/andordada)

"Ludic Society Tagging game" (http://ludic-society.net/tagged/)

"Ingress. The Game" (https://www.ingress.com)

"wardive 1.o" (http://www.and-or.ch/wardive_wintermute)

Co-producing

From flâneur to co-producer

The performative spectator

IMANUEL SCHIPPER

In the 1842 drawing, Le Flâneur, we see modern man[1] – well dressed, standing[2] with his hands in the pockets of the long, baggy but still elegant trousers, shirt and coat, a stick under his left arm, a hat on his head, his face tilted towards the sun. Much ink has been spilled over this strolling figure, this aimless walker of 19th-century Parisian streets, as he was a central figure in literary works by Poe, Joyce, Baudelaire, Döblin, and Proust. This romantic figure takes us – the readers – by the hand for a stroll into the city and shares all that he discovers with us. But the flâneur does much more than just discover secrets in the arcades of early modernity and cultivate his idleness. He is the prototype of the modern urbanist, a new sort of city goer as there were and are many types around. The flâneur dwells in the streets with "cool but curious eyes" (Rignall 1989: 112); he is the constant observer of the ever-changing spectacle that emerges around him. "Have we seen enough of the flâneur, the Parisian idler who sampled the sights and sounds of the city as he strolled with no destination in mind?" asks Gregory Shaya (2004: 46) in his essay:

1 In most images and stories, flâneurs are male, as is echoed by the male form adopted or cited in this text. Most theories on flâneurship are in this sense problematic; see the feminist crique on this discourse (cf. Wolff 1985; Van Godsendthoven 2005; Scalway et al. 2006).

2 Paul Gavarni: Le Flâneur, 1842.

"He was a common figure of the nineteenth century, essential to any picture of the streets of Paris. The flâneur was the man of leisure who went into the street in search of some satisfaction for his overdeveloped sensibilities. He was, by various accounts, a gastronome, a connoisseur, an idler, an artist [...]." (Shaya 2004: 47)

The later attribution is the one that might be interesting in contemporary discourses: the flâneur as an artist, an actor, and a writer. Let us go back to Garvin's little image.

Figure 1: Le Flâneur

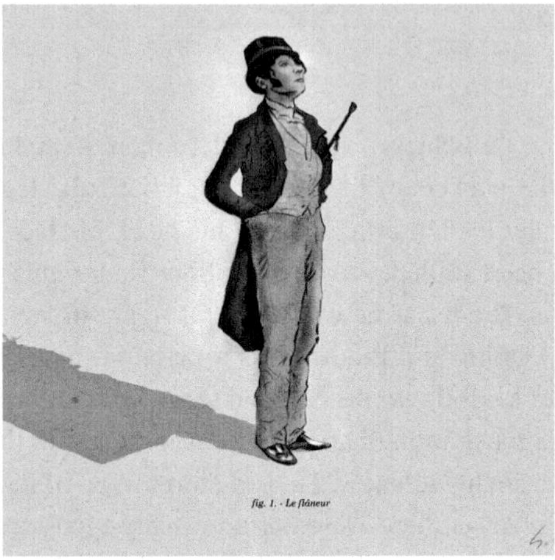

© Paul Garvarni, 1842

The elegant man with his stick, standing still for a moment and looking up in the air – where is he looking and what is he seeing? A bird, a tree in blossom, a lady behind a window? Or is he just enjoying the sun as hinted at by the shadow behind him? We do not know and actually it is not of importance WHAT he is looking at but how that looking-at-whatever-it-is constitutes his specific experience and makes him important enough to become a *sujet* for the painter. In other words: this flâneur is both a spectator and an actor in a play called 'the flâneur'.

As Cees Noteboom notes (1995), flâneurs are artists even if they do not write, because they are witnessing that what is going on in the city, "they are the eye, the protocol, the memory, the judgement, the archive, in flâneurs the city becomes aware of itself" (Noteboom 1995: n. pag.; my translation).

It is this double action of flâneurship that is of interest. By walking through the streets and collecting impressions, the flâneur is constantly producing a story of his lived experiences while being an *acteur* in the play he is currently watching. Although Rancière is not voting for theatrical actions that force the audience to become physically active, he describes the constant activity of the spectator even in a classical setting of theater:

"The spectator also acts [...]. She observes, selects, compares, interprets. She links what she sees to a host or other things that she has seen on other stages, in other kinds of place. She composes her own poem with the elements of the poem before her. She participates in the performance by refashioning it in her own way – by drawing back, for example, from the vital energy that it is supposed to transmit in order to make it a pure image and associate this image with a story which she has read or dreamt, experienced or invented. [...] This is a crucial point: spectators see, feel and understand something in as much as they compose their own poem, as, in their way, do actors or playwrights, directors, dancers or performers." (Rancière 2009: 13)

I agree with Rancière that bringing the audience out of theater buildings would not necessarily mean an emancipation of the spectator, but I would argue that a specific mode of walking in the city (the flâneur-mode) comes very close to what Rancière would call emancipated spectatorship. The flâneur is not just an observer or passive spectator of a finished play, he is more a coproducer of that very city life. He is in a mode that is described as "a historically specific mode of experiencing the spectacle of the city in which the viewer assumes the position of being able to observe, command, and participate in this spectacle all at the same time" (Schwartz 2001: 1733). It was Walter Benjamin who introduced the concept of the flâneur into academia in 1929 with Die Wiederkehr des Flâneur (1991[1929]: 194-199), reviewing Hessel's Spazieren in Berlin and later in 1935 sketches of The Arcades Project (1999[1935]), where he pointed out that the flâneur is an active producer of the urban scenery he lives in: "It [the city] opens up to him as a landscape, even as it closes around him as a room" (Benjamin 1999[1935]: 417). For Benjamin, the city not a fixed thing anymore but a space that changes its appearance and functionality constantly depending on the action and choices of its visitor, user, inhabitant, actor. And the city even becomes a strange and unknown place: "To the flâneur, his city is – even if [...] he happened to be born here – no longer native ground. It represents for him a theatrical display, an arena" (Benjamin 1999[1935]: 347). Benjamin, reflecting Baudelaire here, propose to see the city as theater that is set up and used by actors, which in this case are flâneurs, but are increasingly all members of urban society in general.

In other words: in the city that works here as a medium (cf. Kittler 1996) it is the citygoer, the passant, the active and emancipated spectator (cf. Rancière 2009) that turns the urban landscape into a "theatre of social action" (Mumford 2015: 93), a "theatre whose setting is the street" (Brecht 1987[1930]: 176)[3] or a performance (cf. Schipper 2014a). The assemblage of collected impressions are merged into a texture of experiences, a storyboard of the film that we live at the same time. Or more generally and in the words of the human geographer Doreen Massey: "We are constantly making and re-making the time-spaces through which we live our lives" (Massey 1999: 23). Massey not only discusses the inseparable relations of space and time but in her core argument points to the production of identities through the concept of relational aspects of space: "We cannot 'become', in other words, without others. And it is space that provides the necessary condition for that possibility" (Massey 2005: 56). The very performative notion of space – that it is not a fixed thing to walk through but more a mean or medium in which things and settings become possible – has been discussed by many scholars such as Lefebvre (1974), Certeau (1980), Merleau-Ponty (1945), Deleuze and Guattari (1980). I do not intend to dig deeper into relational space theories or the politics of space. However, it is obvious that these approaches to space and space production have an effect not only on how we receive space as such, but actually form the way we behave in that space and even what and how we see and understand things, objects, situations and actions in that space. In other words – the space we produce will structure the life-time we spend in it.

This is a highly performative approach to describing space and its narrative – the relational space production gets a kind of dramaturgical agency for the play that is called "my life". Recalling our flâneur as a starting point and heading to questions of theatrical performances that use digital technologies and urban space, it seems to be useful to remember the dramaturgical importance that space production has. (cf. Schmidt 2010, Schipper 2014, Fischer-Lichte/Wihstutz 2013 and Merx this volume) Now – I do agree that the flâneurs, the dwellers, the strolling figures, are not in completely the same role as a member of a classic theater audience, as this is mostly sitting on a given seat in a dark indoor space, staring at the illuminated stage. Theater producers have employed these conditions to concentrate the attention of spectators towards hot spots of action and debate since the late 18th century. This primacy of emphasizing the event may

3 In his 1930 poem "On Everyday Theatre", Brecht invites the actors ("[…] you artists who perform plays / In great houses under electric suns […]") to step down from the stage and visit the city and its theater in the streets. (cf. Brecht 1987: 176–179, Rokem 2010: 158-160)

be the crucial point that has changed in contemporary performances investing in the use of digital technologies.

DIGITALITY

What makes a theater production that belongs to digital culture different from one that does not? Of course, that raises the question of what digital cultures are at all, and engenders many possible answers[4]. In this essay, I closely follow the concept of Felix Stalder in his recent publication on the culture of digitality, where he proposes three quite general qualities that together constitute together of what could be called digital culture: referentiality – the use of existing cultural material that has to be selected and merged, communality – the autonomous or heteronomous collective actions in networks, and algorithmicity – automatic processes that make data sets visible and usable for human beings. Stalder's tryptichon is very helpful for the analysis of performances as it addresses questions of materiality (text, actors), structure (dramaturgy), and reception (audience), yet it lacks one important aspect of the latter: the multiple, strong and completely changed position and responsibility of the individual member of the audience.

In this paper, I discuss this issue by arguing that a focus on audience experience is of utmost importance. More specifically, I will look at the mode of participation and coproduction the audience is given and how much this will transform the simple spectator to a coproducer of the performance that he/she is attending. Following the example of the flâneur in the city, I will discuss two examples of how digital technologies emphasize the changed concept of spectatorship. Both examples need an audience that works as a coproducer; both move the spectators around and ask them to perform actions. And although in neither example is the audience seated in a theater, but has to move around in space, nor is the plot presented by actors, but the content delivered by an audio stream over headphones, the kinds of approach to spectatorship are quite different in each of the two performances. Walking the City by LIGNA is a site-specific audio-guided tour in an urban landscape and Situation Rooms is more a multiplayer video game in a labyrinth-like installation. In both performances the compositions of the experiences are related to the choices of the spectator, although there

4 See the video interviews *DCRL Questions: What are digital cultures?*: http://www.leuphana.de/en/research-centers/cdc/digital-cultures-researchlab/projects/dcrl-questions.html

does exist a stream of rules and hints delivered to the audience through an audio voice or video clips. In these cases, the digital devices do not mainly replace the stage or deliver the content but serve as a hand that guides the user through the experience. I chose these examples in order to discuss the ways the role of the audience is formed by the specific use of digital devices.

In an essay on new media dramaturgy, the authors ask the question: "What job can or does the spectator do?" (Eckersall/Grehan/Scheer 2015: 376), stating that the digital cultures are not just an additive to that which happens on stage but are a radical change to every aspect of performance, and especially the spectator. They argue that performances working under the paradigm of new media dramaturgy change "everything for the spectator. The landscapes of production and reception are unrecognizable in the sense that the use of space and the demands on our attention as spectators are radically different than they have been up until now." (ibid.) Even while a huge change has been brought about, there remains a situation where there is an attention produced by the production and demanded of the spectator. But what about performances where the demand is not produced by the artistic team but by the users-spectators, or the attention has to be given by the so called actors and not the audience? What about productions that will only take place if the audience is much more active than the production team? There are performances that evoke computer games more strongly than dramatic plays, and sometimes, there is literally nothing more for an audience to see than what you would see as a flâneur. The state of coproduction is already beyond that what Bishop discusses in her conclusion of Artificial Hells:

> "From the audience's perspective, we can chart this as a shift from an audience that demands a role [...], to an audience that enjoys its subordination to strange experiences devised for them by an artist, to an audience that is encouraged to be a co-producer of the work." (Bishop 2012: 277)

WALKING THE CITY

In 2013-14, the Hamburg-based performance collective, LIGNA, invited the audience to an audio-guided stroll through eight different cities in *Walking the City*. LIGNA consists of three media- and performance artists who describe their work as "creating temporary situations that employ their audience as a collective of producers" (LIGNA n.d.), they are the inventors of the *RadioBallet* (2002), that "provides radio listeners with a choreography of excluded and forbidden gestures in formerly public, now controlled spaces like train stations or shopping malls. [...] More recent works like *Secret Radio* (2014) or *The Great Refusal* invite the participants to stage a complex interaction in public space or on stage, which discloses itself to them only gradually." With *Walking the City* LIGNA asks different questions about walking, inspired by the one strong question from Balzac (2011 [1833]: 33):

"Is it not truly extraordinary to realise that ever since men have walked, no-one has ever asked why they walk, how they walk, whether they walk, whether they might walk better, what they achieve by walking, whether they might not have the means to regulate, change or analyse their walk: questions that bear on all the systems of philosophy, psychology and politics with which the world is preoccupied?"

Walking the City is a performance without actors that invites the audience to stroll through a pre-existing ready-made urban space and experiment with it in particular ways and, in doing so, read it afresh. Of course, there are constant, well-composed and registered acoustic invitations to perform actions. They are sent by a radio transmitter to a personal radio receiver, which are handed out at the beginning of the show. Nevertheless, the audience would only get half the experience if they didn't set themselves into action and actually – walk:

"At the starting point, I am handed a small radio receiver with headphones. A voice tells me to walk toward the Spalenberg district in the old town. On the way, my acoustic guide repeatedly draws my attention to my gait, the steps my companions and I are taking. The voice instructs me to move closer to my fellow peripatetic researchers, link arms with them and walk down the alley in coordinated rhythm. Our steps echo off the narrow house fronts like those of marching soldiers; bemused passers-by stop and stare at our procession. You can see them asking themselves: what on earth are they up to? What's the demonstration all about? Altered by the visual and acoustic intervention, the space becomes unsettling. For a brief moment, Spalenberg is transformed from a charming and sleepy little shopping street that can feel somewhat lonely even on the busiest days, into the walkway for a potentially violent corps of loudly marching people. The group takes possession of the space, pushing pedestrians towards its edge; and suddenly the street seems to close in. One is reminded of the Morgenstraich – the parade that forms part of Basel's carnival celebrations – or a troop of soldiers returning to barracks after a march-past. I am right in the middle of it, part of it. I too am causing this change. Later I am alone once again with the voice in my ear instructing me to conduct various investigations into the act of walking. The scene changes yet again; the street is at once a laboratory and an object of inquiry. I read the asphalt and flagstones as a map for future paths, the holes and dirt in them as the traces of past activities. I walk on, staring down at the ground, then gazing only at the sky and interpreting the clouds; finally, I advance with my eyes closed. As I walk, I link the locations I have passed through – the places of the past – into a network that potentially contains future places. I experience this space and the way the past flows through the present moment into a future. A space defined by temporal and social coordinates takes shape. Led and guided by the voice from the radio, my body and my movements, evidently less smooth and more halting that just a couple of years ago, become an instrument for measuring this space-time experience. Finally, the voice leads me zigzagging from one side of the road to another. I rebound through the streetscape marked out by my experience like a rubber ball, until I am instructed to bring my solitary excursion to an end. Filled with my newly-detailed knowledge of the streets of Spalenberg, I return the radio receiver." (Schipper 2014b: 27)[5]

Figure 2: Walking the City, Poitiers

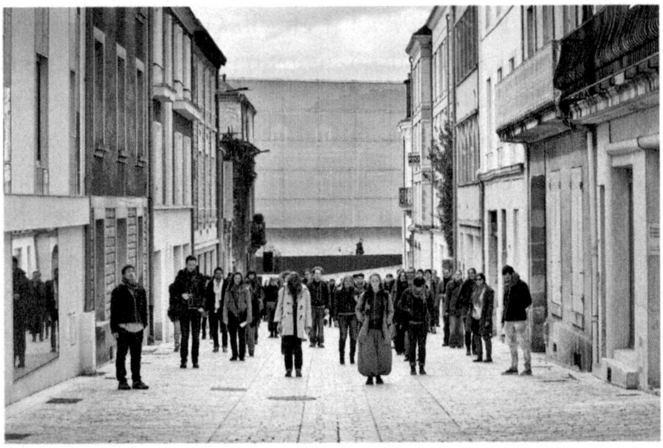

© Arthur Pequin for LIGNA, 2013

"The City Is a Medium" stated Kittler and Griffin in 1996, actually pointing to the functions of information, data and networks that the built infrastructure inhabits. But in *Walking the City,* it was exactly not the buildings, the streets or the pavement that was constructed there years ago. The essentials of that experience were the traces of past lives, the echo of walkers from many hours ago, the imagined possibilities of the multilayered spaces. These experiences were not told through the written text that was played directly into my ears. What was preproduced had very little to do with what I, as one individual member of the audience, was producing during the show: dancing, standing, running, searching,

5 This quote and the one in the later section are borrowed from an article on scenography I wrote for the Swiss Culture Foundation Pro Helvetia (Schipper 2014b).

jumping, marching… and of course walking – these were actions that I was asked to do – but the text (or texture) of what I lived and lived through was not given to me. And obviously the own biography, the own taste, they own interests are strong guides of your individual experience. How does the experience of a spectator participating o the performance differ from that one could have if we would just walk through the city in a different manner? Or in other words: what is the distinction from a spectator to a flâneur?

Both made the choice to walk through the city in a way that is not only dedicated to the fastest way to get your body from point A to point B. Both have the privilege to spend time to experience themselves in that specific mixture of spaces called the city and to collect and assemble impressions after their own rules. But besides to some similarities there is still some important differences: While the flâneur is completely driven by no specific interests and no specific aim to reach - the LIGNA-walker has a kind of a temporal and also spatial structure that works like a set of rules of a sport game or the invisible agenda of a wedding ceremony. And not unlike a sport game that looks every time completely different even though the rules are exactly the same, this performance is not only different on every show every single day and in every single city but also for every single audience member. The set of rules that we know from sports but of course even more from all games is the stable structure for all shows that incorporates as the two sides of a medal: stay exactly the same and allows only the multiplicity of experiences.

This is a fundamental shift in the history of theater and the concept of the theater audience: where an architecturally designed focus of a theater guided all senses to the stage, now there are radio receiver earphones, so close to your brain. Because they are stuck literally in your ears, earphones are no longer even visible; they are so light, awareness of the technical intervention fades after just a few minutes. A technical infrastructure is voluntarily adopted. This kind of 'cyborg light' makes auditory sense very sensitive to the messages that come out of the radio transmitter. But the optical sensorium and the infinite possibilities for movement are completely free of the limitations of theatrical infrastructures.

In other words: in this case the voice and the body of one actor (or many actors) is divided in this digital-spatial performative network into two actors (at least): One is the technological device that incorporates the set of rules of that interactive encounter by delivering acoustic invitations or framing actions in the given borders of time and space. This representative of the digital world also suggests at one moment to take an individual tour and at another to team up with some fellow city-walkers to march in formation. The voice is the leader and guide through the game. Dramaturgically, it is a structural voice but not a voice that conveys content. It is voice that answers more the question of 'how' (the play looks) than the question of 'what' (the play is about).

Another aspect of normal theater that is played by the actor is that of providing the body for the performance. In *Walking the City,* this role completely delegated to the audience. Each participant embodies the actor that will act in the show he is attending. Theatrical events like this – walks, audio guided tours – often work with this theater-historical game-changer – there is no actor to do all the work; no audience to sit and passively witness. In this production there is nothing to see unless the spectator puts himself into action. This play goes a step further than just presenting an invitation to participate – it gives clear instructions to follow in order to see the play. Already in the title – *Walking the City* – it says what is expected from you. Some may decide not to follow the invitation or prefer not to accept the rules of the game. Their decision would only effect their own experience and would not have any impact on others who decide individually to follow the instructions.

This radio play works in very sophisticated way with the possibilities of grouping and separating players as it starts with a collective body of walkers in the street, followed at some point by separation from the group to follow individual paths. And again: the actions that you decide to perform dictate what kind of experience you have. In addition to the rules and invitations from the device and the physical and sensual experiences derived from your actions, there is a third kind of agency in the game that is quite important: the unpredictable. Other people, action on the street, buildings, traces of previous city goers – these are all random elements that are neither in the hands of the production of theater pieces nor really selectable for the recipient. It is an *agency of chance* that is staged here along with a *technological agency* (that of the devices and the voices) and a *human agency* (that of individual choices).

The audio stream that is broadcast to the audience as a radio emission has the function of a master of ceremony, an 'acteur' that sets rules, decides and controls the timeframes and invites guests (the audience) to investigate the topic (walking the city) by proposing different actions. It also delivers some extra historical and site-specific information, plays music and reminds you to get back on time. Even while the hands of the users/players/spectators are free and the guiding voice sits in the ears, this set-up still produces a strange feeling of being taken by the hand.

SITUATION ROOMS

Let's change the scenery. We are going back into a closed venue, not really a theater space, but one of the many industrial-era factories repurposed into cultural spaces. In the middle of a hall stands a huge installation that looks like the back side of a film set, dark panels and a dozen yellow doors, each with a big number on it. It is the installation of *Situation Rooms* made by the German/Swiss collective *Rimini Protokoll* in collaboration with the scenographer Dominic Huber.

Figure 3: Model and draft for Situation Rooms A & B

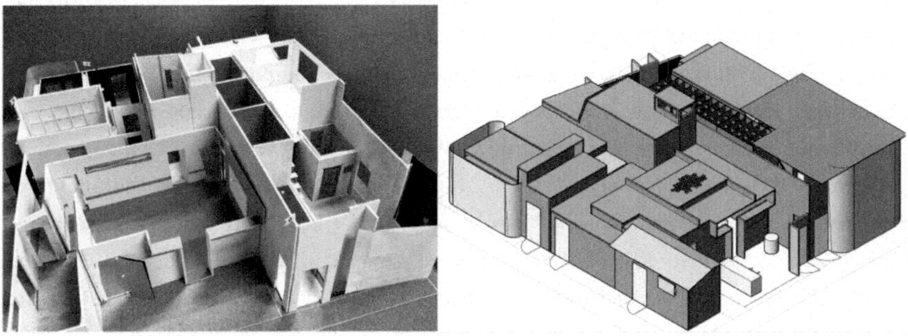

© Dominic Huber, 2013

Situation Rooms is a production about war, the international network of arms trades, the uses of arms and the impact of what the use of arms could have. Viewers are led to consider what the content and the aesthetics of that play could have been. (cf: Schipper (2014), Oberender (2015), Birgfeld/Garde et al. (2015), Whistutz (2015) In this paper I am interested in the way the concept of augmented reality is used and how that impacts the mode of spectatorship. But first, another subjective impression:

"In the space of three short hours, I am twenty different people. On one occasion I am nine years old; on another I am in my late sixties. I hail from thirteen different countries and find myself in as many different theaters of action. Each time I follow my hand, which holds an iPad on which short film sequences are replayed. The films were made using the same device, carried by a protagonist in the arms and war trade. I watch the screen and attempt to replicate the movements previously made by the person behind the camera. When the film shows me a hand opening a door, I open that actual door in front of me. Every seven minutes the screen goes dark, and the journey into the world of the absent protagonist is interrupted. I am myself once again overwhelmed by the stranger's life in which I was just immersed, and disconcerted by the momentary duplication of the present. I am aware that I am standing on a stage set made up of separate, interlinked rooms, all of which are depictions of a reality. As a former helicopter pilot in the Indian army, I ascend to a lookout point affording views over the wide expanses of Kashmir with unmanned drones keeping watch for terrorists. At the same time, this imaginary tactical lookout opens up a real view of the complex set design. Spotlights hang from the ceiling, flickering in choreographed pattern. Here I can make out the photographic mural of the oriental city, there the huddle of tents making up the field hospital, artfully illuminated from outside. I can also see the black stage wall sections, professionally assembled in sequence to divide up the space. I look down from above on the intermingled, superimposed spaces and worlds below: a sight that conveys peace and order but at the same time makes clear that this peace exists only outside the system. It is a glance behind the scenes of this machinery of war and weapons. I meet possible arms buyers, take aim at potential terrorists, shake hands with politicians, examine wounded patients and put on a bulletproof vest. I experience first hand how a weapon manufactured in peaceful Europe causes me life-threatening injuries in the space next door. With the voices of the absent protagonists in my ears and their fields of view on the iPad in my hand, I move in their stead through hyper-realistically recreated copies of their worlds. […] I travel through countries, places, spaces and times, before finally I am disgorged once again into the auditorium. What remains are the stories, the images and the physical experiences such as a handshake, lying in the field hospital, the smell of borscht – and the disquieting feeling that so many things are linked to other things, and that behind local theaters of conflict there is a global space of responsibility and consequences." (Schipper 2014b: 28)

There are a number of similarities in the way the audience is addressed in *Walking the City* and *Situation Rooms* – and some important differences. Here too, the visitor is equipped with a digital gear, in this case with headphones that are connected to an iPad mini that is installed in landscape mode on a wooden holder. This installation lets you hold the display in a way reminiscent of the use of selfie sticks, but actually the spectator is asked to use it in a way familiar from some augmented reality apps, where you hold the image of your device in visual coordination with the real world in front of you. It is a performative gesture that is broadly known from situations where we compare a materialized image (painting, photo prints, sketches, …) with the original sujet.

Once the user has understood this main rule of the game, he is taken into that multilayered installation of 20 characters and their stories and 15 highly real interiors. All the Spaces look like film settings, which is what they actually are. On the devices you see film clips that were shot with the camera of the very iPod that the audience holds in their hands in that very film set / installation.[6] This is an interesting transfer: Though the user only sees a pre-produced video clip on the screen of the iPad, he behaves as if it were an augmented reality application by constantly overlying the devices image with the real world. Using AR in urban surrounds you get an overlay of actual (and reproduced) information a live camera image that you have to transfer to the actual real world. In *Situation Rooms,* the medially material is all pre produced – the image on the device, the information you get and even the 'real world' is only a pre-produced film set. Though some documentary material is included, the main function of the film clips is guiding visitors through the labyrinth of the installation, bringing them to a previously foreseen position in the room and directing their field of vision towards the director's proposition.

This complete set of visual instructions that moves bodies, faces and eyes is superimposed with the voice of the protagonist (which changes every seven minutes) that tells his/her story in a way that addresses you directly, like the beginning of the clip of Amir Yagel, Israel Defense Forces, 50th Batallion, 2007-2010:

"I just finished high school. I was 18. My dream in this age was to have sex already with a girl. I didn't know back then that the south, the north, the east and the west, the railways, the buses and the junctions of Israel will all look totally different to me from now on. [A video clip is showed on the] This is in Hebron 2009 five AM and the Muezzin is calling. This video was shot by soldiers I knew during the time I was in the army. How was the army for me? At first, I had to get used to speak with plural and not in singular form. We were always together. […]" (Rimini Protokoll: 2013)

Or Andreas Geikowski's, a sport shooter in Germany:

"This is the shooting range in Wannsee, Berlin. I work between 8-10 hours here every day. And train the police and competitive shooting athletes. That's me 22 years ago, training for the Berlin police force. That was the first time I came into contact with a live firearm. And that's me today: Andreas Geikowski, 45 years old, active shooting athlete for 23 years. I'm the sponsored marksman for the companies Heckler & Koch, H&N Geschosse and Triebel Berlin." (Rimini Protokoll: 2013)

In other words: the way the spoken text is written and spoken by the protagonist invites or actually forces the visitor to play the lives of the protagonists for seven

6 The filming was done simultaneously with all 20 protagonists.

minutes. This is supported with the visual field of a subjective camera that was shot by the protagonist and the hyper-realistic reconstructed copy of the protagonist's space. The combination of text, voice, film clip and physical space produces an immersive experience that visitors almost cannot escape from.

Figure 4: In the role of Irina Panibratowa, a Russian nutrional engineer in a weapons factory

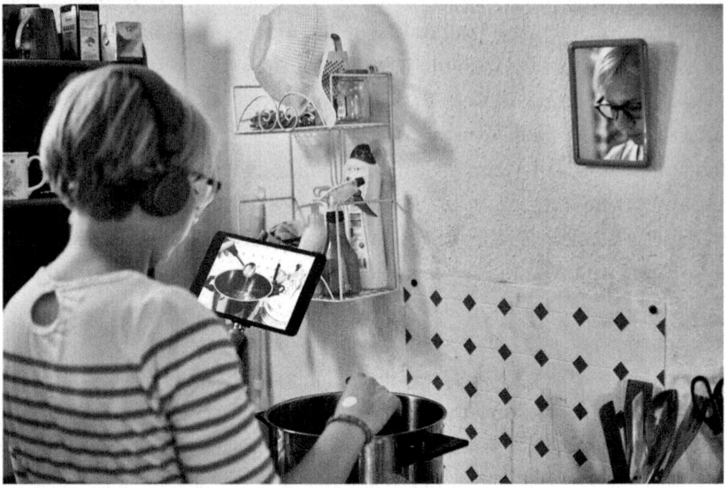

© Jörg Baumann, 2013, for Ruhrtriennale & Rimini Protokoll

Digital technology here affords a closer taking-by-the-hand than in *Walking the City*. The System of the game works like a clock. It does not stop. Either you are following the trace and the pace or you are out. The grade of freedom in the offer to participate is small here – it is more an invitation to step into a pre-produced role than to explore different possibilities. The devices help the visitor to take the position of the protagonist – like a prompter guides an actor through the performance.

While the user/gamer/visitor/spectator follows the visual instructions on the device, they listen to the stories of the protagonists and enter one room after the other. They sometimes meet other visitors, also equipped with iPad and earphones. On the screen, however, they see the another protagonist filming their own tour. For this reason, a single space can be for one visitor the canteen of an arms factory in Switzerland; for another, an apartment in Russia; for a third, the solitary room of a detention center for asylum seekers in Germany. The Rooms are defined not just through their built existence, but also by Situations and by those who play their roles within them. As you visit different rooms from different places of the world and incorporate different positions in that deadly network you get a broad, diverse and multiple view on that field.

The *human agency* seems to allow less freedom in that piece than in the work of LIGNA as each movement in the installation and every position in the spaces is choreographed by the directors, acted and filmed by the protagonists and reenacted by the audience. It is this feeling of standing in place of somebody in a naturalistic reconstruction of an original venue that works better if you try to copy the point of view of the protagonist as perfectly as possible. Obedience to clear rules seems to promise a stronger experience. In *Situation Rooms,* the spectators are not only asked to follow the path of the protagonists but also to interact with other users – to shake hands, to serve soup, to take coats. By doing so, they serve the story of another visitor by using their bodies – in other words: they became an actor and perform with and for other spectators/actors. Concerning the *technological agency* we can add the following: the films are shot on iPads with a wide-angle lens framing a section of the world that demands actions and positions. They lay the path that the users will follow in order to reenact a historical situation. What brings us to the *agency of chance* that is marginal here as I compared this system with a clockwork. In fact, everything is set up so that, in theory, each session of seven minutes looks the same and works in exactly the same way. Nevertheless, there is a strange and unpredictable situation produced if we consider the moment of the after-performance, when the audience has given back the technical equipment, have met in the foyer and started to talk. Then a new play starts. Questions are asked, "Who were you?", "where were you?", and "what did you experience?", questions that show once more how the 'job' of the audience has changed: chatting after the show is now carried out from an actor's perspective – not of that of an audience.

To finish this reflection let us look at the final scene: All twenty users are brought into a conference room and gather around a table, some standing, some seated. Like as in the preceding hour, they all follow their displays and listen to the music that is played. The video clip moves around in the room, showing all other protagonists. After a while a message on both the display and the audio stream asks users to turn the display around so that it faces outwards; each visitor now holds a portrait of the protagonist infront of himself, against his chest. An image reminiscent of a Facebook profile, a screenshot from a Skype conversation or an ID-card on a lanyard that says: See, that is me. All users gathered collectively they show who they are in that situation – a spooky presence of all the missing people. However, after a short while the images began to switch screens, circulating the group at increasing speed, then finding themselves in a black screen – the end: "please leave the installation". The visitors that became these ten other persons and finally meet all the others are dismissed from their duty as actors and sent back to their life as theater goers – a debriefing that will actually take some more time as the stories will stay for a while. Situation Rooms is a wonderful example of a performance in digital culture if we reconsider the triptichon of digital culture of Stalder: Assembling the historic and personal stories of twenty protagonist of the international network of weapon trading (referentiality), having twenty users reenact them together (communality), sophisticatedly guided by an in-ear audio stream and a hand-held video display controlled via Wlan from a central server (algorithmicity) – these elements construct not one but many narratives of that hybrid field.

CONCLUSION

The role of the spectator has changed dramatically. Not only how we consider its presence and activity in the classical theater setting (as Rancière proposed) but also in what is expected of them from the artists and producers when they propose performances that rely completely on a willingness to coproduce. It demands much more than openness and awareness – it needs a readiness to follow the rules even if there is no explanation of where it might lead. Start walking – we will guide you. The romantic and nostalgic vision of the flâneur was the starting point for my argument of how the role of the audience in some contemporary theater changes and what part technologies and practices of digital cultures hold in it. It is the walking, the looking at things and the assemblages of stories – biographical and autobiographical, images and memories that evoke not only a participation in a performance but a coproduction of the very performance attended. In both examples, the impact of the acoustic source of the audio voice being very close to the ears of the recipients (earphones) and the direct addressing of visitors/users/spectators in second person language, are strong. Digital devices take the role of a guide, they take the visitor by the hand and stay with them until the end of the show.

Both the acoustic setting and the taking by the hand produce an individual approach to and for each member of the audience and help them produce their individual experience of the performance – the performances were literally different for each participant. On the other hand, there are still activities and situations that were made together, in a collective of co-players, co-producers. A common production through individual decisions and recalculated by technological devices? Or a production of individual acting and common sociality at the same time – mediated and orchestrated by algorithms, as Stalder writes in his book on the culture of digitality?

In Benjamin's works, a society is evoked only by the fact that there are people on the streets, in the cities. How is that nowadays in the streets of our cities – what kind of societies are appearing and shaped by the use of devices? Reviewing this article, the streets of European cities are occupied by multiple societies: In Istanbul, a mob, mobilized by a TV broadcast of a video call of Erdogan, ready to use violence, is confronting tanks and soldiers. In London, ten thousand followed a social media invitation to demonstrate against Brexit. And in Hamburg, hundreds of teenagers who normally sit in front of computers games rove the streets to hunt Pokemon with their handheld devices.

Contemporary theater practitioners inhale possibilities of digital cultures and adapt how technologies and their use are changing the viewing habits for their productions. The strongest impact of digital cultures on the field of theater is documented by the fact that the audience has become more and more a real coproducer of the performance. If that is a sign of a stronger emancipation of the spectator (Rancière) or a (maybe neoliberal) imperative to creativity (Reckwitz 2012) or an increase of gamification is still to be discussed – what is obvious is that spectatorship is a highly performative mode of constructing worlds and cultures.

REFERENCES

Balzac, Honoré de (2011[1833]): "Theory of Walking." (T. Infold, trans.), In: Being Alive: Essays on Movement, Knowledge and Description, London: Routledge, pp. 33.

Benjamin, Walter (1991): Gesammelte Schriften, Band 3. Frankfurt: Suhrkamp.

Benjamin, Walter (1999[1935]): The Arcades Project (H. Eiland/K. McLaughlin, trans.), Cambridge: Harvard University Press.

Birgfeld, Johannes/Garde, Ulrike/Haug, Helgard/Kaegi, Stefan/Wetzel, Daniel (2015): "'Eine Wechseldusche zwischen direkter Begegnung und vermittelter.' Ein E-Mail-Interview mit Rimini Protokoll über *Situation Rooms.*" In: Johannes Birgfeld/Ulrike Garde/Meg Mumford (eds.), Rimini Protokoll Close-Up: Lektüren, Hannover: Werhahn Verlag.

Bishop, Claire (2012): Artificial Hells: Participatory Art and the Politics of Spectatorship, London/NewYork: Verso Books.

Brecht, Berthold (1987 [1930]): "On Everyday Theatre." In: J. Willet/R. Manheim/E. Fried (eds.), Poems 1913-1956, London: Routledge.

Certeau, Michel de (1980): "L'invention du quotidien." In: Union Generale d'Editions 1, Arts de Faire, pp 10-18.

Deleuze, Gilles/Guattari, Felix (1987[1980]): A Thousand Plateaus (B. Massumi, trans.), Minneapolis: University of Minnesota Press.

Eckersall, Peter/Grehan, Helena/Scheer, Edward (2015): "New media dramaturgy." In: Magda Romanska (ed.), The Routledge Companion to Dramaturgy, London: Routledge, pp. 375-381.

Fischer-Lichte, Erika/Wihstutz, Benjamin (eds.) (2013): Performance and the Politics of Space, London: Routledge.

Gavarni, Paul (1842): Le Flâneur, Painting.

Kittler, Friedrich /Griffin, Matthew (1996): "The City Is a Medium." In: New Literary History 27/4, pp. 717-729.

Lefebvre, Henri (1974): La production de l'espace, Paris: Anthropos.

LIGNA (n.d.): "Projekte". June 15, 2016 (http://www.ligna.org)

Massey, Doreen (1999): "Power-geometries and the politics of space-time." In: Hettner-Lecture 1998 2, Heidelberg: Dep. of Geography, University of Heidelberg.

Massey, Doreen (2005): For Space, London: Sage.

Merleau-Ponty, Maurice (2005[1945]): Phenomenology of Perception (C. Smith, trans.), London/New York: Routledge.

Mumford, Lewis (2015): "What is a city? Architectural record (1937)." In: Richard T. LeGates/Frederic Stout (eds.), The City Reader, London/New York: Routledge, pp. 91-95.

Noteboom, Cees (1995): "Die Sohlen der Erinnerung." In: DIE ZEIT, 49/1995, June 30, 2016 (http://www.zeit.de/1995/49/Die_Sohlen_der_Erinnerung).

Oberender, Thomas (2015): "The audience takes over." In: Anne Fournier/Paola Gilardi et al. (eds.), Mimos 2015: Rimini Protokoll, Bern: Peter Lang.

Rancière, Jacques (2009): "The Emancipated Spectator." In: Jacques Rancière (ed.), The Emancipated Spectactor, London/New York: Verso, pp. 1-23.

Reckwitz, Andreas (2012): Die Erfindung der Kreativität, Berlin: Suhrkamp.

Rignall, John (1989): "Benjamin's Flâneur and the Problem of Realism." In: Andrew Benjamin (ed.), The Problems of Modernity: Adorno and Benjamin, London: Routledge, pp. 112-121.

Rimini Protokoll (2013): Situation Rooms, unpublished manuscript.

Rokem, Freddie (2010): Philosophers and Thespians, Standford: Stanford University Press.

Scalway, Helen (2006): "The contemporary flâneuse." In: Aruna D'Souza/Tom McDonough (eds.), The Invisible Flâneuse?: Gender, Public Space, and Vis-

ual Culture in Nineteenth-century Paris, Manchester: Manchester University Press, pp. 164-172.
Schipper, Imanuel (2014a): "City as performance." In: TDR/the Drama Review 58/3, pp. 18-26.
Schipper, Imanuel (2014b): "Performing place and space." (G. Spearing, trans.) In: Passagen 63/2, Zürich: Pro Helvetia, pp. 27-30.
Schmidt, Theron (2010): "Unsettling representation: Monuments, theatre, and relational space." In: Contemporary Theatre Review 20/3, pp. 283-295.
Schwartz, Vanessa R (2001): "Walter Benjamin for historians." In: The American Historical Review 106/5, pp. 721-743.
Shaya, Gregory (2004): "The Flâneur, the Badaud, and the Making of a Mass Public in France, circa 1860-1910." In: The American Historical Review 109/1, pp. 41-77.
Stalder, Felix (2016): Kultur der Digitalität, Berlin: Suhrkamp.
Van Godsendthoven, Karen (2005): Women's Passages: A Bildungsroman of Female Flânerie, PhD diss, University of Gent.
Wihstutz, Benjamin (2015): "Unbekannte Räume, Grenzen, Schwellen." In: Jörn Schafaff/Benjamin Wihstutz (eds.), Sowohl als auch dazwischen: Erfahrungsräume der Kunst, München: Wilhelm Fink.
Wolff, Janet (1985): "The invisible flâneuse: Women and the literature of modernity." In: Theorie, Culture & Society 2/3, pp. 37-46.

Instituting

Performing institutions

A catalogue of performative practices

MELANIE MOHREN AND BERNHARD HERBORDT

The world is constantly reconfigured. Concepts are defined, and rules for potential action are devised. Universities, academies and independent research institutions enhance and communicate knowledge. Libraries and archives attend to its administration. Parliaments create laws for living and working together. Art may toy with these social machineries and realize their potential to differ.

Therefore, we question the grand narrating machines of society with artistic means: archives, universities and theater – institutionalized concepts of producing history, knowledge, a public community. What emerges is a continuously extended catalogue whose entries are not written down, but are rather staged instead with experimental settings: for instance, the archive project *All That I Have* (2010-2012), the eleven-day performance *The Institution* (2013), the theater production *The Audience* (2015) or the theatrical outing to the countryside with *The Theatre* (2015).

As these performative experimentations are essentially volatile, new potentialities may continuously appear: potentialities that take shape in encounters with guests and visitors. The entries in our scenic catalogue are not conceived as new definitions or even designs of better institutions, but rather they contribute to a continuously extended collection of performative practices which are able to seize and enhance patterns of social action – patterns that have become part of a society's set repertory by means of institutionalization. Through these patterns, a society obtains reassurance, ways of administration and continuation. Playing with these patterns enables us to react to social processes of transformation, to influence or even to generate them: *Performing Organizations, Institutions and Societies*.

The experimental settings that are based on these considerations are described below. They focus on physical encounters of performers, guests, visitors and research material, but always take place in surroundings that become rhythmical and enhanced through digital processes such as light, sound and video programming. Pre-produced as well as newly-recorded material is transmitted into the theatrical space; it interweaves with the current action and articulates a new temporality. A space that does not (yet) exist emerges in the thresholds between programmed, rehearsed and unpredictable processes, between virtual and actual infrastructures.

ARCHIVING

Since 2010, performances and walk-in installations have showcased the archive project *All That I Have*[1]. The starting point is a collection of images, sketches and texts, printed on square and labeled documents. Each document relates to one of 170 questions. For instance: 'Who is speaking?', 'What are worlds made of?', or 'Are we alone?'. The questions function as the archive's register. The rest of the material that has been added to the archive during international research and interview travels, relates to one of these 170 questions. In the excerpts taken from texts and interviews, in sketches and photos – by now more than a thousand – different elements are listed: movements, stories, talks, sounds, people, places, and both visible and invisible things. The material is arranged in alphabetical order, is continuously extended, and eventually assembled into films, object collages, books, choreographies, texts, audio guides and space constellations. Each entry in the catalogue again relates to at least one of the numbered questions. Each performance, installation or publication that is based on the documents, objects and lists will be archived again. Visible (and invisible) information is thus translated and multiplied again and again, and becomes part of a ramified network of found (and invented) references.

The visitors of archive exhibitions and performances may trace single questions within this network; they may, with an audio guide, follow stories through the archive (which are sometimes contradictory on purpose); they may find new connections between the archive material; they may wander aimlessly through cross-references, get lost between them; or they may expand the material with their own memories. In a strict sense, *All That I Have* is not an archive. It does

1 'All That I Have' (2010-2012). Performance series by Herbordt/Mohren, Akademie Schloss Solitude Stuttgart, Künstlerhaus Mousonturm Frankfurt/Main, Museum for Contemporary Art Novi Sad, Sophiensaele Berlin, Württembergischer Kunstverein Stuttgart, and others, www.die-institution.org/index.php/en/2010-the-archive/.

not document, order and offer accessibility to an actual present. Rather, it collects gazes, descriptions and notations which deliberately enhance the given material. It documents possibilities of things being different, and it overrides the gap between existing knowledge and potentialities to come. These long lists are registers of possible protagonists, of stories that could be told, sounds that could be heard, things that are not (yet) to be seen. *All That I Have* is an inventory of how it could also continue; now, in this moment, and in any other.

Figure 1: 'All That I Have'

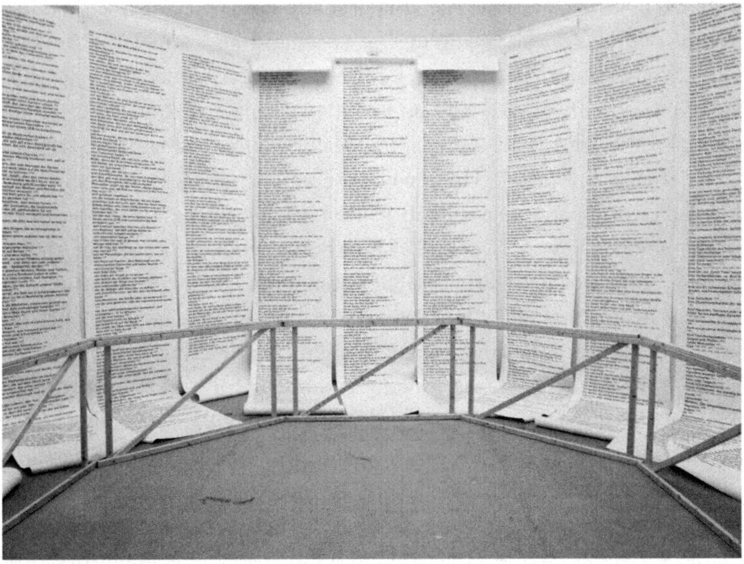

© Herbordt/Mohren

DECENTRALIZING

Our main goal is to establish an extended concept of theater with respect to format, spatial scope and participation. We imagine a theater which integrates other art forms effortlessly, and which for each project focuses on specific aspects according to the context. A theater that may take place anywhere, but that searches vigorously for new configurations of theatrical principles. A theater that purposefully rearranges the dividing lines between those who watch and those who are being watched, those who know and those who don't, those who are involved and those who are not. At the center of its debates, a decentralizing theater takes the peripheries of the institution of the theater, of urban spaces, and of clear-cut concepts of 'oeuvre' and 'author'.

For instance: *The Theatre*.[2] Every other Sunday, a group of theater visitors sets out for a one-and-a-half-hour bus ride to visit a small village. The honorary village representative welcomes them to the new establishments: a walk-in village chronicle, a guest house, a cinema, a museum for contemporary art and a theater. Each of these miniature institutions is installed in vacant buildings, taking place on the threshold of art and everyday life; the responsibility is mainly in the hands of the villagers. The art museum initiative, for instance, is a platform for local and associated artists. The village centre initiative constructs a new centre, part of which is a cake sculpture[3] in constant transformation. The Michelbach Symphony initiative performs a farewell symphony,[4] specifically composed for the village and its visitors with up to 100 participants. No musical training is necessary. At the same time, the visiting theater audience experiences the whole village as if it were staged. They may observe the village square through the window panes of the community hall while listening to sounds and stories with their headphones. They try to distinguish fact and fiction in the village chronicle, they watch a film about a fictitious village community in the cinema, they follow the traces of people that might have passed through the village in the guesthouse, or they even book a room there – for a night, or for a few months – free of charge and with breakfast at the friendly neighbour's included. A series of discursive festivals at the cooperating theater[5] and in the village[6] accompanies these initiatives and activities. The visitors, together with guests from the arts and humanities, discuss how participation may be introduced as a critical practice, which potentialities can be recognized in the withdrawal of communal institutions in rural regions, and how art may accompany and initiate transformational processes in this context. The project creates decentralizing and self-organized

2 'The Theatre' (2015). Performative outing to the countryside by Herbordt/Mohren, Theater Rampe Stuttgart/Michelbach an der Lücke, http://www.die-institution.org/index.php/en/theatre/.

3 'Cakeskape' (2015). Steel sculpture by Michl Schmidt, Michelbach an der Lücke.

4 'Michelbach-Sinfonietta' (2015). Composition by Gordon Kampe, Michelbach an der Lücke.

5 'The Village Festival' (2015). Staged symposium by Herbordt/Mohren, Theater Rampe Stuttgart, October 24, 2015, http://www.die-institution.org/index.php/en/2015-the-village-festival/.

6 'The Theatre Festival' (2016). Staged symposium by Herbordt/Mohren, Michelbach an der Lücke, May 22, 2016, http://www.die-institution.org/.

versions of grand machineries of narration in the countryside. The audience travels to the village from all over the place and observes the village's communal structures and everyday practices as art. In these processes, new interdependencies emerge between town and countryside and between invented and existing infrastructures.

Figure 2: 'The Theatre'

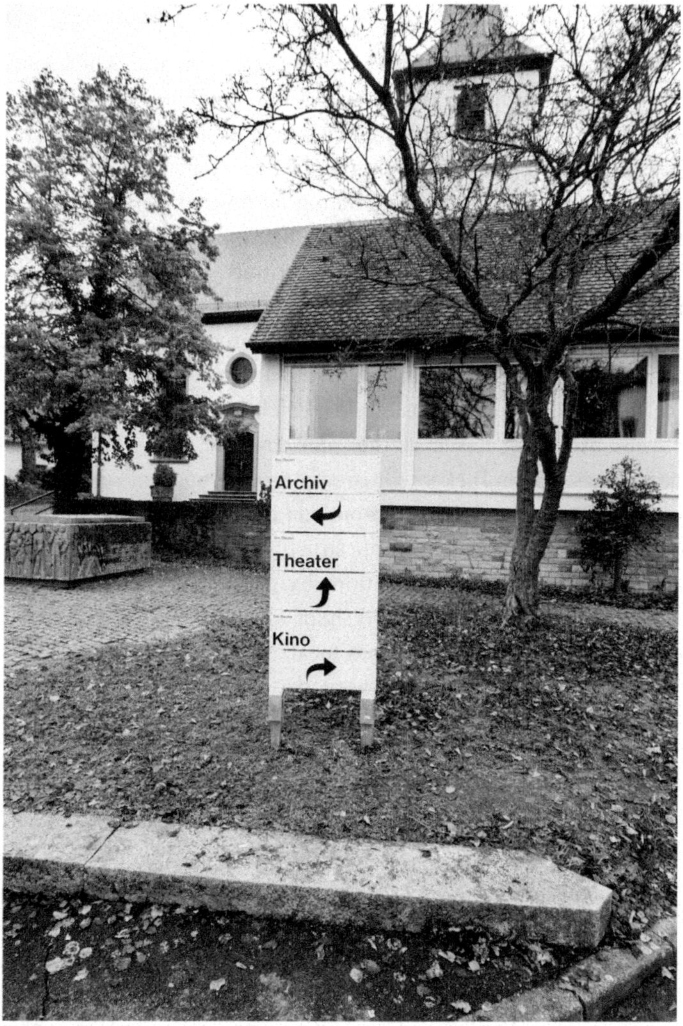

© Florian Model

ESTABLISHING

We stage *The Institution.*[7] It takes place in a centrally located apartment and lasts for 11 days, six hours a day, with around 70 active participants: actors, musicians, researchers, artists, visual arts students, a cook and many more. The term 'institution' is understood in its broadest sense: from a set of rules (for instance, to design ways of living and working together in a society) up to the concept of a consolidated organizational, programmatic and architectural narrative (such as the institution of theater).

Yet our institution remains elusive. It is a performance which plays with these definitions. It invents strategies for how to continuously determine anew what an institution could look like. In concrete terms this means: a second floor plan is built into the existing one – slightly shifted against the first one, only rudimentarily realized, and potentially pointing far beyond the original plan, as an exhibited architectural model reveals – including indoor garden, guest room, archive and debate room. For 11 days, the performers make use of the rooms in ever-changing ways and change its characteristics. In an endless combination of tasks (as guest, host, visitor, or witness), places (archive, public square, theater, or home), and situations (work, inhabit, invite, disappear, show, or observe) they play along the lines of a set of basic rules which continually change the rhythm of movements. All sequences have the same timeline. Every eight minutes and thirty-one seconds, a light flickers for twenty-nine seconds and an electronically-distorted sound played back into to room can be heard.[8] At the same time, *The Institution*, positioned in this space-time structure, becomes rearranged every day in its narrative and functional attributions by guests and visitors (artists' interventions, music clubs' rehearsals, workshops and seminars, neighbours' meals). Everything that happens – be it a shared meal, a lecture or a performative play – becomes accessible and criticizable as a performance through these external

---

7 'The Institution' (2013). Durational performance by Herbordt/Mohren, project space of Akademie Schloss Solitude Stuttgart, http://www.die-institution.org/index.php/en/the-play/.

8 "Light takes about eight minutes and thirty-one seconds to travel from the sun to the earth. If the light of the sun suddenly expires, eight minutes and thirty-one seconds remain for one last inventory. Eight minutes and thirty-one seconds in order to construct a future that continues differently, or a different history, in order to observe how it becomes darker and darker, and how, after twenty-nine seconds, everything starts again." Excerpt from 'The Institution' (2013). Durational performance by Herbordt/Mohren, Stuttgart, http://www.die-institution.org/index.php/en/the-play/.

markings. Every thirty minutes, a visitor is guided through the rooms. They can observe what happens, and, at the same time, listen to factual background information to invented stories on headphones, find themself alone in an automatized guest room, meet the hosts in the archive, and finally withdraw to the veranda for a private opening celebration.

The Institution combines possible qualities of a (theatrical) institution: It is theater (in which actors stage something for an audience), rehearsal room (where neighbouring music societies rehearse the interpretation of an eleven-day composition), meeting point (for instance, for a neighbour's meal), archive (where its fictive history is invented, collected and continued), seminar room and gallery. It provides a preliminary working context that cooperates with a number of regional and supra-regional institutions of the arts and sciences, as well as with local initiatives – while largely remaining self-organized.

Figure 3: 'The Institution'

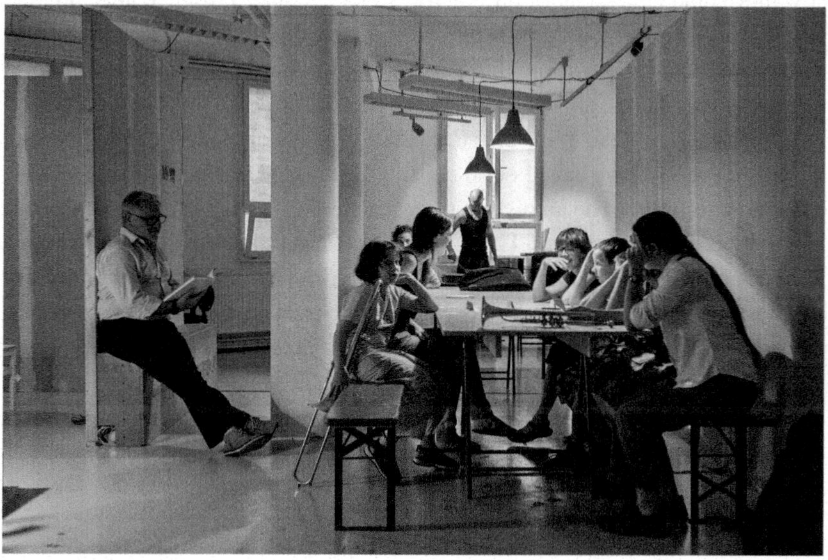

© Bernhard Kahrmann

IMAGINING

Performative practices produce a form of something that is (yet) to come. It provides a (preliminary) reality for something that is only imagined by performing it as concrete.

> "What I think is fascinating in projects like these is that they are concrete drafts of what establishing could also be. You remain in the conditional here, but in a concrete one. You could, because you can. Because you can do this here temporarily, one could." (Badura 2015: 292)

A series of workshop talks with guests from the arts and sciences called *Performing Institutions*,[9] accompanies *The Institution* and serves as a platform for discursive preparation and critical reflection. The brief talks and discussions ask for the tasks and goals of institutions, for the criticism they might undergo, and how they could be thought of differently. So far, examples from architecture, the visual arts and from law have been debated, as well as the question of institutional critique in the performing arts. The talks are an inherent part of the performance; they merge art with the reflection of art, and they question the staged host institution in turn. With the succession of different contributions invented institutions meet upon staged ones, existing institutions encounter their possible criticism and future. The ambiguity of 'vorstellen' (imagine, perform, represent) lies at the core of the project. The fictitious host institution turns the tables on its visitors and asks them with each of its arrangements: Which other concepts could we think of as institutions? How could we arrange our living and working together? Which other strategies could we find to change these structures?

9 'Performing Institutions' (2013-2015). Series of talks of the Young Academy at the Berlin-Brandenburg Academy of Sciences and Humanities and the German National Academy of Sciences Leopoldina, initiated by Herbordt/Mohren, Berlin, Frankfurt, Mülheim, Stuttgart, and others, http://www.die-institution.org/index.php/en/2013-the-conversation/, http://www.diejungeakademie.de/en/home/.

Figure 4: 'Performing Institutions'

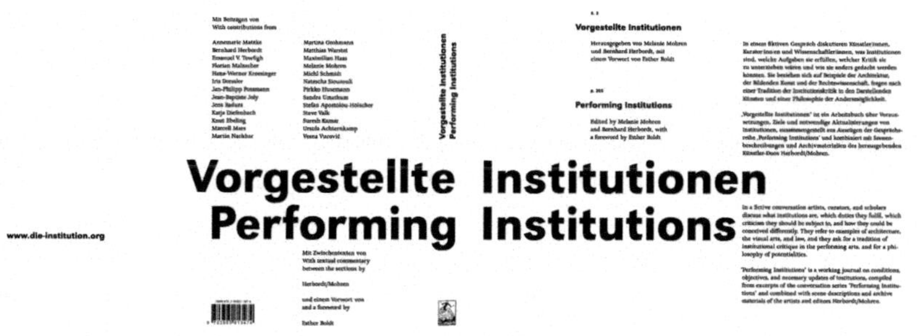

© Demian Bern

TRANSLATING

The concept that holds together the catalogue entries and the performances emerging from them is that of translation. 'Translation' here becomes representative for the following entries that are (still) missing: 'confusing', 'constructing', 'disappearing', 'documenting', 'filling', 'inventing', 'recording', 'remembering', 'repeating', 'reporting', 'representing', 'shifting', 'transforming', and so on. Concepts, themes and scenes are translated from one medium to the other. Facts are translated into fictional documents and vice versa. Observations are translated into memories, memories into texts, texts into movements, movements into social issues, social issues into politics, politics into art. Information multiplies. Perspectives become doubled. Distinctions become blurred. Systems (and their institutions) become rearranged.

WATCHING

The audience may watch what is going on from a safe distance, like in the theater; they may participate in the open space of the stage; and they may also continuously decide between the two options. In this scenic arrangement, clear-cut divisions between watching and participating cannot be drawn. Rather, there is a constant process of negotiation between the two, and they cannot be considered separately. This blurring of boundaries is the project's intention; it demands a constant self-questioning and readjustment of positions from the audience. This is what *The Audience* (2015)[10] is about, another performance in the series of *The Institution.* Initiatives and societies that form civil society alternatives to federal and communal institutions gather on stage. They act side by side, they each follow individual goals, but together they build the model of a different city within the city. The performances trigger informal processes of discussion, exchange and collaboration that continue beyond the context of the performances. The theater audience is invited to enter the staged, alternative model of a city, to follow its rhythms and routines, to participate in them or to observe them from a distance. A composed sound structure that connects the light and video work, frames the performance. A staged film team films a fictitious documentation of these activities. In the auditorium, headphones and screens broadcast sound and image of the live documentation. The spectators turn into *The Audience* in both senses of the word: as a public participating in its city while critically observing it at the same time – like in the theater.

The contributions, in this text only collected in extracts, form an archive of potentialities of being different; they readjust prevalent structures of retaining and ordering knowledge; they come up with different architectural and organizational solutions for social tasks; they translate that which is present into that which is not yet present; they perform things only imagined as if they were real, and they blur the distinction between watching and participating, between civil society action group and art. The contributions collected in this text present performative actions that might be capable of expanding social structures. They may be described with the term of 'performative practices'. The series around *The Institution* sketches such practices, creates a catalogue whose entries are not linked to definitions, but to scenic arrangements.

In this context, it is always central to implement thresholds of indeterminacy. These thresholds between everyday life, research and aesthetic experience, do not clearly show where representation starts, where the accompanying criticism ends, and where an unexpected encounter, a factual model experiment begins. With the help of digital technology, additional virtual and actual infrastructures of things present, past, and still to come, are connected. And yet, the conditions of all encounters described are staged. They follow an assigned timeline; when a certain period has ended, specific events occur; nothing happens by chance. Such systems of rules, which organize encounters of most different agents, can be called institutions.

10 'The Audience' (2015). Performance by Herbordt/Mohren, Theater Rampe Stuttgart, http://www.die-institution.org/index.php/en/home/.

When institutions start to protect the awareness of potentialities in their routines and decisions – instead of insisting on solutions once determined – they might turn out to be better institutions:

"SV Institutional change, new models of institutions are possible. It is actually possible to break up institutions and to make something new. (Valk 2015: 303)

ID To dare to have utopian concepts, to risk to make yourself vulnerable or even ridiculous. When you do certain things, you can of course do something wrong, but sometimes it's better to do something wrong than to play it totally safe. (Dressler 2015: 297)

VV To me it seems essential to be able to answer this: If institution is an answer, what was the question? Which social function does an institution have? Which kind of public does it produce? (Vuković 2015: 298)

BH What we would need is not 'no institutions', but rather better ones." (Herbordt 2015: 250)

Within the quotes above, the necessity to perform institutions in alternating ways is marked. The artist's book they are extracted from is called *Vorgestellte Institutionen / Performing Institutions* (Herbordt/Mohren 2015). It concludes:

"In their last minutes, they will carefully establish a square meter for a single visitor one last time. One last time, they will take a circuitous, but nonetheless purposeful route, although there would be a much easier one. They will believe they have indeed briefly seen things in passing, which, however, isn't true. They will report to others about their plans. They won't worry about what of these plans will really happen. At eleven o'clock at night, they will arrive in the entrance hall. They will recount a performance. They will see each other again and it will be a proper celebration. On an easily visible brass plate in the middle of the entrance hall, they will be able to read: The cornerstone of this institution was laid among the esteemed presence of visitors, guests, witnesses, and hosts. Someone will have said: We are not at the end of history. We shouldn't give up writing it, but rather start writing in the first place! They will step into the entrance hall and everything will be brightly lit.
A succession of unexpected sounds.
A change of lighting and a new beginning.
Everything is brightly lit." (Herbordt/Mohren 2015: 306-307)

Translated by Sandra Fluhrer and Nadine Feßler

Figure 5: 'The Audience'

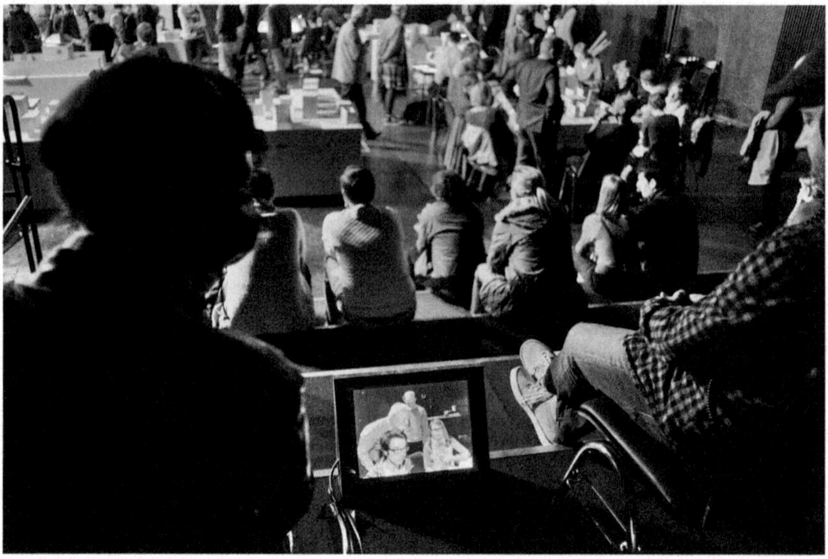

© Luzie Marquardt

REFERENCES

Melanie Mohren/Bernhard Herbordt (2015): Vorgestellte Institutionen / Performing Institutions, Berlin: Alexander Verlag Berlin.

All Quotations within the text, in alphabetic order of the prenams, from: "Performing Institutions. With contributions from Annemarie Matzke, Bernhard Herbordt, Emanuel V. Towfigh, Florian Malzacher, Hans-Werner Kroesinger, Iris Dressler, Jens Badura, Jean-Baptiste Joly, Jan-Philipp Possmann, Katja Diefenbach, Knut Ebeling, Martina Grohmann, Maximilian Haas, Melanie Mohren, Marcell Mars, Martin Nachbar, Michl Schmidt, Matthias Warstat, Natascha Siouzouli, Pirkko Husemann, Stefan Apostolou-Hölscher, Suresh Kumar, Sandra Umathum, Steve Valk, Ursula Achternkamp, Vesna Vuković." In: Mohren, Melanie/Herbordt, Bernhard (Eds.) (2015). Vorgestellte Institutionen / Performing Institutions. Berlin: Alexander Verlag, p.217 – 307.

Badura, Jens, p. 297.
Dressler, Iris, p. 297.
Herbordt, Bernhard, p. 250.

Mohren, Melanie/Herbordt, Bernhard, p. 306.
Valk, Steve, p. 303.
Vuković, Vesna, p. 298.

Organizing

'The machine could swallow everything'

Satin Island and performing organization

TIMON BEYES

> The machine could swallow everything, incorporate it seamlessly, like a giant loom that reweaves all fabric, no matter how recalcitrant and jarring its raw form, into what my hero would have called a master-pattern – or, if not that, then maybe just the pattern of the master.
> MCCARTHY 2015: 34

Satin Island, the latest novel by artist and writer Tom McCarthy, is set in the strange world of organization in digital cultures. The book is woven around the experiences, observations and reflections of its protagonist, "U". U is an anthropologist, whose fieldwork and subsequent doctoral thesis on club culture was mainly lauded not for its insights into the clubbing scene, but for its methodological meditations on ethnographic research and the performativity of the researcher. The thesis brought him enough attention – "a famous anthropologist […] is about as well known as a third-division footballer" – to be plucked "from the dying branches of academia" and grafted into "the febrile hothouse" of a consultancy firm in London (McCarthy 2015: 28-29). "U" reads as 'you', of course: The figure of the corporate anthropologist or 'semiotic engineer', as employees of Silicon Valley firms who hold humanities degrees have been called (Lewis-Kraus 2015), represents a contemporary 'organization (wo)man'. U's anthropologist "hero", referred to in the opening quote, is Claude Lévi-Strauss (McCarthy 2015: 33). Yet the ethnographic discovery of social-cultural patterns is now put to work for "the Company", as U's employer is called throughout the book, with a capitalized 'C'. Peyman, the boss of the consultancy firm, tasks the protagonist with writing the "Great Report": "Not just *a* book: *the* fucking *Book*. […] Sum the tribe up. Speak its secret name" (ibid.: 55; orig. emphasis).

Satin Island, then, is a novel on the problem of reporting on, and from within, the conditions and effects of today's ubiquitously networked – and thus pervasively organized – spheres of life; at one point in the book, the novel itself is presented as the remnants of the impossible Great Report, the "offslew of the real unwritten manuscript" (ibid.: 103).[1] In this chapter, I read the text as a report on contemporary organization and, more specifically, on the performativity of organization in the time of ubiquitous and pervasive media technologies. To do so, I first discuss existing encounters of organization theory and performance (studies). On this basis, I reflect on different layers of performativity and organization as they are enacted in *Satin Island*. Perhaps the most significant layer concerns the effects of digital technologies and networked infrastructures. Some of the novel's most striking passages, or so I argue, reflect a 'posthumanist performativity' (Barad 2003) and therefore instigate a posthumanist theorizing of organization.

ORGANIZATION THEORY AND THE QUESTION OF PERFORMATIVITY

What comes to the fore when one approaches organization through the notion of performativity? As the use of these terms in general and in the book this chapter appears in demonstrate, performance and performativity have become all-purpose "carry-home concept[s]", widely applicable and taking many forms (Loxley 2007: 29). In this spirit, the study of organization, too, was recently diagnosed to have taken its own "performativity turn" (Gond et al. 2015: 18). Without aspiring to a complete overview, I distinguish between three broad encounters of organization theory, performance studies and performativity. The first relates to questions of organizational efficiency and performance management; the second consists of theatrical and dramaturgical approaches to organization; and the third is marked by a turn to the performativity of different

1 A version of Satin Island's cover already plays with the novel's 'open form' and its shifting boundaries with other textual genres: Scattered across the page are both coloured dots of different shapes and sizes and possible 'qualifiers' or denominators of what the book 'is', all of them crossed out: "~~a treatise~~", "~~an essay~~", "~~a report~~", "~~a confession~~", "~~a manifesto~~". Only "a novel" is (momentarily?) not crossed out – "and I think that would be the space of literature, which is neither one nor the other; it's this messy, unresolved between" (McCarthy: 2016: 50).

processes of organizing, where organization becomes a provisional phenomenon and a precarious effect of diverse performative practices.

First, there is a strong current of understanding organizations as machines of efficiency, measured and acted upon through performance criteria – and the critique of such an understanding and its consequences. This is what performance theorist Jon McKenzie (2001) refers to as 'organizational performance'.[2] Such 'performance studies' reproduce what Lyotard, in *The Postmodern Condition* (1984), discussed as the proliferation of 'performativity criterion' and 'performativity principle' as a legitimizing practice, which here means achieving desired outcomes effectively and generating desired returns. Part and parcel of "a generalized spirit of performativity" (1984: 45), such a notion of organizational performance is closely connected to the marketization or 'mercantilization' of many, if not all walks of life (and prominently includes the educational sector, as Lyotard foresaw).

Second, there is what one could call the theatricality of organizational practice as interpreted through theatrical and dramaturgical metaphors. Drawing upon Goffman's seminal work on identity formation and presentation of the self, but also the social anthropology of Turner and even Burke's 'dramatistic pentad', organizational life here is analyzed in terms of theatrical performances and according to dramaturgical principles (cf. Mangham 1986; Cornelissen 2004). All organization is a stage, on which rituals, quotidian dramas and role-playing is performed. What mainly comes into view in this line of thought, then, is the everyday performances in organizations and how to think of organizations as made up of such mundane performances. Moreover, there is also work on theaters as well as theatrical performances or interventions as cases of organizing (Beyes/Steyaert 2006), for instance by investigating the practice of Rimini Protokoll (Biehl-Missal 2012; Beyes/Steyaert 2013; Schipper, this volume).

Third, echoing the wider performative turn in the cultural and social sciences – and, correspondingly, the expansion of what falls into the field of performance studies – the notion of performativity has more recently inspired a number of

---

2 While originating from – and still strongly influenced by – sociological thought, the study of organization has come to be shaped to quite some extent by the institutional power of business school-interests. It is thus often, albeit not exclusively, limited to a certain type of bounded organizational form, usually capitalist firms, and it is prone to an instrumental and oddly normative logic of coming up with knowledge that not only helps us to better understand such organizations but to help them performing better economically, i.e. with insights 'for' management and for questions of steering and control (Beyes, 2007).

studies and approaches according to which organization is continuously performed and produced through various actions and processes. It is therefore this loose group of texts that constitutes organization theory's minor 'performativity turn'. Following Latour, Czarniawska (2008: 6-7) distinguished between "ostensive" and "performative" approaches to organization. Whereas ostensive definitions look at organizations as distinct, presupposed units, into which actors are placed and which are therefore assumed to exist independently of everyday social and material processes of organizing,[3] a performative sensibility sees organization as something that is continuously effected.

In this register, studies that explicitly enlist notions of performativity have drawn upon what are usually regarded as the main strands of performativity theory (Gond et al. 2015). Based on Austin's speech-act theory and its ramifications, organizational scholars have inquired into performative utterances as perlocutionary acts, i.e. into how organizations come into being through communicational flows (Cooren 2004). Following Callon's 'performation program', others have traced how theories of economy and management are brought into being and translated into organizational practice (Muniesa 2014; Schröter, this volume). Inspired by Butler's work, organizational researchers have interrogated

3 Broadly speaking, the first two 'schools' of performance and organization studies that I have mentioned – organizations as theatre, organizational performance – tend to reproduce the entitative/ostensive view of organization. The third, performative view overlaps with the much-discussed processual shift in organizational theorizing: It entails a replacement of 'what?'-questions (what is an organization?) with 'how?'-questions (how is organization assembled, or how does organizing take place?). In other words, this in itself heterogeneous approach deviates from "a Cartesian habit of mind" (Barad 2003: 807), according to which organizations exist as entities with inherent, presupposed attributes – and anterior to their representation.

It follows that what is at stake, too, is a shift from the study of organizations as bounded, stable entities (the company, the nonprofit-organization, bureaucracy) to a focus on processes of organizing between, beyond, after or before the bounded notion of an organization. Cooper's work is seminal in this respect. As he wrote, "if we insist on thinking in terms of *organizations*, we miss the bigger question of how *organization* as a generic process both structures and destructures our world, how our minds and bodies are caught up in its complex, reflexive dynamics. To think of *organizations* is to think of specific objects external to us. To think of *organization* is to recognize a more general force which includes us in its perpetual movement between order and disorder, certainty and uncertainty" (1998: 154; orig. emphasis). Hence this chapter's title: 'performing organization' rather than 'performing organizations'.

the performative making of gendered identities in organizations (Tyler and Cohen 2010) and pondered the potential of queer theory to disrupt mainstream accounts of organizational life (Parker 2001). Importantly, the notion of performativity has not only been linked to discursive formations of organizational realities and the production of identities, but also to the very material and affective forces of organizational spaces (Beyes/Steyaert 2012) and to its objects and technologies (Orlikowski/Scott 2014; Nyberg/Wright 2015). Moreover, the performativity of organizational scholarship itself has been discussed both methodologically (Beyes/Steyaert 2011) and politically, the latter primarily by way of the development of, and debates on, the notion of 'critical performativity' (Spicer et al. 2009; see McKenzie, this volume).

In sum, organization studies' minor 'performativity turn' has spawned a number of promising approaches for investigating the 'doing' of organization, and it has helped ushering in an appreciation of, and a sensibility for, organization as a processual, material, situational and contested accomplishment. And yet, forays into the performative effects of digital technologies are recent and few, and they tend to presuppose formal organizations, in which IT systems 'do things' to organizational processes and its actors. The subsequent discussion of *Satin Island* and its layers of 'performative organizing' builds up on organization theory's 'performativity program'. It briefly touches upon the performative force of communication and the performativity of concepts before arriving at the agency of objects and technologies. As I try to show with and through the novel, however, the entanglements of digital technologies and human conduct deserves further scrutiny.

BLACK BOX ORGANIZING: DOING ORGANIZATION IN *SATIN ISLAND*

Beyond the figure of Peyman, the somewhat charismatic boss, McCarthy's depiction of the nameless Company barely touches upon formal hierarchies, structures of organizational decision-making or organizational members. Rather, it is infrastructures, media and materialities as well as U's experience of – and reflections on – these organizational environments and atmospheres that dominate the ethnographer's narrations. For instance, the Company's London premises' glass walls created

"an expansive vista in which sketches, diagrams and other such configurations of precious data, lying faced-up on curved tabletops, pinned to walls or drawn on whiteboards or, occasionally (and this made the data seem all the more vulnerable, fragile even), on the glass itself, seemed to dialogue with one another in a rich and esoteric language, the scene conveying (deliberately, of course) the impression that this was not only a place of business but, beyond that, a hermetic zone, a zone of alchemy, a crucible in which whole worlds were in the mix." (McCarthy 2015: 20-21)

Yet what kinds of worlds are in the mix remains unclear. Alongside having to write the Great Report, the protagonist participates in the large-scale "Koob-Sassen-Project", "supra-governmental, supra-national, supra-everything" (ibid.: 110), in which the Company has a role among hundreds of other players. The Project's aim and content are never clarified – for legal reasons, as U explains, but also because he and, apparently, the other people involved, simply do not know what the project involves. It is a "black box" (ibid.: 60): "Sometimes it seemed enormous, like an emperor's mausoleum; at others it appeared no larger than a trunk, or coffin; at others still, the size of a child's toy- or music-box. The only constant or unchanging aspect of it was that it was black: black and inscrutable, opaque" (ibid.: 70). The Project is amorphous and shape-shifting; it crosses the boundaries of formal organizations; "it has to be conceived of as in a perpetual state of passage, not arrival – not *at*, but *in between*" (ibid.: 74; orig. emphasis). *Satin Island* can thus be read as a novelistic reflection – or a report – on the performativity of organization understood as process, as an unstable and at least partly diffuse phenomenon that perpetually needs to be accomplished through different layers of performative agency. In the following, I tentatively distinguish between three layers enacted in the book: communicative performativity, the performativity of concepts and the performativity of media technologies that is tied to digital devices and algorithms.

PERLOCUTIONARY ACTS

"They discussed [the Project] not as people discuss things they know about, subjects whose properties and parameters are given, but rather as they try to ascertain those of a foreign object, one that is at once present – omnipresent – and elusive: groping after its dimensions; trying, through mutual enquiry, to discern its composition, charge and limit. When, in the course of my professional activities, I asked people to provide a visual image that, for them, most represented it, I got answers varying from hovering spaceship to rabbit warren to pond lilies." (McCarthy 2015: 63)

Precisely because it is perceived as shape-shifting and inscrutable, the Project has to be performed into its (amorphous) being by way of incessant talk. The anthropologist's "in-transit-metaphor" and "perpetual-state-of-passage-analogy" (ibid.: 117) itself becomes a performative ploy, used in Company memos and project representations. The ethnographer is convening meetings with civil servants, asking them to "discuss their sense of what the Project entailed, or more subtly, implied" (ibid.: 50). Yet the civil servants are too clever for ethnographic tricks, knowing full well they are being observed and studied – the ethnographer, of course, knows that his interlocutors know – and in response they conjure up catchphrases such as "'excitement' (one hundred and eighty-two occurrences over three hours); also 'challenge' (one hundred and four); 'opportunity' (eighty-nine); 'transformation' (seventy-eight); and, as an upscale variant on the last word, 're-configuration' (sixty-three)" (ibid.: 50). (McCarthy is a brilliant satirist.)

Yet fittingly, nobody else is performing organization through speech acts such as Peyman, head of the Company. McCarthy presents him as a man without qualities of and for the present: as a cipher for organizational management as a kind of art of fabulation. If he (Peyman) had to sum up what the Company did, he would "choose not *consultancy* or *design* or *urban planning*, but *fiction*" (ibid.: 45; orig. emphasis).

"The city and the state are fictional conditions; a business is a fictional entity. Even if it's real, it's still a construct. Lots of the Company's projects have been fictions that became real. [...] We should view all propositions and all projects this way." (ibid.)

Peyman's aphorisms, slogans and imperatives sound clever yet are sometimes hard to decipher in terms of their constative or ostensible meaning, part of the Company's "rich and esoteric language" referred to above (ibid.: 21). Both illocutionary intent and perlocutionary effects of such fabulation seem to reside in attracting and seducing (potential) clients as well as impressing and partly dumbfounding colleagues and underlings.

Performing concepts

Peyman's talk already touches upon a second and related layer of how organization is performed in *Satin Island*: the performative force of theories or concepts themselves. McCarthy enacts a dark satire of the translation of aesthetic and allegedly critical theories into contemporary selling propositions. Such theories and concepts seem perfectly attuned to a culturalized or aesthetic economy in which the emphasis shifts to the creation or staging of worlds in which objects and subjects exist (Lazzarato 2004) – a state of affairs that calls for expanding the categories of use value and exchange value with 'orchestration value' or 'staging value' [*Inszenierungswert*] (Böhme 2016). Apart from the heavy-handed irony of having the corporate anthropologist and ardent admirer of Lévi-Strauss consult the jeans-maker Levi Strauss, McCarthy's U makes good use of his schooling in continental theory and scholarly self-reflection, yet for the sake of the market, "feeding vanguard theory [...] back into the corporate machine" (McCarthy 2015: 34). 'For' the client Levi Strauss, U stole a concept from the French philosopher Deleuze:

> "for him, le pli, or fold, describes the way we swallow the exterior world, invert it and then flip it back outwards again, and, in so doing, form our own identity. I took out all the revolutionary shit (Deleuze was a leftie); and I didn't credit Deleuze, either. [...] I did the same thing with another French philosopher, Badiou: I recycled his notion of a rip, a sudden temporal rupture, and applied it, naturally, to tears worn in jeans, which I presented as the birth-scars of their wearer's singularity, testaments to the individual's break with general history, to the successful institution of a personal time." (ibid.)

PERFORMING MEDIA TECHNOLOGIES

In *Satin Island*, the performances of human communication, self-styling and concepts are embedded in a narrative of apparatuses and data streams. Stalder (2016) recently suggested three mutually interwoven characteristic forms or qualities that mark digital culture: 'referentiality' [*Referenzialität*], collectivity or communality [*Gemeinschaftlichkeit*] and, importantly, 'algorithmicity' [*Algorithmizität*]. With regard to the novel's organizational performativity, the dimension of referentiality is at work in the mash-up of theory and (business) practice enacted in the Company. The quality of communality could then be connected to the on-going task of communicatively performing and relating what is occurring, to bring into being different versions of what is taking place. Yet today, both qualities are pervaded and shaped by digital networks and their automated procedures of decision-making that handle data, extract information as well as offer and perhaps pre-determine modes of action. Such is the invisibility and inscrutability of the Koob-Sassen-Project:

"It was a huge, ambitious scheme, he said, on the same scale as poldering and draining land masses of thousands of square miles, or cabling and connecting an entire empire – and yet, he continued, the most remarkable thing about it was that, despite its massive scale, it would remain, in an everyday sense, to members of the general populace, invisible [...]. It was a feat, rather, of what he called *network architecture*. He went on for a long time about networks, convergence, nodes and relays, interstices – it was very abstract." (McCarthy 2015: 31-32; orig. emphasis)

It seems that what could be called the algorithmic performativity of organizing, which is enabled by network infrastructure, is what drives the Project and what provokes the experiences of opacity and not-knowing (Beyes/Pias 2014). Moreover, this kind of performativity leads the ethnographer to deeper suspicions about the nature and possibility of a Great Report. As U, the good reader of Lévi-Strauss, very well knows (McCarthy 2015: 104), the problem might not be that the Great Report is an unwritable fantasy and thus a quixotic quest in the first place. Rather, the report has already been written or it is continuously being written, albeit not by field researchers, anthropologists or sociologists, but by software. U experiences a kind of epiphany:

"Write Everything Down, said Malinowski. But the thing is, now, it is all written down. There's hardly an instant of our lives that isn't documented. Walk down any stretch of street and you're being filmed by three cameras at once – and even if you aren't, the phone you carry in your pocket pinpoints and logs your location at each given moment. Each website that you visit, every click-through, every keystroke is archived: even if you've hit *delete*, *wipe*, *empty trash*, it's still logged somewhere, in some fold or enclave, some occluded avenue of circuitry. [...] And as for the structures of kinship, the networks of exchange within whose web we're held, cradled, created [...]: well, those networks are being mapped, that task performed, by the software that tabulates and cross-indexes what we buy with who we know, and what they buy, or like, and with the other objects that are bought or liked by others who we don't know but with whom we cohabit a shared buying- or liking-pattern." (ibid.: 107; orig. emphasis)[4]

4 McCarthy-the-satirist has U fantasizing about the possibilities of resistance and resistance movements against the 'automatic writing' in general – which would reduce us to "no more than actions and commands within its key-chains" (2015: 108) – and the Project in particular. It is worth quoting, even if reflecting upon the limits and potential of resistance is beyond the scope of this chapter: "And then my cohorts, that semi-occluded network of covert anthropologist I'd dreamt into being already: they could join me in the cause. Together, we could turn Present-Tense Anthropology™

The novel here reflects a debate that, as far as I can see, the study of organization is only beginning to confront: how the performativity of algorithmic ordering is a common feature of today's processes of organizing beyond the boundaries of formal organizations. To quote the media theorists Galloway and Thacker (2007: 29), there is a new "new physics of organization" that enacts 'protocological' forms of control and entrainment. Such performativity is indeed central to contemporary organization in that it encourages and partly shapes social and individual conduct (Neyland 2015). Part of the problem is the fact that access to – and modulation of – the digitally generated data masses of, for instance, social media platforms, is both restricted to, and everyday practice in, the research departments of, say, Google and Facebook; this kind of data is unavailable for public research (Baxmann et al. 2016).[5]

BUFFERING

The 'being-written' of human/non-human networks points to a final and important aspect or layer of performativity that lurks in the question of the effects of digital infrastructures and algorithms, yet cannot be reduced to these effects. Socio-material analyses (of organization) tend to fall back upon the distinction between human and machinic actors or objects in trying to make sense of the agency of objects and technologies on the one hand, and human agency on the other hand. They enact, in Barad's terminology, 'agential cuts' in order to

---

into an armed resistance movement: I pictured them all scurrying around to my command, setting the charges, using their ethnographic skills to foment riots, to assemble lynch-mobs, to make urban space itself, its very fabric, rise up in revolt. I saw manholes erupting; cables spontaneously combusting; office wi-fi clouds crackling the way to audibility, causing hordes of schizoid bureaucrats, heads given over to a cacophony of voices, to flee their desks and tear about the streets, blood trickling from their ears […]." (ibid.: 111)

5 In 2014, a study on "Experimental evidence of massive-scale emotional contagion through social networks" caused a minor scandal. Co-authored by a researcher employed at Facebook, the study analysed the results of an experiment with and on nearly 700'000 Facebook users (without their awareness) that entailed the purposeful manipulation of newsfeeds in order to find out if and how moods are transferred and travel across social networks (Kramer et al. 2014). It is surprising that some people were genuinely surprised that Facebook would do this kind of thing, i.e. to instrumentally try to induce changes in users' emotions.

delineate and perform objects, algorithms and subjects as distinct entities (Barad 2003). They thus tend to skirt the problem of thinking together the human and technology. Yet the mapping of the great report through a kind of foundational entanglement of algorithmic agency (which reacts to, and informs human conduct) and human agency (which reacts to, and informs algorithmic communication) hints at a different kind of agency, an 'intra-agency', that "calls into question the givenness of the differential categories of 'human' and 'nonhuman', examining the practices through which these differential boundaries are stabilized and destabilized" (ibid.: 808).[6] Barad's notion of posthumanist performativity thus instigates scholars to explore the processes and practices through which such hybrid entanglements, roles and meaning are performatively brought into being, without departing from a-priori assumptions of either human or machinic agency.

In this sense, *Satin Island*'s most striking passages enact a kind of poetics of intra-action that surpasses a 'mere' satire of late capitalism's capture of practices and concepts of cultural and scholarly production. That processes are material and immaterial, human and non-human at the same time, part of the same mangle of practice, seems to inform the descriptions of organizational spaces such as the Company's headquarters or an airport lounge that sets the scene at the book's beginning. Relatedly, the phenomenon of buffering is a recurring theme in the novel, perhaps offered as a counterpoint to the bleak diagnosis of software's great report, which influences how human actors move and communicate yet is readable only by other software. U frequently experiences bouts of buffering that resemble provisional interruptions, suspensions or recesses, in which, for a moment, "the entire time of the world and of your subjective agency is put on hold", as McCarthy commented after the novel's publication (2016: 45). By way of Barad's posthumanist account of performativity, one can grasp these 'liminal spaces' as phenomena – for her, phenomena, not things or objects, are primary ontological units (2003: 818) – that are produced through intra-action. That is precisely why these small in-between moments of buffering, when what will

6 The neologism of 'intra-action' takes the place of the well-worn notion of 'interaction', which according to Barad would presuppose the prior existence of entities that are then related, such as technological object and human being. Instead, "[i]t is through specific agential intra-actions that the boundaries and properties of the 'components' of phenomena become determinate and that particular embodied concepts become meaningful" (ibid.: 815). In other words, the concept of intra-action helps thinking the 'agential cut' that effects the separation – and thus the emergence of relata like subject and object.

happen next becomes dubious, afford "a sense of bliss" as well as "a kind of dread" (2015: 64):

> "I'd spend long stretches staring at the little spinning circle on my screen, losing myself in it. Behind it, I pictured hordes of bits and bytes and megabytes [...] I pictured a giant *über*-server [...] pumping out information non-stop, more of it than any single person would need in their lifetime, pumping it all my way in an endless, unconditional and grace-conferring act of generosity. *Datum est*: it is given. It was this gift, I told myself, this bottomless and inexhaustible torrent of giving, that made the circle spin: the data itself, its pure, unfiltered content as it rushed into my system, which, in turn, whirred into streamlined action as it started to reorganize it into legible form" (ibid.: 63; orig. emphasis).[7]

CONCLUSION

The layers of performing organization that are gathered and interwoven in *Satin Island* present a challenge to rethink and complexify the relation of organization and performativity. There is perhaps an irony in turning to the 'old' artistic medium of the novel to ponder processes of organizing (in) digital cultures. Yet it seems to me that the open and speculative form of a novel such as *Satin Island* allows for explorations of the complexity and performativity of organizational processes that are not, or only rarely, to be found in the methodologically controlled and thus less daring proceedings of the social sciences.

In any case, organization in *Satin Island* does not, or only marginally, rely on criteria such as contractual membership, corporative legal form, formal hierarchical power or routinized decision programs – although these classic definitions of what constitutes an organization can of course be studied in terms of their communicative and material performativity, too. Neither does performativity merely reside in organizational efficiency programs or the everyday dramas of

7 U proceeds to derive a speculative theory of experience from the phenomenon of buffering, according to which affect theory's missing half-second (see Angerer, this volume) is part and parcel of the necessary buffering of experience: „[i]t dawned on me that what I was actually watching was nothing less than the skeleton, laid bare, of time or memory itself. [...] We require experience to stay ahead, if only by a nose, of our consciousness of experience – if for no other reason than the latter needs to make sense of the former [...] and, for this purpose, has to be fed with a constant, unsorted supply of fresh sensations and events." (McCarthy 2015: 64)

organizational life and its mise-en-scènes. For instance, it remains unclear where and how decisions about the Project are made, other than the suspicion that they are shaped in conjunction with the data streams of its network architecture. And although the reader is confronted with U's organizational experiences and actions, McCarthy is clearly not interested in presenting organizational life as one of role-playing and everyday dramas. Rather, organizational effects are perpetually accomplished through talk and speculation; through translating concepts and theories into organizational imperatives and selling propositions; and, significantly, through organizational practices that rely on digital infrastructures and data streams just as much as on the material spaces of organizing and its human actors. At times, U's experiences point to a posthumanist performativity that influences organized life, where the presumed agency of human actors and/or algorithmic infrastructures is blurred into more indistinguishable forms of intra-action that produce phenomena.

It makes sense, then, to perceive U as a revenant of "K", whom Kafka sent into the contingent and impenetrable, uncanny and violent machine of bureaucratic ordering and organization, so often not deemed more than rationally and functionally ordered. As Benjamin (1999: 803) commented, the issue of the "organization of life and work in the human community" would inform Kafka's oeuvre, in which organization itself had taken the place of fate in modernity. As *Satin Island* shows, the late capitalist and pervasively mediated and networked world of organizing engenders its own obscurity and uncanniness, a fate that requires further and deeper engagements with organization's posthumanist performativity.

References

Barad, Karen (2003): "Posthumanist performativity: toward an understanding of how matter comes to matter." In: Signs: Journal of Women in Culture and Society 28/3, pp. 801–831.

Baxmann, Inge/Beyes, Timon/Pias, Claus (eds.) (2016): Social Media – New Masses, Berlin: Diaphanes.

Benjamin, Walter (1999): "Franz Kafka." In: Michael W. Jennings/Gary Smith/Howard Eiland (eds.), Walter Benjamin, Selected Writings Vol. 2, Cambridge, MA: Belknap Press, pp. 794-819.

Beyes, Timon (2007): "Organisationstheorien von Agamben bis Žižek: Auf dem Basar der Organization Studies." In: Thomas Eberle et al. (eds.), Fokus Organisation: Sozialwissenschaftliche Perspektiven und Analysen, Konstanz: UVK, pp. 65-86.

Beyes, Timon/Pias, Claus (2014): "Transparenz und Geheimnis." In: Zeitschrift für Kulturwissenschaft 8/2, pp. 111-117.

Beyes, Timon/Steyaert, Chris (2006): "Justifying Theatre in Organizational Analysis: a Carnivalesque Alternative?" In: Consumption, Markets and Culture 9/2, pp. 101-109.

Beyes, Timon/Steyaert, Chris (2011): "The ontological politics of artistic interventions: Implications for performing action research." In: Action Research Journal 9/1, pp. 100-115.

Beyes, Timon/Steyaert, Chris (2012): "Spacing organization: Non-representational theorizing and the spatial turn in organizational research." In: Organization 19/1, pp. 45-61.

Beyes, Timon/Steyaert, Chris (2013): "Strangely familiar: The uncanny and unsiting organizational analysis." In: Organization Studies 34/10, pp. 1445-1465.

Biehl-Missal, Brigitte (2012): "Using artistic form for aesthetic organizational inquiry: Rimini Protokoll constructs Daimler's Annual General Meeting as a theatre play." In: Culture and Organization 18/3, pp. 211-229.

Böhme, Gernot (2016): Ästhetischer Kapitalismus, Berlin: Suhrkamp.

Cooper, Robert (1998): "Interview with Robert Cooper." In: Robert Chia (ed.), Organized Worlds: Explorations in Technology and Organization with Robert Cooper, London: Routledge, pp. 121-164.

Cooren, François (2004): "Textual agency: how texts do things in organizational settings." In: Organization 11/3, pp. 373–393.

Cornelissen, Joop P. (2004): "What are we playing at? Theatre, organization, and the use of metaphor." In: Organization Studies 25/5, pp. 705-727.

Czarniawska, Barbara (2008): A Theory of Organizing, Cheltenham: Edward Elgar.

Galloway, Alexander R./Thacker, Eugene (2007): The Exploit: A Theory of Networks, Minneapolis: University of Minnesota Press.

Gond, Jean-Pascal et al. (2015): "What do we mean by performativity in organizational and management theory? The Uses and abuses of performativity." In: International Journal of Management Reviews, published online before print, 12 June, 2015 (http://onlinelibrary.wiley.com/doi/10.1111/ijmr.12074 /epdf).

Kramer, Adam D.I./ Guillory, Jamie E./Hancock, Jeffrey T. (2014): "Experimental evidence of massive-scale emotional contagion through social networks." In: Proceedings of the National Academy of Sciences 111/24, pp. 8788–8790.

Lazzarato, Maurizio (2004): "From capital-labour to capital-life." In: ephemera 4/3, pp. 187-208.

Lewis-Kraus, Gideon (2015): "Negative capability." In: Bookforum, Feb/Mar 2015, June 15, 2016 (http://www.bookforum.com/inprint/021_05/14155)

Loxley, James (2007): Performativity, London: Routledge.

Lyotard, Jean-François (1984): The Postmodern Condition: A Report on Knowledge, Manchester: Manchester University Press.

Mangham, Iain (1986): Power and performance in organizations, Oxford: Blackwell.

McCarthy, Tom (2015): Satin Island, London: Jonathan Cape [Epub].

McCarthy, Tom (2016): Recessional – Or, the Time of the Hammer, Berlin: Diaphanes.

McKenzie, Jon (2001): Perform Or Else: From Discipline to Performance, London: Routledge.

Muniesa, Fabian (2014): The Provoked Economy: Economic Reality and the Performative Turn, London: Routledge.

Neyland, Daniel (2015): "On organizing algorithms." In: Theory, Culture & Society 32/1, pp. 119-132.

Nyberg, Daniel/Wright, Christopher (2015): "Performative and political: corporate constructions of climate change risk." In: Organization, published online before print, June 15, 2016 (http://org.sagepub.com/content/early/2015/02/25/1350508415572038.full.pdf+html)

Orlikowski, Wanda J./Scott, Susan V. (2014): "What happens when evaluation goes online? Exploring apparatuses of valuation in the travel sector." In: Organization Science 25/3, pp. 868–891.

Parker, Martin (2001): "Fucking management: Queer, theory and reflexivity." In: ephemera 1/1, pp. 36-53.

Spicer, André/Alvesson, Mats/Kärreman, Dan (2009): "Critical performativity: The unfinished business of critical management studies." In: Human Relations 62/4, pp. 537-560.

Stalder, Felix (2016): Kultur der Digitalität, Berlin: Suhrkamp.

Tyler, Melissa/Cohen, Laurie (2010): „Spaces that matter: gender performativity and organizational space." In: Organization Studies 31/2, pp. 175–198.

Crashing

Performing the economy, digital media and crisis

A critique of Michel Callon

Jens Schröter

Milton Friedman, who received the Nobel Prize in economics in 1976, published a famous and controversial essay in 1953. In "The Methodology of Positive Economics" he wrote:

"Positive economics is in principle independent of any particular ethical position or normative judgments […]. Its performance is to be judged by the precision, scope, and conformity with experience of the predictions it yields. […] [T]he belief that a theory can be tested by the realism of its assumptions independently of the accuracy of its predictions is widespread and the source of much of the perennial criticism of economic theory as unrealistic. Such criticism is largely irrelevant, and, in consequence, most attempts to reform economic theory that it has stimulated have been unsuccessful." (Friedman 1966: 4 and 41)

Friedman argues that only the *predictions* of a given model, not its *assumptions*, have to be correct. This argument was and is used to defend different, more or less orthodox ('neoclassical') economic models, based on problematic assumptions (e.g. methodological individualism, *homo oeconomicus*, money as neutral 'veil', the 'auctionator'[1]). Friedman explicitly states that this kind of 'criticism is largely irrelevant'. Unfortunately, it also fails to support orthodox economic models, insofar as most of them predict that markets tend towards a state of equi-

1 There are lots of critiques on these points, see especially with regard to Friedman Keen (cf. 2001: 148-153). See Keen (2011) for a general critique of mainstream economics.

librium. This is not to say that there are no theoretical extensions and refinements that discuss the possibilities of market failure and of course the notion of 'neoclassical' is too narrow to describe what remains of pluralism in 'mainstream' economics. But since 2008, there's a growing feeling that 'orthodox' or 'mainstream' economics is somehow incorrect. Economist Kenneth Rogoff, former member of the International Monetary Fund, admitted that the "very elegant economic models that dominated academic science for decades turned out to be very useless in practice".[2] There was a "complete failure of neoclassical economics to anticipate the crisis" (Keen 2011: xi). Today it seems that only theoretical models that predict crises are correct.

It is significant that at least some economists criticize their own models – while Michel Callon says, admittedly five years before the crisis: "There are [...] positions we have to abandon. The first is the idea of critique of hard economists, which is intended to show them that [they] are wrong" (Barry/Slater 2002: 301). This statement by Callon, implies that he follows the potentially obsolete models of 'hard economists' without any critique, already points to the necessity of analyzing his approach of the 'performativity of the markets' more closely.

Why Callon? He is one of the leading proponents of Actor-Network-Theory (ANT), which is highly fashionable at least in contemporary media studies. The aim of this paper is to show that ANT has no explanation for the economic crisis, not even a notion of it. In showing this, a deeper theoretical problem is addressed. In criticizing Callon's approach, I would also like to criticize what has recently be called the *practice turn* in media studies (often using ANT) and I will try to defend what one could call 'the logic of specific logics'. To avoid misunderstandings: It is of course to be welcomed that media studies analyze media practices empirically, e.g. using ethnographic methods, and do not just deduce abstractly potentials of a given medium from its alleged essential properties. But if this orientation on practices is radicalized, if it is stated that the media are simply an effect of practices and if a 'non-media centric media studies' is developed, as recently done by Shaun Moores and David Morley (cf. Krajina/Moores/Morley 2014), then we cross the line towards what I call *praxeo-*

---

2 „Neuorientierung der Wirtschaftswissenschaften" see: http://www.handelsblatt.com/unternehmen/management/koepfe/star-oekonom-fordert-neuorientierung-der-wirtschaftswissenschaften/6097068.html
Cf. Keen (2011: 12-15) on the very few economists that predicted the crisis from 2008 (although the neo-marxian approaches are not mentioned).

centrism, in which the practices of presupposed human actors are privileged.[3] Callon's theory of the performativity of economics is quite exemplary for this problem – in forgetting the scripts of money and digital technologies and how these two non-human actors interact.

In her famous 1992 text on the "De-scription of technical objects", Madeleine Akrich, herself a central proponent of ANT, demanded a two-step analysis. *Firstly* there had to be the analysis of the technical object, the opening of the black box, the reading of the *scripts* of the object, a move also demanded by Bruno Latour (2005: 79-82), the most important author of ANT. Only then, as a *second* step, practices should be analyzed – because without knowing the scripts, one could not even know if a practice was a 'misuse' of the object or exactly the intended, prescribed use. One could not even know if there was room for different practices at all. Often the human actors are themselves, not aware of the contingency and historicity of the technological scripts. Ethnographic methodologies, as used by Morley for example, pay more attention to the actions of people because technical objects don't reveal their scripts if you simply observe them visually from the outside. The symmetry proposed by ANT between human and non-human actors tends to be dissolved by privileging human actors. Instead of 'non-media-centric media studies', it seems, a non-praxeocentric praxeology is required.

1. CALLON, PERFORMATIVITY AND CRISIS

The central slogan of ANT is: 'Follow the actors' and at least Latour (2005: 54) names Harold Garfinkel's (1967) ethnomethodological approach as one of his central intellectual sources. In this sense, ANT observes the ongoing, processual, performative production of 'the social' through ever changing networks of human and non-human actors. "The performativity program starts with an ethnography of socio-technical *agencements*" (Callon 2005: 5).

3 Of course in Callon this is more complex: human actors are themselves defined by relations and theoretically humans are not the fundamental unit of ANT-analyses (see Callon 2007: 346). But de facto human practices are often privileged above non-human actors, as I will try to show.

In 1998, Callon published the anthology, *The Laws of the Markets*, in which he presented his concept of the *performativity of* economics (Callon 1998a).[4] The main idea is that economics, – the science describing economical processes – does not just describe the economy but also *produces* it.[5] That means an entity like 'the market' is not given, but continuously produced[6] and one of the ingredients of these, as he calls it, (with a notion that can already be found in the work of Gilles Deleuze and Felix Guattari,) *agencements,* are economic theories (for a critique cf. Brisset 2016).

I begin my reading with the observation that Callon surprisingly reinvents some basic concepts already invented by Marx. I insist on that point, because what is really problematic is that there is no notion of crisis, the word does not

4 It is not possible here to detail the history of notions like 'performativity' and 'praxeology' – but it is also not necessary, I will stick to the versions given by Callon and his followers, but see Reckwitz (2003).

5 The first obvious question arises already here: Callon just speaks of 'economics' and of 'economists' (see the quote above) without specifying *which* economics he means. That suggests he simply accepts the reigning mainstream economics, that is, simply put, neoclassical theory (mentioned e.g. in Callon 1998b: 22; cf. also Mirowski/Nik-Khah 2008: 96 and 117). He refers to "standard economic theory" (1998c: 247) and marginalist analysis (ibid.: 247-248), which is of course part of 'standard' neoclassical theory. This already negates the conflict in economics between this mainstream and so-called heterodox economics (cf. Keen 2001 and 2011 for a scathing critique of the neoclassical mainstream; cf. Lee 2009 on the history of heterodox economics; see also http://paecon.net; Callon (2005: 11) at least mentions "heterodox or even radical currents" – but gives no clear explanation why he implicitly and explicitly prefers the orthodox one. One has to assume it is because it is dominant – but that would presuppose what has to be explained).

6 Here the next question arises. Fine (2003: 480) observes that markets of course existed long before economy as an academic discipline existed (as Callon 2005: 8 himself admits). So why is analyzing economics particularly important or relevant in order to understand how markets are performed? Of course one could argue that market participants have something like implicit theories of what a market is (cf. ibid.: 9), but then one should analyze these instead of academic economics (cf. Mirowski/Nik-Khah 2008: 99, they especially insist in the case of the so-called 'FCC auctions': "*Corporate imperatives played the decisive role in determining the auction*" (ibid.: 112; original emphasis) – and not 'performing economists').

even appear in the index of *The Laws of the Markets*[7] and at least Marxian theory, whatever else its flaws may be, has developed some ideas for the cause of economic crisis. This is a particularly pressing problem: Keen's controversial study, *Debunking Economics,* begins with the observation (2001: 1), that mainstream economics in the last decade was indeed very often involved in constructing ('performing') markets and economies – and that this went awry quite often. It is difficult to conceive how crisis comes about when the markets are 'performed' – and it is not very convincing just to say, well, performing something can also go wrong, or as Callon (2007: 326) puts it: "But the performation may well fail, and the conditions of felicity may not be fulfilled." But why and how does performation fail?

One of the rare examples for crisis in Callon is the crash of October 19, 1987, connected to the Black-Scholes Formula, a mathematical tool, developed in the early 1970s to calculate and therefore price risks of given assets (cf. Taleb 2010). Callon (2007: 321) writes: "Yet failure can occur when events take place that are incompatible with the formula and its world. Financial crisis is a crisis for the formula."

Firstly, this implies that the crisis is in a way an unexpected and unwanted event, a 'failure'. Although this may seem self-evident, it is not – especially in a framework in which the thesis is that the economy is performed and this 'performation' is described as the "construction of a world" (ibid.: 333). There are at least some conspiracytheory-style economists (cf. Bichler/Nitzan 2014; similar arguments can be found in Post-Operaism) who would argue that the crisis is wanted by 'the capitalists' and that 'unemployment' is one of their 'weapons'. So there should at least be an argument, why the crisis was not an *intended effect* of the 'formula' but its failure. Why should 'performing the economy' mean producing a successful economy? And by which criteria 'successful'?

Secondly, even when we exclude this first possibility, Callon's quote suggests that a better formula (with less "technical shortcomings", Callon 2007: 323) might not have failed – crisis is not a *structural property* of non-human ac-

7 Callon can, of course, not be criticized, for not mentioning the dot.com crisis of 2001 or the financial meltdown of 2008 in *The Laws of the Markets* from 1998. But the crash of 1987 is not mentioned once, the crash from 1929 is only mentioned three times (1998a: 78 (twice), 205). It seems that in a very 'neoclassical' fashion crashes and crises are ignored as purely contingent, external phenomena. Even after 2008, this didn't change in the Callon school. In Fabian Muniesa's book *The Provoked Economy* from 2014 there is one mentioning of the 1987 crash (77) and one of the 1929 crash (16). No theoretical explanations are given why such crises exist.

tors like money or capital (as Marxists would have it), but a mistake made by human actors, like financial mathematicians.

Thirdly, this formulation leads to deep problems in the overall makeup of the argument. Underlining the performative character of economics, Callon insists that the formula *produces its world*, otherwise it wouldn't be performative, that is producing what it only seems to describe. When "a world is put into motion by the formula describing it" (ibid.: 320), how then can "unexpected events" (ibid.: 326) appear? And if they occur, doesn't that point to an unperformed outside? Is 'crisis' not *by definition* the limit of the constructive activity[8] implied by the notion of performativity? And what exactly does it mean when Callon (ibid.: 323) then observes, that "it is not the formula itself that can cause that world [...] to exist. Other forces, other interests are involved"? If the formula can be disrupted by those 'other forces', shouldn't they be of primary interest? And how is this boundary, between the performed world and its outside, to be described? To answer this, one would need a theory that does not perform, but describe (a possibility explicitly rejected by Callon[9]), because if this meta-theory would again perform, how could an un-performed outside be described by a performing theory? Wouldn't the meta-theory then perform the boundary between the performed and the un-performed? And how could this be understood – wouldn't this end in

8 As already quoted, Callon (2007: 333) speaks explicitly of "construction of a world". But admittedly it is not clear in the discussion on performativity if 'performing' something is the same as 'constructing' it (especially the work of Judith Butler 1993: 4-12 is a case in point). But in relation to Callon, MacKenzie, Muniesa and Liu write, that "he proposes considering economics not as a form of knowledge that depicts an already existing state of affairs but as a set of instruments and practices that contribute to the *construction* of economic settings, actors, and institutions" (2007: 4, emphasis added, JS).

9 Callon (1998b: 29, emphasis added, JS) writes: "Social science is no more outside the reality it studies than are the natural and life sciences. Like natural science, it actively participates in shaping the thing it describes." If describing a thing means producing it 'performatively' then this is also the case with Callon's approach itself. When he writes that the notion of "framing [...] enables us to think and describe the process of 'marketization'" (19, emphasis added, JS), doesn't that mean that his notion of 'framing' not only describes 'marketization', but also shapes and produces it? Doesn't Callon's theory shape all things it describes as performative? And how then can he state in the title of Callon (2007: 311) that "economics is performative" (emphasis added, JS), as if this were an ontological (that is: non-performed) fact outside of his own theory?

a massive self-contradiction, a theory performing the un-performed? And so forth.

It is not possible here to read all passages of Callon and his followers closely to point to the somewhat vague character of the notion of performativity. A few remarks will suffice:

Firstly, the possibility of failure or "misfire" (Callon 2010) is central to the debate of performativity, already in an early text by Derrida (1988) on Austin's notion of the 'performative', which is relevant for Butler's (1993) arguments on performativity. In his debate with Judith Butler (2010), Callon insisted that "the general rule is a misfire" (2010: 164) and agrees with Butler's idea that "the risk of breakdown and disruption are constitutive to any and all performative operations" (ibid.: 165, quoting Butler 2010: 152). I cannot go into why exactly performative operations are in a way structurally prone to breakdown – in my view this question isn't clearly answered by Butler, Callon or Derrida. But even if we assume it to be correct, it still fails to demonstrate why the economy sometimes works (or at least: seems to work) and sometimes is in a state of manifest crisis – again the questions of the 'conditions' or the 'outside' which produce resistance to the performation becomes pressing.

Secondly, Callon writes:

"MacKenzie proposes the notion of counterperformativity to denote these failures, because in this case the formula produces behaviors that eventually undermine it. [...] What Popper called refutation is another name for counterperformativity or what I have called overflowing." (2007: 323)[10]

Now it is the formula that produces what undermines it – how does this relate to the 'unexpected events' cited above? When 'counterperformativity' is the same as 'refutation' by Popper – which means that theories can never be positively confirmed, but only definitely be falsified by experimentation – why then is this complicated notion of 'performativity' necessary at all? Wouldn't it then be enough to say – as Keen (2001; 2011) does – that a certain model to describe the economy, let's say neoclassical economics, doesn't fit to the observed facts (the crisis) and therefore is simply wrong?[11] Of course, Callon (2007: 320) insists

10 The concept of 'overflowing' is discussed in more detail in Callon (1998c). Basically it's the "irrepressible" (ibid.: 250) result or side-effect of 'framing' – it is that what necessarily evades framing.

11 It is interesting that Callon (2007: 330) writes: „The Black and Scholes formula or the theory of general equilibrium, confined to the academic world can find its appropriate

that "the concept of performativity has led to the replacement of the concept of truth (or nontruth) by that of success or failure". But if a scientific theory makes a prediction that is confirmed by observation – then we call it a *successful* theory and also a 'true model', as long as (in accordance with Popper) it is not refuted by new observation. Otherwise "a prediction proves false" as Butler (2010: 153) puts it in a critical discussion of Callon's approach. So the difference of 'success' and 'truth' is not quite convincing. It is not clear that Callon's notion of the performativity of economics offers a 'successful' model to understand crisis.

2. CAPITALISM AND KAPITALISM

If we follow Friedman's methodological musings, meaning only theories predicting crisis are correct nowadays, the absence of a coherent theory of crisis points to fundamental problems in Callon's approach. My thesis is that *the praxeocentric reduction of the inner logic of non-human actors* is the reason for Callon's inability to cope with the crisis. *And the two non-human actors whose interior logic is erased are two media technologies: money and the digital computer.* Callon (2007: 354) writes:

"I use the word Kapitalism, with a capital K, to denote the reality imagined by everyone who considers the Western economic system to be a homogeneous reality, endowed *with its own logic* [emphasis added]. The assumption of a homogeneous economic reality is made by those who criticize capitalism[12], thus defined, as well as by those who defend it

milieu, its felicity conditions. But when they move over to the Chicago derivatives exchange or to ministries responsible for economic planning, they may encounter or even trigger resistance, for their felicity conditions are not filled. [...] Within the academic world, marginalist analysis thrives without any problem. As soon as it leaves that world of textbooks and students, which suits it so well, it gets into trouble." 'General equilibrium' and 'marginalist analysis' show that Callon is talking here about so-called mainstream, neoclassical economics – but when 'marginalist analysis' gets into trouble when its confronted with the real world, doesn't that simply show that it is wrong (as Keen [2001; 2011] at least for some forms suggests)? And isn't it revealing that nowadays lots of students of economics demand 'real world economics' – obviously economics fitting better to the world (see: http://www.real-world-economics.de; http://paecon.net)?

12 See Callon (in: Barry/Slater 2002: 297): "Capitalism is an invention of anti-capitalists". In a way this statement isn't very helpful because it is obvious that a

by talking of the market and its laws, in general. Experiments[13] in past decades have shown that Kapitalism could only be a fiction: no program has managed to make Kapitalism exist nor to overthrow it. There are only capitalisms."

A typical move for praxeocentric discourses is to deny the possibility of an 'inherent logic' in relation to non-human entities – the argument is always that entities are situated in historical and local practices and therefore are different without any underlying homogeneous logic (see Callon 2005: 15: "I don't believe in *A* Kapitalism that could be reduced to *AN* impersonal logic").

Firstly, it is simply wrong that the critics of capitalism, against whom Callon's argument is obviously made (explaining the German sounding "Kapitalism" with a capital 'K'[14]), postulate a homogeneous entity called 'capitalism'. 'They' always admitted that capitalism has had historical phases e.g. imperialism and state-monopolistic capitalism or in another theoretical vein, Fordism and post-Fordism or that there is uneven development etc.[15] They just postulated that capitalism has one or more fundamental principles that remain in place below historical and local differences, that is why Marx analyzes capitalism in "its ideal average" (1991: 970).

Secondly and far more importantly, Callon seems to at least gesture to the existence of such a principle too: How could he even speak of 'different capitalisms'? He presupposes a fundamental principle common to all these capitalisms or otherwise he couldn't even classify the different phenomena under one label 'capitalism'.[16] See this symptomatic quote by Callon (2005: 5):

---

notion like 'capitalism' is the result of a description that is based on a theoretical model (e.g. differentiation theorists like Niklas Luhmann wouldn't use it, he would speak of 'functionally differentiated society'). And you can use such a model to criticize what you describe. But that's of course true of all descriptions (also of that describing economics as performative) and insofar it makes no sense to say 'Capitalism is an invention of anti-capitalists' as if that would be a valid critique.

13 The 'experiments' seems to be Callon's word for so-called 'real socialism' (cf. Callon 2007: 349).

14 I guess that this is related to the German tradition coming from Marx.

15 The literature on these points is far too extensive as to be summed up here.

16 Of course different theorists (like Niklas Luhmann) would doubt that there is such a thing like 'capitalism'. For Luhmann there would only be different subsystems (one among them economy) whose difference is the unity of society, but ANT is no differentiation theory and Callon himself introduces the question of capitalism, therefore he has to live with the question how to define capitalism (and even in differentiation

"Instead of assuming, for example, the existence of a spirit of capitalism or an overall logic of a mode of production, we can relate certain forms of economic activity to the more or less chaotic, regular and general upsurge of calculative agencies formatted and equipped to act on the basis of a logic of accumulation and maximization."

At first, the idea of an 'overall logic of a mode of production' is negated – but then self-contradictorily 'a logic of accumulation and maximization' (that is of course, the logic of capitalist accumulation[17]) is reintroduced.

This logical flaw typical of praxeocentrism is repeated over and over in his texts and it finds its most radical expression in a statement he quotes approvingly: "Rationality is always situated" (Callon 1998b: 48). For Callon, it seems to be universally rational to assume that rationality is never universal, but always situated – that is self-contradictory. A radical praxeocentrism dissolving everything in locally and historically situated occurrences is logically impossible, because it could not even compare two different occurrences to highlight their local specificity, because to compare them, a general principle of comparison (here: that both occurrences are 'practices') has to already be taken into account. It makes no sense to say, 'there is no such thing as photography but only photographic practices', because even to select two practices to compare them as different *photographic* practices, presupposes an implicit knowledge of what photography is, otherwise the practices could not even be selected.

Coming back to Callon: One of the main goals of his whole approach, and one I find quite appealing, is to show that markets are nothing natural and that the calculative agencies required in markets have to be constructed. Although Callon (1998b: 6) rejects "sociocultural frames", he mentions such things like the law and the state, which also were named as preconditions for markets in the Marxian tradition (cf. Pashukanis 2002). But he insists particularly on the way in which the *homo oeconomicus* is produced. While this would perhaps be subsumed under the problematic notion of 'ideology' in the Marxian tradition, Callon is more interested in the concrete tools and operations that produce 'calculativeness' on the side of the human actors and 'calculability' on the side of the objects. The question immediately arises, *what* is calculated and *why* there is calculation at all. "Competition between calculative agencies [...] is largely de-

theories like systems theory there is a controversial discussion nowadays if economy is really just a subsystem among others, cf. Pahl 2008: 55-63). See also the discussion between Barry, Slater and Callon (in: Barry/Slater 2002: 296), where they discuss the question of a "fundamental aspect" of capitalism.

17 See Marx (1990: 742): "Accumulate, accumulate! That is Moses and the prophets."

termined by the respective qualities of the calculating devices. The probability of gain is on the side of the agency with the greatest power of calculation […]" (Callon 1998b: 45). Competition and the goal of 'gain' are presupposed here and explain why calculation is used. That means: Callon presupposes a social form in which any entity, besides their specific and unique use-value, also has an *abstract exchange value*, because only such an abstract value can be calculated. Although he doesn't use these Marxian notions, one of his examples is very telling (cf. Callon 2007: 336-339): Norwegian fishers that are turned into economic subjects by transforming the fish into calculable 'cyborg-fish', that is: commodities. This is nothing other than a reinvention of what Marx (1990: 873-907) called 'primitive accumulation', in which objects are violently transformed into objects that have exchange value (and besides, may be useful).[18] For Marx, primitive accumulation is the precondition of the establishment of capitalist societies. But Callon does not use the term 'value' systematically in *The Laws of the Market*, sometimes he speaks of "usage value" (1998b: 33) or "use value" (ibid.: 35), "exchange value" is only to be found in a quote (ibid.: 19), so basically it remains unclear *what* exactly is calculated in Callon's approach.[19] Interestingly, in another text he writes: "As the old Marx so clearly saw: there is no exchange value without a use value, and no use value in a market regime without the production of an exchange value" (2005: 6).

---

18 Holm (2007: 239) is very explicit about that: "When the cyborg fish is in place, the most violent acts of dispossession against coastal communities have already been undertaken; the fisheries commons have already been closed; the heritage of the coastal people has already been parceled and laid out, ready for the auction. With the successful introduction of fisheries resource management, most of the organizational and institutional apparatus that could have served as a power base for those who want to resist ITQs has already been squashed." We read of 'violence' through which the 'commons' (*Gemeingut* or *Allmende* in German) of the fishermen are closed and thereby the fishermen are 'dispossessed'. This is *exactly* the process of primitive accumulation as described by Marx. See also Callon (1998b: 24 and 27) on "extending the spaces of calculation". See also Holm/Nielsen (2007) again on the 'cyborg-fish'.

19 The word 'value' is sometimes used in Callon (1998b: 38, 50) in a vaguely moral sense, 'values' that are opposed to the market.

3. CALCULATION AND MONEY

At this precise point we have to return to the question of a 'specific logic'. Shouldn't we say that the reduction of everything to exchangeable, calculable abstract quantities, a process that is also implied in Callon's central notion of 'framing' (see below), is *specific* for capitalism? This is at least the answer Marxian theory would give – capitalism is most generally to be understood as the total reign of abstract value-form, represented in money, meaning that everything, especially labor-power, is turned into exchangeable commodities with an exchange value that is measured or at least represented in its price (cf. Larsen et al. 2014).[20] Due to his praxeocentrism, we should expect that Callon denies this, especially since it would force him to accept the existence of Kapitalism (with a capital 'K') and this is indeed the case:

"[T]here is no Great Divide between societies populated by calculative agencies and societies in which the agents do not calculate. Even Deleuze and Guattari were on the wrong track with their concept of deterritorialization, that extraordinary faculty bestowed on capitalism for breaking all ties and undoing solidarity [...]. So-called traditional societies are populated – sometimes even over-populated with calculative agencies." (Callon 1998b: 39)

Callon argues that there is *no* great divide between societies with and without calculative agencies, because there are no societies that do not calculate: there was always calculation and as a consequence, there is nothing special about capitalism – if capitalism can be equated with or related to calculation (see below), a connection Callon infers by referring to Deleuze and Guattari on capitalism next to his musings on calculation. We would either have to abandon the term 'capitalism' or we would have to call all societies, even 'so-called traditional societies', capitalist, acknowledging that there are indeed different capitalisms and no Kapitalism with any underlying principle. But this argument leads Callon to argue against himself: By stretching the principle of calculation to all societies and thereby erasing any (great) 'divide', he is the one who homogenizes unduly. It is difficult to understand why he rejects, on the one hand, a homogenizing principle

20 I'm ignoring here the difficulties of relating values and prices, whose relation turned into a difficult problem in the Marxian tradition. Keen (2001: 269-299) devastatingly criticizes Marxian economics on this 'transformation problem' as others do, but there are also defenders of Marx and authors who argue that this whole debate is completely beside the point (see Kliman 2007).

('Kapitalism') that allows to relate different 'capitalisms' to each other and on the other hand introduces an even wider homogenizing principle – a calculation as such – that surprisingly and a-historically unites 'traditional societies' (by which, I guess, he means so-called 'primitive societies') and modern industrial capitalism under one category. But his argumentation is not only logically but also historically unconvincing. If we assume that Callon relates the question of calculation to the existence of money (because he talks about the economy and not about mathematics), he would have to argue (if calculation is his homogenizing principle), that the sheer existence of money already means that there is capitalism. As Jacques Le Goff (2012) and others have shown, however, even the existence of money (as a materialization of calculation) does not make a society capitalist.[21] Money is much older than capitalism.

The question is, if a society is *centered* around money and, to use Akrich's term, its scripts. Only when the basic script is M-C-M', meaning that money (M) is used to produce commodities (C) that are sold for more Money (M') and when this script is fundamental for all activities (cf. e.g. for a recent and especially pointed argument Lotz 2014), then we can speak of capitalism. At least this is a definition that avoids the confusion created by Callon. This script (M-C-M') is the definition of capital, according to Marx (1990: 247-257): Capital is the *process* of making more money out of money.[22] Marx (ibid.: 166-167) writes: "They

---

21 As these remarks suggest, there is a profound lack of historical thinking in Callon. One can see this already at the very beginning of his introduction of *The Laws of the Markets*, where he writes: "The aim of the present book is to contribute to the analysis and understanding of the subtle relationships between economics and the economy; not within an historical perspective, although some chapters do include historical material, but within a deliberately anthropological one." (Callon 1998b: 2) It is of course legitimate to choose an anthropological perspective, but as I suggested (and will go on arguing) this produces severe problems of understanding 'the economy'. But worse, just one page after he explicitly rejected a 'historical perspective' he writes: "[T]he market is a process in which calculative agencies oppose one another, without resorting to physical violence, to reach an acceptable compromise in the form of a contract and/or a price […] Hence, the importance of the historical dimension which helps us to understand the construction of markets and the competitive arrangements in which they are stabilized, for a time and in a place." (ibid.: 3) The least one can say is that Callon's relation to history is somewhat unclear. See also Callon (2007: 347) on his ideas for a "history of economics".

22 My reading of Marx follows recent neo-marxian approaches like the 'critique of value' (cf. Larsen et al. 2014) that focus not on class struggle but on the autopoietic

do this without being aware of it." Marx' definition implies that there is a script to money regulating our practices. Money is not just a transparent means for human ends existing independently of money – as a praxeocentric theory would have it (and by the way, also neoclassical economics has it, in which money plays nearly no role, cf. among a lot of other authors Pahl 2008: 9-16).

Insofar as money is pure abstraction, that is: pure quantity, its quantum can only diminish or grow. It is not surprising that in its practical use, its quantum diminishes or grows. And therefore it is also not surprising that economic actors 'calculate', as Callon rightly insists, because money can *only* be calculated. Callon argues in a typically praxeocentric matter, that there are only *different* markets: "The idea of the market as a unified category and institution is progressively disappearing" (Callon, in Barry/Slater 2002: 291)[23] but of course no one would trade and calculate on markets if the outcome wasn't *more money* than the amount invested. Again: This script disappears and although Callon implies, as I have argued above, the goal of 'gain' as central for markets (1998b: 45) the ex-

---

movement of value in the form of money as central for capitalism. One point might seem problematic here: If the tendency of money to become more money would lie – as I suggested – in its purely quantitative character, shouldn't the existence of money automatically lead to capitalism and how can there be societies with money but without capital (understood as infinite process of accumulation of money)? Although this is a complex question, which cannot be answered here in detail, it seems that firstly in many 'traditional' societies money-commodity-relations are marginal (compared to subsistence) and secondly that the disruptive script of money was deliberately repressed, e.g. by the ban of interest (as in Islam) or giving money such a heavy and cumbersome materiality that it cannot be accumulated easily, as in the classical case of the 'stone money of Yap' (cf. Gillilland 1975).

23 The context of the quote is: "But the market is not this unified category as it was in the nineteenth century, or even in the first half of the twentieth century. I think that the paradox is the following: everybody agrees that the market is a very effective institution, but now it seems to me that more and more people consider that there are various ways of organizing concrete and specific markets. So it's a very different situation because you now have an abundance of ways of seeing economic markets. The idea of the market as a unified category and institution is progressively disappearing." Again: that different forms of markets may exist is plausible – but that doesn't mean that there isn't an underlying principle (a 'unified category') that makes it possible to address this different phenomena *as markets* in the first place. Interestingly, Callon argues that the idea of the market 'as a unified category' is 'progressively disappearing', although he gives no hint what the reasons for that might be.

plicit "imperative of profitability is absent" (Fine 2003: 480), because this would explicitly (and rightly so) introduce a unifying principle.

Callon (1998b: 12) states: "The agent is calculative because action can only be calculative." For one, this statement fails to differentiate economic practice ('action') from every other practice and thereby again underlines the status of calculation as Callon's homogenizing principle. Moreover, Callon deduces calculativeness from *action* ('because action can only be calculative'), that is: from practice and not from the central role of a medium whose script is pure calculability. Although the role of devices, technologies etc. is so central for Callon's argument, they are suspiciously often reduced to useful tools in the hands of human actors. This is especially (and very significantly) the case for money – it seems that Callon, implicitly following (and not criticizing, as was noted above) the economical mainstream, also follows the neoclassical mainstream's exclusion and oblivion of money.[24] We can expect that this discursive operation appears as a reduction and erasure of the pure quantitativeness, calculability and abstraction of money. That is exactly the case.

4. MONEY, COMMODITY, PRODUCTION

Callon (1998b: 21-22) begins with describing the script of money:

"To be sure its main contribution was to provide a unit of account without which no calculation would be possible. However the essential is elsewhere. Money is required above all – even if this point is often overlooked – to delimit the circle of actions between which equivalence can be formulated. It makes commensurable that which was not so before. [...] It provides the currency, the standard, the common language which enables us to reduce heterogeneity, to construct an equivalence and to create a translation [...]. It is the final piece, the keystone in a metrological system that is already in place and of which it merely guarantees the unity and coherence. *Alone it can do nothing* [emphasis added, JS]; combined with all the measurements preceding it, it facilitates a calculation which makes commensurable that which was not so before."

24 See also Orléan (2014: 4) who underlines that for the „neoclassical theory of value [...] money is a peripheral fact, a secondary device, a mere adjunct to utility that exists solely as a means of facilitating transactions". It should be noted that in Latour's theory of 'immutable mobiles' there is also a reduction of money to just one 'immutable mobile' amongst others, so this repression of money seems to be common to different authors from ANT, cf. Schröter (2011: 229-241).

At first sight, Callon seems to acknowledge the script of money – but with a significant twist: Money is added as the endpoint of a metrological chain of measurements onto a world before money. There is a world performatively roduced as calculable by measurement and then money comes in – 'merely' as a 'final piece'. But this doesn't explain how 'equivalence' is achieved, how money is related to 'measurement', that is: *what it measures*. Therefore, as was already stated above, some theory of value would be needed, which is not provided by Callon.[25]

But to reduce money to the 'final piece' also negates that in the world we live in, everything is already produced with regard to money. Nothing is produced that doesn't at least potentially yield more money than was invested – and this rule even shapes the commodities in a very concrete way, think of so-called 'planned obsolescence' (cf. Bulow 1986). In Callon's model,[26] money is added as a market device to a production devoid of money: production does not appear.[27] But if production is already structured with regard to money, money is not just a practical means of exchange. Commodities are things that have a price, that is, they are equivalent to some amount of money. Being a commodity means being a thing *and* being money.

Callon (1999: 189) writes about the being of a commodity: "[T]o transform something into a commodity, it is necessary to cut the ties between this thing and other objects or human beings one by one." The central notion here is 'framing':

> "[A] clear and precise boundary must be drawn between the relations which the agents will take into account and which will serve in their calculations, on the one hand, and the multitude of relations which will be ignored by the calculation as such, on the other." (ibid.: 186-187; see also Callon 1998c)

---

25 Callon (1998: 22) writes: "Money establishes an ultimate equivalence between the value of a human life and that of investment in pollution abatement." He makes this statement in relation to an example, in which the "negative externalities, for example the effects of pollution produced by a chemical plant" (ibid.: 21) are concerned. But the question arises: How can such different things be compared and made equivalent? 'Measurement' alone cannot be the answer, because you need something to be measured – that is 'value'. But Callon does not define 'value' (see above).

26 And it is a model, even when Callon (cf. 1999: 194) insists that ANT is not a theory.

27 To be sure, "producers" are mentioned a lot (Callon 1998b: 18, 19, 20 and passim), but there is no description or theory of production.

The objects simply seem to be there, out of nothing, and framing seems to mean ripping them out of emotional contexts to sell them. This looks more like a flea market than like a real economy in which commodities *are produced as commodities for the markets*. When Callon (1999: 189) writes: "one is not born a commodity, one becomes it",[28] this is not quite correct for the vast majority of objects surrounding us (the processes of primitive accumulation mentioned above set aside here, because in primitive accumulation, objects that weren't commodities are turned into commodities). Although the book is called, *The Laws of the Markets,* Callon speaks right on the first page of the introduction of "economy" (1998b: 1), as if markets and (capitalist) economy were identical. He only talks about markets. This is also typical of the neoclassical approach, which tends to focus on exchange (cf. e.g. Orléan 2014: 37). To argue that way is to erase production, which means to erase capital from the picture, understood as M-C-M' in which production of commodities is part of the movement of value, where commodities and money are in a way the same, namely metamorphoses of capital (cf. Marx 1990: 255). It seems that Callon has this theoretical (Marxian) argument in mind when he writes:

"Money seems to be the epitome of the commodity; it is pure equivalence, pure disentanglement, pure circulation. Yet, as Viviana Zelizer showed so convincingly, agents are capable of constantly creating private money which embodies and conveys ties [...]. This is the case of grand-mothers who gives her grand-daughter silver coins, or supermarkets

28 See also Callon (1998b: 19), where he develops basically the same argument, quoting anthropologist Nicolas Thomas on the definition of 'commodity': "Commodities are here understood as objects, persons, or elements of persons which are placed in a context in which they have exchange value and can be alienated. The alienation of a thing is its dissociation from producers, former users, or prior context." Interestingly enough, Callon doesn't take his definition of 'commodity' from economic theory (as one might expect, given his argument that economic theory performs the economy), but from an anthropologist. Firstly that shows that he consequently follows his line of equating traditional societies and industrial capitalism (by means of 'calculation'). But secondly, and in line with my critique of this being ahistorical, this is highly problematic. To me it simply makes no sense to describe commodity production in industrial capitalism with a notion like 'alienation' in the sense that the product has to be torn away from its producer – products (commodities) in industrial capitalism *are made to be given away*, no one is emotionally attached to them.

which give fidelity vouchers to their customers." (Callon 1999: 190; he is alluding to Zelizer 1998)[29]

Or see a similar quote from another publication: "Earmarking is deployed as much in the domestic sphere, with silver coins which a grandmother gifts to her grandchildren to put in their piggybanks in memory of her, as in systems of mass distribution, with vouchers, fidelity or credit cards and other such devices" (Callon 1998b: 35).

This is highly symptomatic: The coins grandma gives her granddaughter are treated as 'private money' – although these coins cannot be exchanged against commodities. Grandma can give as many coins as she wants to her granddaughter, she could even produce new 'private money' by writing the word 'money' on paper snippets as much as she likes, but she shouldn't try to go to a supermarket (even to one that emits vouchers) and try to acquire commodities with the private money.[30] 'Private money' is not money at all (there is no 'private money' as there is no 'private language'), even if the human actors name it 'money' – which demonstrates that there's an irreducible script that cannot be easily changed by different practices.[31] Callon (1998b: 35 and 54, FN 6) gives an example of a prostitute who writes the day and the date of an especially beautiful night with a client on a banknote – this is an example that "the banknote is an excellent medium for the exercise of rewriting". Apart from the fact that the banknote here is explicitly called a medium the argument seems to be that money is not abstract and that its "official attachments" can be 'overloaded' with

29 It is strange that Callon defines the commodity by framing, that is untying (1999: 189: "cut the ties between this thing and other objects or human beings one by one"); but doubts that money is 'disentanglement' and follows Zelizer on 'money which embodies and conveys ties'. With this argument he separates again commodities from money (because only commodities seem to follow the basic operation of 'framing'), although commodities can only be understood *as* commodities in relation to money. Giving away a thing on the market (and in that sense 'untying' it from me as the seller) means exchanging it against money – money is the force that allows generalized 'untying' and in that sense it is 'pure disentanglement'. It is a basic move in Callon to tear apart money and the commodity – to erase the basic logic of capitalism.

30 This shows that money cannot easily be understood as a 'sign' (on the sign-theories of money see Hutter 1995).

31 Callon mentions the law – and the law, the state, the police and ideological state apparatuses have exactly to ensure the stability of the script, or to put it precisely: one set of aspects of the potentiality of the script.

"new, private, messages" (ibid.: 35). But what does this mean? Of course, I can use a banknote as a medium of writing, but it would be outlandish to suggest that the role of money is thereby changed from the universal equivalent, pure calculability to something personal and individual (as the individual banknote might be). In a similar way, you could say that you can change the rules of soccer by writing some personal notes on the ball. *The script of money is repressed in favor of practices by human actors. ANT's own principle of symmetry is violated.*

To sum up: Money is severed from the notion of commodity.[32] This means that Callon, contrary to his talk of performativity which implies processuality, erases the endless processual character of money changing into commodities and back, a movement that Marx (1990: 255) called the "automatic subject" of society – and which is perhaps the 'outside' of the performation of the economy in Callon's sense.

5. LABOR AND COMPUTERS

If production is erased from Callon's discourse, then labor of or in production is erased too. The word 'labor' is not mentioned once in *The Laws of the Market* (except from some titles in bibliographies); not surprisingly, for ANT, the word 'laboratory' is much more frequent. The erasure of production also means that digital technologies can only play a role on the level of the markets, that is on the level of distribution and circulation – and it's even more radical: In *The Laws of the Markets* (1998) the computer is only mentioned a few times and in *Market Devices* (2007), the word 'computer' shows up only once; the word 'digital'

32 It is interesting that one of the paradigmatic examples for Callon is an experimental strawberry market in southern France (cf. Garcia-Parpet 2007). As Callon (1998b: 20) underlines this was a "market with characteristics corresponding to those described in political economy manuals" – meaning a demonstration of the performativity of economics. But this strangely constructed market adhered indeed closely to neoclassical manuals, in that it was a market with an 'auctioneer' in the Walrasian sense (cf. Keen 2011: 178-180). Firstly, real markets don't have 'auctioneers' (cf. Binswanger 1990: 345), insofar this example doesn't show that real markets can be constructed according to neoclassical manuals and secondly the Walrasian market is a market *without money* (cf. Binswanger 1990). Although Callon discusses money right next to the strawberry market (cf. 1998b: 21) he doesn't mention with a word the exclusion of money in Walras' model of markets. Again money is reduced and repressed.

doesn't appear at all (cf. Mirowski/Nik-Khah 2008: 118 for a critique of Callon leaving out "the notorious quasi-material shape-shifter the computer").

We can sum up: Callon severs money from commodities and in this way, from capital, and he represses production and therefore, on the one hand, labor, and on the other hand, the role of computers or digital technologies in production. I insist on that point, because by excluding money, labor and digital technologies from his picture of the "economy" (1998b: 1),[33] Callon excludes the relationship that gives at least *one* explanation for the moments of crisis we witness – at least if we follow the 'critique of value' (cf. Larsen et al. 2014). The thesis is – to put it in highly simplified terms – that the unavoidable competition results in individual companies needing to produce commodities more cheaply in order to succeed in the market. In order to achieve this, increasingly advanced technologies must be used, hence increasing productivity. This means *firstly*, that increasingly large advance investment in infrastructure is required – the first reason for the increasing inflation of credit, i.e. the financial superstructure.

Secondly, so-called 'rationalisation' gradually eliminates labor. A primary historical compensatory mechanism for this was provided by the fact that the reduction in prices for products caused by increased productivity used to result in expanding markets (e.g. nowadays, many people have a car). Even if the increased productivity undermined the creation of surplus value, provided the absolute quantity of commodities increased, then more surplus value could still have been produced.

One argument of the 'critique of value' at this juncture is that, with the introduction of new digital technologies, for the first time in history, the elimination of labor is proceeding faster than markets can expand. The argument, that in the past technological progress didn't lead to structural unemployment and therefore this won't happen now, is flawed. Digital technologies are much more flexible and can substitute cognitive work, too. The script of digital computers is their programmability, leading to flexibility. One might say that the medium of money is struggling against digital technologies – they do not coexist or 'co-perform' (cf. Callon 2007: 335) peacefully.[34] Their scripts come into conflict, independent of human practice. Marx knew this too, in a surprising anticipation of automa-

33 Or at least reducing them.

34 Another aspect is the discrete digital code, which can in principle be reproduced without loss – meaning the digital products are more and more difficult to 'frame' as commodities, to use Callon's words. These are products for which Callon's thesis "one is not born a commodity, one becomes it" (1999: 189) does really apply and he doesn't even mention them.

tion: after all, if people increasingly only relate "watchman and regulator to the production process itself", then (at least for most of them) labor will cease to be a "great well-spring of wealth". The less that production depends on "labour time and on the amount of labour employed than on the power of the agencies set in motion during labour time [...], the general state of science and on the progress of technology", the more "production based on exchange value breaks down" (Marx 1993: 704-705). In 2005, the world's 200 largest companies already accounted for over 25 per cent of global economic activity, but are only able to employ 0.75 per cent of all people (cf. Kurz 2005: 81). It is therefore revealing that there have been, especially in the last years, several publications addressing exactly this problem. In 2009, the computer entrepreneur, Martin Ford, published a much-discussed book, *The Lights in the Tunnel*. The book's blurb already poses unmistakable questions: "Where will advancing technology, job automation, outsourcing and globalization lead? Is it possible that accelerating computer technology was a primary cause of the current global economic crisis?" (Ford 2009). In one chapter (ibid.: 67-73) he emphasizes that a significant number of cognitively more complex tasks can be taken over by the growing artificial intelligence of our 'smart' devices (which is of course why they are called 'smart'). Mental labor is rationalized, too. Erik Brynjolfsson, a professor at MIT and Director of the MIT Center for Digital Business[35], published in 2011 with Andrew McAfee a book titled *Race against the Machine. How the Digital Revolution is Accelerating Innovation, Driving Productivity, and Irreversibly Transforming Employment and the Economy*, where the authors also discuss the potential disappearance of labor.[36] Finally, I want to mention a current study that predicts that up to 47 per cent of all jobs in the United States will be prone to rationalization (cf. Frey/Osborne 2013).

After all, a jobless person consumes less, i.e. products that are manufactured cannot be sold (domestic market crisis) or consumers have to take up credits to maintain their lifestyles, the second reason for the inflation of debt. People who don't have work may be unable to pay taxes. Therefore the state, which is supposed to provide the legal, educational, etc. framework for the market. cannot

---

35 See http://ebusiness.mit.edu/erik/

36 This is especially interesting because Brynjolffson (1993) wrote an overview on the 'IT productivity paradox'. If even he admits, as he does in *Race against the Machine*, that there is a problem, it really has to be serious.

continue to function without credits – third reason for the inflation of debt.[37] If it is no longer possible to consume and produce, then – to put it in simplified terms – it is also not possible to valorize value: one consequence is the flight to 'fictional capital', as Marx (1991: 525-542) called it, meaning, the inflation of financial markets: if you can't make profits with production, you may make profits with assets. And the inflated financial markets can collapse, but the collapse from 2008 was not the cause of the crisis, but one of its symptoms (cf. Lohhoff/Trenkle 2012 for a very firm, but surely controversial position).[38] The expansion of computer-based technologies, the increase in structural mass unemployment and the ever-denser chain of financial crises, large and small, since the late 1970s, stand in an internal, systematic relationship. Even if one doesn't accept *this* explanation for the crisis, it is at least *an* explanation for the crisis, whereas Callon has none.

Interestingly enough, he writes (Callon 2007: 315): "Without assistance, economic agents are not able to produce [...] all the innovations that will guarantee them a competitive advantage. They need chemists, physicists, or biologists working in universities." Here, production and the role of 'science' and 'technology' for competitive advantage - basically by reducing costs through reducing labor – is at least implicitly addressed. And: "Competition between calculative agencies, focused on their ability to have their decisions recognized and accepted (for example, to propose a given product on a given market segment), is largely determined by the respective qualities of the calculating devices. The probability of gain is on the side of the agency with the greatest powers of calculation" (Callon 1998b: 45). Similarly, if you understand the 'powers of calculation' as those computing powers that help companies to reduce costs and to increase productivity, you could come close to a theory of crisis – but Callon doesn't develop this any further.

---

37 Of course these are not linear developments, there are lots of digressions and counter movements (e. g. there are nowadays also lots of savings; in some countries like Germany the unemployment rate falls due to successful export economies etc.).

38 For English-speaking readers here's the translated introduction to the book: http://www.krisis.org/2012/the-great-devaluation-introduction. Interestingly Butler (2010: 153) writes in her debate with Callon: „The present recession in some ways highlights this failure at the heart of financial performativity" – meaning she really tries to connect the discussion on the performativity of economics to the crisis of 2008, although she also seems to locate the reasons for the crisis in the financial realm without asking why there is such an inflated financial superstructure in the first place.

6. CONCLUSION

My readings of Callon's texts on the performativity of economics tried to show that there is a privileging of human practices in Callon's discourse, contrary to the alleged symmetry of human and non-human actors.[39] Perhaps the most blatant example of this is the idea – following Viviana Zelizer – that earmarking money can somehow change the script of money (or that actors can produce 'private money'). This *praxeocentric* erasure of the specific logic or script of the non-human actor of money is consistent with the erasure of the idea of 'specific logics' in general, which leads to inconsistencies in Callon's argument. The praxeocentrism of his (and Latour's) discourse is masked by the alleged 'agnosticism' of ANT-style description: "I consider that social scientists don't have special access to a truth that would be inaccessible to actors themselves" (Callon 2005: 12). This idea of a pure description of the actors themselves (cf. also Latour 2005: 46-50 and 147) has the problem, besides others,[40] that the non-human actors cannot speak for themselves.[41] The descriptivist discourse of ANT

39 It seems that Butler (2010: 153) basically critiques the same point: „My worry is that the cultural constructivist position thinks performativity works and that it imputes a certain sovereign agency to the operation of performativity."

40 A 'pure description' without any premises is impossible (Hands 2001: 208-210 underlines the role of economic metaphors in ANT, meaning that there is always already a specific framework in place); even if it were impossible, it is never completed, because networks are infinite; and even if it were possible and it could be completed in a meaningful way, the question still remains what exactly the use is in simply doubling and mirroring an existing practice. Purely doubling the practices of actors makes social science superfluous – Callon, by the way, admits that: After having written 'that social scientists don't have special access to a truth that would be inaccessible to actors themselves' some lines later he states: "The role of the anthropology of (the) econom(y)ics is, I believe, to make these anthropological struggles explainable in their theoretical and practical dimensions, by *identifying and revealing the forces* that, in a more or less articulated way, challenge the dominant models and their grip on real markets." (Callon 2005: 12, emphasis added, JS). Here, the social scientist or anthropologist 'reveals' (and 'identifies') something, meaning that it obviously has been hidden and misunderstood before, hidden to the actors involved and misunderstood by them. Obviously, scientists also in Callon need access 'to a truth that would be inaccessible to actors themselves' – otherwise they simply would be no scientists and couldn't 'explain' anything, a notion Callon uses in the quote.

41 And even human actors might not know exactly what they are doing and why.

leads automatically to a praxeocentric reduction of non-human actors, contrary to all alleged symmetry.

Moreover, this theoretical structure makes it impossible for Callon to develop a consistent theory of crisis, a theory which allows for the 'crisicity' of crisis, if you allow this strange neologism – meaning a notion of crisis, in which it is not a mistake of human actors (e.g. developing unfortunately flawed formulas), but a result of the failing 'co-performation' of non-human actors, that is money and digital technologies,[42] beyond all human intentions. That's why humans then experience the crisis as incomprehensible disruption, as happened in 2008. Only a non-praxeocentric praxeology, as might be implied by the 'value-critical' reading of Marx, can be an appropriate theory of this.[43] Marx' notion of the "automatic subject" (1990: 255) of capital – a non-human actor – is interestingly enough confirmed by a much-discussed paper by Gode and Sunder (1993), in which they made simulations of markets with 'zero intelligence traders'. Although the simulated actors had no intelligence at all, the allocative efficieny of the markets was stable – meaning that no human practices, no human knowledge, is necessary at all. The structure alone ('the rules') determines the output, which is a clear indication that human practices should not be overemphasized. Instead of this – with Marx – the social forms (structural dynamics) have to be analyzed and perhaps criticized.

Although more should be said on that topic, finally a few words on the political implications of Callon's discourse. Although we already heard that Callon doesn't want to criticize the economists, that doesn't mean that he just and only follows the mainstream discourse – he tends to argue for "diversity":

> "[S]aying that economics, with the multiplicity of frames of analysis and theoretical models that it develops, contributes to the constitution of the object that it studies, means implicitly claiming that there is no single way of organizing the economy and moreover of organizing it satisfactorily or even effectively."

42 One could perhaps translate this failing co-performation into the conflict between forces of production and the relations of production, which are so important for the Marxian tradition.

43 It would be interesting to read Marx' notion of the "automatic subject" (1990: 255), which is decidedly processual and is 'performed' unknowingly by (and 'through') human actors everyday with Butler's non-subject-centered notion of performativity (cf. Butler 1993: 7ff.). I will develop this in another essay.

But this diversity and pluralism is not very far-reaching:

"In itself the thesis of diverse modalities of organization of economic life is by no means new or revolutionary – no more than that of the diversity of market configurations. What the performativity thesis does add, is that there is no one best way, no single form of organization that imposes itself naturally and compellingly, so to speak, as the only one able to ensure the optimal functioning of markets."

The form of the market, "to stick to this very specific economic form of organization" (Callon 2010: 163), is simply presupposed as – it seems – natural form.[44] The actors are not asked. No choice beyond the dichotomy of state and market (cf. Callon 2007: 349), although the 2009 Nobel Prize for economics was awarded to Elinor Ostrom, who showed that there might be solutions beyond state and market, solutions which, by the way, might lead to forms beyond Kapitalism.[45] Why not let these insights perform the economy?

There is one passage in Callon (2007: 330) which sounds like an explicit allusion to Friedman's 'Methodology of Positive Economics', with which my text began: "All of the economists who say that the unrealism of their propositions are of no concern to them have chosen their world, a world of papers, colleagues, and students – the one that suits their theories." Apart from the point that here he surprisingly criticizes 'hard economists', one cannot avoid the conclusion that this also applies to Callon himself.

44 It is puzzling that Callon states: "To be sure, the market can be put to the service of political action". This seems quite unrealistic given the neo-classical and neo-liberal hegemony – on the contrary, we have to read about 'market-conforming democracy' (cf. Berger 2013).

45 To be sure, Callon (2007: 350/351; with reference to Gibson-Graham 2003) also mentions in passing experimentation in cooperative forms, but not surprisingly the result is: "The cooperative does not propose the alternative solution to a general problem but a particular solution to a series of very specific problems. In so doing it does not help to strengthen the illusion that global forms of organization of the economy exist." For Callon obviously such 'global forms of organization of the economy' do exist – and that are of course the holy markets.

REFERENCES

Akrich, Madeleine (1992): "The de-scription of technical objects." In: Wiebe E. Bijker/John Law (eds.), Shaping Technology/Building Society: Studies in Sociotechnical Change, Cambridge, MA/London: The MIT Press, pp. 205-224.

Barry, Andrew/Slater, Don (2002): "Technology, politics, and the market: An interview with Michel Callon." In: Economy and Society 31/2, pp. 285-306.

Berger, Jens (2013): "Market-Conforming Democracy." March 3, 2016 (http://la.indymedia.org/news/2013/11/262253.php).

Bichler, Shimshon/Nitzan, Jonathan (2014): "How capitalists learned to stop worrying and love the crisis." In: Real World Economics Review 66, pp. 65-73, March 2, 2016 (http://www.paecon.net/PAEReview/issue66/BichlerNitzan66.pdf).

Binswanger, Hans Ch. (1990): "Geld und Gleichgewicht. Ein Vorschlag zur Überwindung von Preis- und Werttheorie." In: Zeitschrift für Wirtschafts- und Sozialwissenschaften 110, pp. 337-358.

Brisset, Nicolas (2016): "Economics is not always performative: Some limits for performativity." In: Journal for Economic Methodology 23/2, pp. 160-184.

Brynjolffson, Erik (1993): "The productivity paradox of information technology." In: Communications of the ACM 36/12, pp. 66-77.

Brynjolffson, Erik/McAfee, Andrew (2011): Race Against the Machine. How the Digital Revolution is Accelerating Innovation, Driving Productivity, and Irreversibly Transforming Employment and the Economy, Lexington: Digital Frontier Press.

Bulow, Jeremy (1986): "An economic theory of planned obsolescence." In: The Quarterly Journal of Economics 101/4, pp. 729-749.

Butler, Judith (1993): Bodies that Matter. On the Discursive Limits of "Sex", London: Routledge.

Butler, Judith (2010): "Performative agency." In: Journal of Cultural Economy 3/2, pp. 147-161.

Callon, Michel (1998a) (ed.): The Laws of the Markets, Oxford: Blackwell.

Callon, Michel (1998b): "Introduction." In: Michel Callon (ed.), The Laws of the Markets, Oxford: Blackwell, pp. 1-57.

Callon, Michel (1998c): "An essay on framing and overflowing: Economic externalities revisited by sociology." In: Michel Callon (ed.), The Laws of the Markets, Oxford: Blackwell, pp. 244-269.

Callon, Michel (1999): "Actor-network theory – the market test." In: John Law/John Hassard (eds.), Actor Network Theory and After, Oxford: Blackwell, pp. 181-195.

Callon, Michel (2005): "Why virtualism paves the way to political impotence. Callon replies to Miller." In: Economic Sociology. European Electronic Newsletter 6/2, pp. 3-20, March 2, 2016 (http://econsoc.mpifg.de/archive/esfeb05.pdf).

Callon, Michel (2007): "What does it mean to say that economics is performative?" In: Donald MacKenzie/Fabian Muniesa/Lucia Siu (eds.), Do Economists Make Markets? On the Performativity of Economics, Princeton: Princeton University Press, pp. 311-357.

Callon, Michel (2010): "Performativity, misfires and politics." In: Journal of Cultural Economy 3/2, pp. 163-169.

Derrida, Jacques (1988): "Signature Event Context." In: Gerald Graff (ed.), Limited Inc., Evanston: Northwestern University Press, pp. 1-23.

Fine, Ben (2003): "Callonistics: A disentanglement." In: Economy and Society 32/3, pp. 478-484.

Ford, Martin (2009): Lights in the Tunnel. Automation, Accelerating Technology and the Economy of the Future, United States: Acculant Publishing.

Frey, Carl Benedikt/Osborne, Michael A. (2013): "The future of employment: How susceptible are jobs to computerisation." In: OMS Working Paper, March 2, 2016 (http://www.oxfordmartin.ox.ac.uk/downloads/academic/The_Future_of_Employment.pdf).

Friedman, Milton (1966): Essays in Positive Economics, Chicago: Chicago University Press.

Garcia-Parpet, Marie France (2007): "The social construction of a perfect market. The strawberry auction at Fontaines-au-Sologne." In: Donald MacKenzie/Fabian Muniesa/Lucia Siu (eds.), Do Economists Make Markets? On the Performativity of Economics, Princeton/Oxford: Princeton University Press, pp. 20-53.

Garfinkel, Harold (1967): Studies in Ethnomethodology, Englewood Cliff, NJ: Prentice-Hall.

Gibson-Graham, J. K. (2003): "Enabling ethical economies: Cooperativism and class." In: Critical Sociology 29/2, pp.123-161.

Gillilland, Cora Lee C. (1975): The Stone Money of Yap. A Numismatic Survey, Washington: Smithsonian Institution Press.

Gode, Dan/Sunder, Shyam (1993): "Allocative efficiency of markets with zero-intelligence traders." In: Journal of Political Economy 101, pp. 119-137.

Hands, D. Wade (2001): Reflection without Rules. Economic Methodology and Contemporary Science Theory, Cambridge: Cambridge University Press.

Holm, Petter (2007): "Which way is up on Callon?" In: Donald MacKenzie/Fabian Muniesa/Lucia Siu (eds.), Do Economists Make Markets? On the Performativity of Economics, Princeton/Oxford: Princeton University Press, pp. 225-243.

Holm, Petter/Nielsen, Kåre Nolde (2007): "Framing fish, making markets: The construction of individual transferable quotas." In: Michel Callon/Yuval Millo/Fabian Muniesa (eds.), Market Devices, Malden, MA et al.: Blackwell, pp. 173-195.

Hutter, Michael (1995): "Signum non olet." In: Waltraud Schelkle/Manfred Nitsch (eds.), Rätsel Geld: Annäherungen aus ökonomischer, soziologischer und historischer Sicht, Marburg: Metropolis, pp. 325-352.

Keen, Steve (2001): Debunking Economics. The Naked Emperor of the Social Sciences, Ananndale: Pluto Press.

Keen, Steve (2011): Debunking Economics – Revised and Expanded Edition. The Naked Emperor Dethroned? London/New York: Zed Books.

Kliman, Andrew (2007): Reclaiming Marx's Capital: A Refutation of the Myth of Inconsistency, Lanham, MD: Lexington Books.

Krajina, Zlatan/Moores, Shaun/Morley, David (2014): "Non-media-centric media studies: A cross-generational conversation." In: European Journal of Cultural Studies 17/6, pp. 1-19.

Kurz, Robert (2005): Das Weltkapital. Globalisierung und innere Schranken des modernen warenproduzierenden Systems, Berlin: Ed. Tiamat.

Larsen, Neil/Nilges, Mathias/Robinson, Josh/Brown, Nicholas (2014) (eds.): Marxism and the Critique of Value, Chicago/Alberta: M-C-M'.

Latour, Bruno (2005): Reassembling the Social. An Introduction to Actor-Network-Theory, New York: Oxford University Press.

Lee, Frederic (2009): A History of Heterodox Economics. Challenging the Mainstream in the Twentieth Century, New York et al.: Routledge.

LeGoff, Jacques (2012): Money and the Middle Ages, New York: Wiley.

Lohhoff, Ernst/Trenkle, Norbert (2012): Die große Entwertung. Warum Spekulation und Staatsverschuldung nicht die Ursache der Krise sind, Münster: Westf. Unrast.

Lotz, Christian (2014): The Capitalist Schema. Time, Money and the Culture of Abstraction, Lanham: Lexington Books.

MacKenzie, Donald/Muniesa, Fabian/Siu, Lucia (2007): "Introduction." In: Donald MacKenzie/Fabian Muniesa/Lucia Siu (eds.), Do Economists Make

Markets? On the Performativity of Economics, Princeton/Oxford: Princeton University Press, pp. 1-19.

Marx, Karl (1990): Capital. Volume I., London: Penguin.

Marx, Karl (1991): Capital. Volume III., London: Penguin.

Marx, Karl (1993): Grundrisse, London: Penguin.

Mirowski, Philip/Nik-Khah Edward (2008): "Command performance: Exploring what STS thinks it takes to build a market." In: Trevor Pinch/Richard Swedberg (eds.), Living in a Material World: Economic Sociology Meets Science and Technology Studies, Cambridge, MA: MIT Press, pp. 89-128.

Muniesa, Fabian (2014): The Provoked Economy. Economic Reality and the Performative Turn, London: Routledge.

Orléan, André (2014): The Empire of Value. A New Foundation for Economics, Cambridge, MA: MIT Press.

Pahl, Hanno (2008): Das Geld in der modernen Wirtschaft. Marx und Luhmann im Vergleich, Frankfurt/New York: Campus.

Pashukanis, Evgeny Bronislavovich (2002): The General Theory of Law and Marxism, New Brunswick, NJ: Transaction Publishers.

Reckwitz, Andreas (2003): "Grundelemente einer Theorie sozialer Praktiken. Eine sozialtheoretische Perspektive." In: Zeitschrift für Soziologie 32/4, pp. 282-301.

Schröter, Jens (2011): "Das automatische Subjekt. Überlegungen zu einem Begriff von Karl Marx." In: Hannelore Bublitz et al. (eds.), Unsichtbare Hände. Automatismen in Medien-, Technik- und Diskursgeschichte, München: Fink, pp. 215-256.

Taleb, Nassim Nicholas (2010): The Black Swan. The Impact of the Highly Improbable, New York: Random House.

Zelizer, Viviana (1998): "The proliferation of social currencies." In: Michel Callon (ed.), The Laws of the Markets, Oxford: Blackwell, pp. 58-68.

Democratizing

Performance and democratizing digitality

StudioLab as critical design pedagogy

JON MCKENZIE

Performance and digitality constitute an onto-historical[1] apparatus or *dispositif* reshaping cultures globally, yet our engagement with these performative circuits remains out-of-sync and ineffective, especially at the levels of knowledge and power, thought and action. Within higher education, modern disciplinary methods, arborescent institutional structures, and logocentric literacies inhibit the critico-creative syntheses needed to engage and resist neoliberal modes of performativity. In contemporary societies of control, universities around the world face daunting economic and political pressures to transform and innovate, while traditional forms of academic research and education struggle to contend with young people's attachments to mobile technologies, social media, and consumer-driven design practices. StudioLab is a critical design pedagogy that seeks to democratize emerging forms and processes of digitality by supplementing seminar-based *critical thinking* with studio-based *design thinking* and lab-based *tactical media-making*. In StudioLab, students roleplay as critical design teams to research and create conceptually-rich projects that address contemporary social challenges through a variety of media forms and events. Critical design teams combine cultural, organizational, and technological performances and learn ways to introduce values of cultural efficacy into structures dominated by organizational efficiency and technological effectiveness, thereby generating creative and potentially transformative micro-transvaluations in themselves and others. This performative matrix of valorizations helps to situate StudioLab's practices of de-

1 This term signals that history and ontology are themselves historical and ontological constructs.

mocratizing digitality and suggests new figurations of thought and action, new experiential architectures.

METHODOLOGICAL CONTEXT: ALL PERFORMANCE IS ELECTRONIC

All P is E, all performance is electronic: Our abilities to study performance in a wide variety of different forms, spaces, and times – from bodies to machines, from theaters to rituals to outer space, from the past to present and future – are tied to Cold War research, as they date from the mid-20th century. It was then that anthropologists and artists, electrical engineers and rocket scientists, managers and sociologists began patching together concepts of performance and cybernetic feedback to understand behaviors of people, technologies, organizations, and systems in general. Indeed, the radical extension of performance measures and systems theory across all disciplines of knowledge was theorized *as* performativity by Lyotard in *The Postmodern Condition: A Report on Knowledge*, an event he dates from the late 1950s (cf. Lyotard 1979: 3). Lyotard situates performativity – the postmodern legitimation of knowledge and social bonds via optimization of input/output matrices – with the rise of computerized societies. It is not just that new methods of power and knowledge arise, but that all methods bend to a new set of legitimating parameters. Postmodern performativity is audit culture, networked society, the postmodern condition: be operational or disappear, perform – or else.[2]

And yet beyond its postmodern, post-disciplinary valences and thus operating at an entirely different scale, performance also enacts *digitality* by instantiating the emergence of a massive onto-historical apparatus (*dispositif*), one whose millennial coordinates can be mapped with those of orality and literacy (cf. McLuhan 1967 Ong 1982; Ulmer 2002). At this scale, performative digitality tears at the Western foundations of *episteme*, at its modes of conceptual training, its alphabetic media, its arborescent infrastructures. From a cultural perspective, performance emerges 'between' ritual and theater for a reason: performance enacts digitality just as ritual embodies mythic forces of traditional oral cultures

2 As I argue in *Perform or Else* (2001), performance is a challenging-forth of humans into a post-disciplinary formation of power/knowledge. This performance stratum can be understood in terms of Lyotard's *Postmodern Condition*, Deleuze's "Postscript on the Societies of Control", and Hardt and Negri's *Empire*. "Perform – or else" is the order word of this onto-historical formation.

and theater represents the histories and fictions of modern literate worlds. Performance quickens the oral repertoires and literate archives described by Taylor (2003) and more importantly the digital databases encoding them both. Digitality entails the performative reinscription of oral, literate, visual, and numerate traces within networked databases and electronically-processed media flows – as well as the enabling mutations in bodily formation, social habitus, and ontological set-ups. Performance and digitality immerse us as grand moiré patterns produced by transhistorical overlayings of ritual and theater, repertoire and archive, orality and literacy. The West's self-defining distinctions of *logos* and *mythos*, *eidos* and *imagos*, dialectics and mimesis, all become unmoored in this remix of onto-historical apparatuses, and it is within this flickering, transmedia milieu that Nietzsche's revelations, Benjamin's flashes, and Ronell's hallucinogenres[3] emerge as untimely modes of thought. If all P is E, what becomes of *episteme*, pedagogy, and method in their unsettling remix with *doxa*, initiation, and ritual?

Figure 1: Teaching Nietzsche's double affirmation in an MBA program

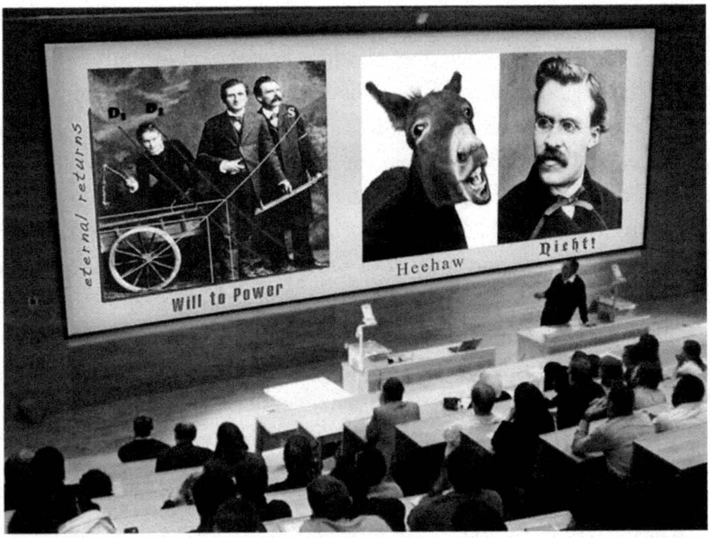

Credit: Author

3 "Hallucinogenre" is Avital Ronell's neologism, a trippy tropic play on hallucinogenics and genres. Smart media, e.g., are modern *pharmakons*, monstrous mashes of different substances.

TEACHING THE UNTEACHABLE

While studying painting and film in the 1980s, I had a fantasy that would come to guide my pedagogical orientation: *how to teach Nietzsche's double affirmation in an MBA program?* This question overcame me while reading Deleuze's *Nietzsche and Philosophy,* and it struck me at the time as truly perverse: how to teach one of the most perplexing philosophical thoughts in one of the most reactionary of institutional sites: a Masters of Business Administration program in Reagan's America? How to translate Nietzsche's prophetic call to affirm both chance and necessity – chance *as* necessity – in a context where both are calculated according to inputs and outputs and driven by utility and the profit motive? How to challenge profits with prophecy?

Unbeknownst to me at the time, the perverse circuits connecting Nietzsche, teaching, and capital had been described decades earlier by Pierre Klossowski, who posed Nietzsche's quest to communicate his revelation of the eternal return in these terms: *how to teach the unteachable?* Klossowski elaborates this question in his comments on *The Gay Science*: "Nietzsche had a nostalgia for disciples and perhaps also for an active, but closed, community. He always dreamed a grand action, of social upheavals or disruptions of political institutions [...] And, to the extent that he estimated the possibility of an understanding, of an affinity with others, he also set forth the infallible law of depreciation of a rare and authentic experience as soon as it enters the habitude of a number of minds [...] But regarding this relation, depreciation has done its work by way of industrial standardization" (Klossowski 2007: 14). Changing gears, Klossowski contrasts two circuits, of phantasm[4] and utensil, of artistic simulacra and capitalist goods, of singular impulses and general communication, circuits whose intersection forms the live wire of one's existence: "Impulsive 'phantasm' – simulacrum; subsistence – utensil fabrication: two circuits which intersect with the individual unity, but which this same unity never manages to break, if only to postpone perpetually the urgency of one or the other circuit" (Klossowski, *Living Currency*, cited by Castanet 2014: 147).

Short-circuiting eternal returns with nervous systems, the quest of teaching the unteachable – along with his poetics of Dionysus and Ariadne, his manifesto of a gay science, and his role as the first typewriting philosopher – make Nietzsche a performative pedagogue of our digital futures. Within the context of performance and digitality, a gay science of teaching the unteachable takes on

4 "Phantasm" is an archaic term used by Klossowski and maintained by his translators and commentators.

many concrete dimensions and raises numerous quests and questions. How to quantify the unquantifiable? How to account for the unaccountable? How to teach a performative transvaluation of values within existing performative values? How to democratize digitality within institutions whose structures, habits, and values are founded on logocentric exclusions and hierarchies that date back to Plato's Academy and whose modern instantiation as Cartesian ideation thereby informs our disciplines, methods, and truths? What kinds of infrastructures, spaces, and events are needed to think and act beyond the cartographies of *eidos*? What sorts of methods and media and bodies are needed?

StudioLab as Critical Design Pedagogy

My long-term research project is StudioLab, a transversal pedagogy that mixes seminar, studio, and lab activities to enable experiments in critical thinking, experience design, and media making. *StudioLab's onto-historical mission is to democratize digitality, just as public education has sought to democratize literacy.* A nomadic, decades-long experiment, StudioLab has traveled from institution to institution, taking different forms depending on the collaborators, infrastructure, and geography. Modular projects, flexible content, emerging technologies, and diverse student bodies have driven the development of its curriculum and spatial configuration. I first developed StudioLab in the mid-1990s at New York University by shuttling students between a Broadway performance studio and a computer lab off Washington Square. Subsequently, at University of the Arts (Philadelphia), Dartmouth College, and the University of Wisconsin-Madison, StudioLab has developed an array of design frames, media workshops, and an architectural form called Media Studio, whose mobile furniture and light tech enable students to mix seminar, studio, and lab experiences within a single space.

StudioLab's contribution to the democratization of digitality lies in its combination of seminar, studio, and lab practices, which allows for the spatialization of conceptual discourses, their transmediation across diverse forms and situations, and the generation of thought and action through collaborative, engaged research. In practical terms, StudioLab has provided backend R&D for the general theory of performance outlined in *Perform or Else* (2001) and subsequent texts, as its courses and projects combine cultural, organizational, and technological performances. Indeed, alongside its mission to democratize digitality, *StudioLab seeks to resist global performativity by interjecting values of critico-creative efficacy into socio-technical systems dominated by neoliberal mixes of efficiency and effectiveness*. The goal is to generate micro- and macro-transvaluations of performative values that move across visceral, affective, and cognitive realms to effect changes within larger socio-technical systems.

From a methodological perspective, StudioLab can be understood as critical *design pedagogy* for democratizing digitality, for inventing and disseminating new forms of post-ideational thought-action. Interaction designers Anthony Dunne and Fiona Raby (2007) introduced the term "critical design" to describe design infused with a politically critical sensitivity, both for designer and end user. HCI designers Jeffry Bardzell and Shaowen Bardzell write that by "inscribing alternative values in designs, critical design cultivates critical attitudes among consumers and designers alike, creating demand for and supporting the professional emergence of alternative design futures". Bardzell and Bardzell (2013: 3299) draw upon Critical Theory and Metacriticism to open up Dunne and Raby's critical design practice for extension into their field of Human Computer Interaction (HCI). In the spirit of democratizing digitality, StudioLab likewise seeks to extend a specific mix of critical design across potentially all fields and social institutions. Like performance and media, design is a transdisciplinary and sometimes incoherent field of practice and study marked by disciplinary borders and territorial disputes. When viewed from the perspective of digitality, however, debates between specialists, as well as tensions between experts and amateurs, can be recast as effects of ideational infrastructures and institutional habits associated with literate, disciplinary knowledge. StudioLab's own metacritical move is to affirm such critical differences by devising creative syntheses across diverse bodies, media, and sites, thereby contributing to the emergence of critical design as a vector for democratizing digitality.

CRITICAL THINKING + DESIGN THINKING + TACTICAL MEDIA

StudioLab's approach to critical design pedagogy combines critical thinking (broader than Critical Theory), design thinking (broader than HCI), and tactical media (broader than writing). This stepping back or broadening of scope situates Frankfurt School Critical Theory, Metacriticism, and other methodological approaches within the larger, disciplinary context of critical thinking in higher education. In the US, *critical thinking* refers to the use of evidence-based, logical reasoning as a guide to ethical decision-making and action, and it is considered an "Essential Learning Outcome" by the Association of American Colleges & Universities. These Essential Learning Outcomes inform the evaluation and assessment of academic programs across the US. The genealogy of critical thinking stretches from Socrates to Descartes to Kant to Marx, and it forms the foundation of disciplinary research and liberal arts education and is thus taught across the breadth of the traditional arts and sciences. From the perspective of digitality, critical thinking is literate, ideational thinking whose methods bring objects clearly and distinctly before subjects, a *dispositif* carefully set up in first-year writing courses. StudioLab's goal is not to replace critical thinking and writing but precisely to supplement and embed literate methods, subjects, and objects within the emerging apparatus of digitality, using media and collaborative problem-solving to connect them with new communities and situations. The *logos* of critical thinking and specialized knowledge remains operational but its efficacy has waned. Given the highly publicized and increasingly politicized crisis of the liberal arts in the US, revitalizing the forms, functions, and sites of critical thinking is crucial to reimagining higher education and advanced research beyond Platonic ideation. StudioLab starts with a simple step: connect the conceptual space of the seminar to the aesthetic and technical spaces of the studio and lab.

To interface seminar learning with studio activities, the second component of StudioLab's critical design pedagogy is *design thinking*, a human-centered design approach to strategic thinking developed by the design firm IDEO and researched by the Hasso Plattner Institutes of Design at Potsdam University, Germany, and Stanford University, USA. Design thinking is a collaborative method for addressing complex organizational and social problems. IDEO CEO Tim Brown argues that designers must "think big", think beyond designing endless objects for meaningless needs and instead tackle complex problems facing individuals and societies, such as healthcare and climate change. Design thinking's transdisciplinary design method balances three constraints – human desirability, economic viability, and technical feasibility – constraints that correspond to the performative values of cultural efficacy, organizational efficiency, and technical effectiveness. Moreover, design thinking's human-centered approach prioritizes human desirability/cultural efficacy, focusing on empathy with various stakeholders to define and reframe the situation at hand. Although design thinking also stresses ideation or the creative generation of ideas as central to its iterative process, this ideation is post-Platonic in that it relies not on top-down, expert knowledge or *episteme,* but rather on empathizing with a variety of stakeholders, that is, on bottom-up, common knowledge or *doxa*. In that sense, it is already critical, though this criticality resides in a matrix of empathy gathered through ethnographic methods of interview, observation, and participation and composed of emotions, knowledge, and values. It is within this matrix that micro-transvaluations can occur at both individual and group levels, revalorizations that produce not exclusions of effectiveness and efficiency but remixes in a different space.

Supplementing critical thinking and design thinking, the third element of StudioLab's critical design pedagogy is *tactical media*, which emerges out of artist activist events and groups in Europe and North America, such as Next Five Minutes (N5M), Critical Art Ensemble (CAE) and Electronic Disturbance Theater (EDT): "The term 'tactical media' refers to a critical usage and theorization of media practices that draw on all forms of old and new, both lucid and sophisticated media, for achieving a variety of specific noncommercial goals and pushing all kinds of potentially subversive political issues" (N5M, cited by CAE 2000: 5). In *Digital Resistance* (2000), CAE situates tactical media within a comprehensive set of practices that go beyond street-based resistance against disciplinary institutions to function as digital resistance within our contemporary performative matrix. Tactical media-making enables StudioLab to supplement the traditional seminar study of argumentative and rhetorical writing with studio and lab work in a full range of media effects: from the Guerrilla Girl's poster, to Reverend Billy's performance protests, to EDT's FloodNet software, to Molle Industria's absurdist games. The digitalization and networking of embodied repertoires and discursive archives are producing forms of procedural rhetoric, diagrammatic semiotics, and transmedia persuasion whose circuits operate at scales too small and too large to perceive.

The elements of StudioLab's critical design approach supplement one another. StudioLab balances the epistemological force of critical thinking's *logos* with the collaborative empathy-driven *doxa* of design thinking and the radical, subversive potential of tactical media-making as *graphe*. At the level of production, critical thinking pedagogies produce individual thinkers and writers, whereas design thinking and tactical media entail the production of critical design teams. Both design thinking and tactical media-making rely on practice-based collaboration, and design thinking produces its own version of tactical media, the "shared media" of sketches and prototypes which emerge as part of its ideational process. Like tactical media, shared media do not report on things but make things happen: they are themselves performative, not constative, though they can become so through iteration. Of course, critical thinking too has its own tactical media: the alphabet, books, and archive, which students spend their entire school life learning. StudioLab is a crash course in designing transmedia thought-action.

The rapid development of design as a critical discourse in the US can be seen in academic courses and programs in *critical design thinking*, including a graduate degree at Virginia Tech University and an undergraduate initiative at Smith College, a small liberal arts college in Massachusetts. "The Smith brand of design thinking envisions design in service of broader social issues of participation, intervention and leadership. Design thinking can be used to question gender, power and ability as dynamics that shape who gets to participate in creating the world we live in." (Smith College 2016) StudioLab's mix of critical thinking, design thinking, and tactical media likewise seeks to intervene in institutions by injecting critico-creative values of social efficacy into processes and structures where values of organization efficiency and technical effectiveness dominate data collection and decision-making. Critical design thinking, in particular, offers students concrete methods for site-specific micro-transvaluations of value, and it is important to note that Smith College's inaugural projects include a campus-wide initiative to rethink the college's work and learning spaces. From StudioLab's perspective, challenging global performativity and democratizing digitality require changing values in order to transform the spaces, media, curricula, and organization of learning that empower students to approach knowledge and power in both critical and creative ways.

CRITICAL PERFORMATIVITY AND INTIMATE BUREAUCRACIES

The fantasy of teaching Nietzsche's double affirmation in an MBA program approaches full-scale actualization in the emerging field of Critical Management Studies (CMS), where researchers have introduced Critical Theory and post-structuralist thought into the discipline of organizational management. Like critical design, CMS explores more subversive forms of critical thinking and does so in institutions ruled by socially dominant values and practices that its scholars have explicitly theorized in terms of performativity. CMS is characterized by "its critical stance towards institutionalized social and intellectual practices, such as the profit imperative, racial inequality or environmental irresponsibility" (Wickert and Schaefer 2015: 108), and within the field, the concept of *critical performativity* offers a nuanced approach to both the efficiency-effectiveness and efficacy circuits of organizational performance.

Spicer, Alvesson and Kärreman (2009) theorize critical performativity by contrasting critiques of Lyotardian performativity (input/output ratios) and resistant practices of Butlerian performativity, understood as subversive resignifications of discourse. "Approaching performativity as possibly subversive mobilizations and citations of previous performances, instead of as an overarching concern for efficiency" (Spicer/Alvesson/Kärreman 2009: 544), they argue for understanding and developing Critical Management Studies as a performative and potentially subversive field, one whose own critical performativity operates through "an affirmative stance, an ethic of care, a pragmatic orientation, engagement with potentialities, and striving for a normative orientation" (ibid.: 546, see Table I).

Table I: An Overview of Performative CMS

Characteristic	**Achieved through**	**Methodological Tactic**
Affirmative stance	Location at close proximity to object of critique in order to identify potential points revision	Affirming ambiguous and mixed metaphors found in organizational discourse
Ethic of care	Providing space for respondents' views, but also seeking to subtly challenge them	Working with mysteries
Pragmatism	Working with particular aspects of an organization	Applied communicative action
Potentialities	Creating a sense of what could be by engaging latent possibilities in an organization	Explorations of heterotopias
Normative	Systematic assertion of criteria used to judge good forms of organization	Engaging micro-emancipations

Adapted from Table 1 of Spicer, Alvesson and Kärreman (2009: 546)

Rather than positioning organizations as objects of critique and researchers as outside performativity, performative CMS envisions workers as actively involved in liberating performative practices that produce resignifications, heterotopias, and micro-emancipations – practices which CMS researchers should actively engage with through participatory methods. The goal of critical performativity is "to not only engage in systematic dismantling of existing managerial approaches, but also try to construct new and hopefully more liberating ways of organizing" (ibid.: 555).

Performative CMS provides StudioLab important critico-creative models for combining cultural, organizational, and technological performances within the context of democratizing digitality and remixing performative values. Resignification entails the queering or refunctioning not only of discourses, but also practices and infrastructures and their simultaneous reinscription within newly imagined heterotopias, spaces with alternative conceptual, physical, architectural, digital, environmental, spiritual, and even cosmic dimensions. Indeed, StudioLab functions as a heterotopia for generating heterotopias. Within this context, making micro-emancipations sustainable and scalable depends upon micro-transvaluations of performative values, augmenting the dominant circuits of efficiency-effectiveness with those of critico-creative efficacy. Here we see how methods of design thinking and tactical media supplement traditional methods of critical thinking by introducing collaborative creativity and interventionist media-making. *Beyond isolated critiques of the bad, collaborative creations of joy.* It may seem counter-intuitive to initiate joyful collaborations at the intersection of cultural and organizational performance, but as CAE argues, the development of tactical media best occurs within tightly-knit activist groups, which depend on the shared generation of ideas and projects, tactical if not strategic thinking, self-organization of diverse talents, and effective project management.

StudioLab approaches art activist groups – as well as artisan guilds, theory schools, rap groups, and other start-ups – both as objects of study and as heuristic models for democratizing the sociotechnical practices of digital culture. Students sometimes extend their model's direction of activism but usually head off in new directions, incorporating conceptual, aesthetic, technical, and organizational insights into their own projects and production processes. Art activist groups such as the Guerrilla Girls, Molle Industria, and the Yes Men, can be understood as *intimate bureaucracies*, a term Saper has coined for modes of "participatory decentralization" (Saper 2012: 1). Intimate bureaucracies enable collective action through common infrastructures, such as the streets, the Internet, and other public services. Saper cites Fluxus art and the Occupy Wall Street political movements and their respective sociopoetic use of the postal service and public parks as primary examples. "These forms of organization represent a paradoxical mix of artisanal production, mass-distribution techniques, and a belief in the democratizing potential of electronic and mechanical reproduction techniques. Borrowing from mass-culture image banks, these intimate bureaucracies play on forms of publicity common in societies of spectacles and public relations. Intimate bureaucracies have no demands, no singular ideology, nor righteous path" (ibid.). Saper highlights the paradox of intimate bureaucracies: the impersonal institutions and procedures associated with bureaucracies are detoured or recircuited by artists, activists, and other community members for more singular, intimate ends. Within the context of higher education, colleges and universities have themselves long served as common infrastructures, providing access to resources and services through libraries, central IT, and physical space, and a large part of education involves teaching students how to use these and other infrastructures.

By combining singularity and institutions, intimate bureaucracies open an infrastructural dimension to StudioLab's quest to teach the unteachable, to short-circuit singular impulses and general communication. In the language of Deleuze and Guattari: intimate bureaucracies function as desiring machines that have evolved from isolated bachelor machines into full-blown collective assemblages of enunciation, scaling up the creation of joy across different social planes by constructing referential universes and planes of consistency that enable sustainability and resonance with other movements. In the terms of design thinking: the creative constraints of human desirability and technical feasibility that define any social innovation find sustenance with those of economic or ecological viability, the ability to survive within a given milieu or environment. If design thinking brings the power of creative processes to large organizations, intimate bureaucracies bring the power of large organizations to creative processes. The student body is the site where these circuits intersect.

Figure 2: "Make a Toy" Exercise

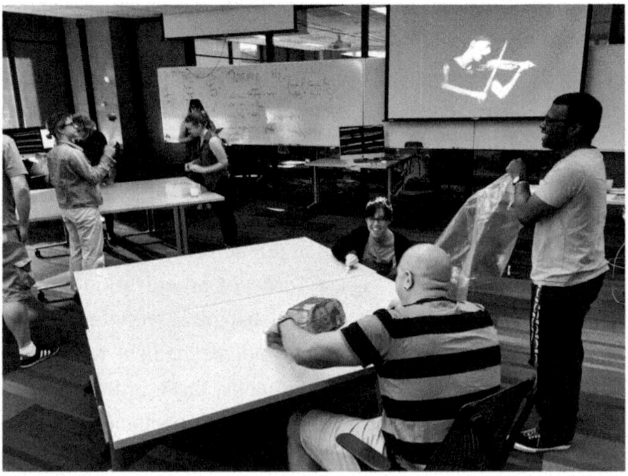

Credit: Author

TRANSVERSALITIES, PROJECTS, AND DESIGN FRAMES

StudioLab's critical design pedagogy synthesizes traditional critical thinking, transdisciplinary design thinking, and interventionist tactical media by moving students transversally through seminar, studio, and lab activities. *Bodies learn differently in each space.* Students combine cultural, organizational, and technological performances and thereby gain hands-on experience engaging the values of efficacy, efficiency, and effectiveness. At the heart of StudioLab are projects and design frames that integrate conceptual, aesthetic, technical, and social learning through individual exercises and larger collaborative projects. In an initial "Make a Toy" exercise, students use common household materials to design and create toys – tiny desiring machines crafted to generate joy in others – while learning principles of experience design, the shaping of interactions, emotions, and thought. Concepts are spatialized, taken back to the drawing board and connected with others, and explored through hands-on engagement. StudioLab's project-based pedagogy unfolds by juxtaposing studio exercises with seminar discussion, lab training, and time for fieldwork, presentation, and reflection. In a subsequent exercise, "Design an Activist Museum", students self-organize and scale-up their desiring machines into critical design teams, role-playing as intimate bureaucracies. Researching art activist groups and miming their different mixes of social activism and tactical media, critical design teams develop names, logos, and mission statements, while drawing on local public commons and transferring their research to issues and situations that resonate with their own lives. Like all StudioLab projects, "Design a Museum" is modular and portable: it can embrace potentially any topic, field, or community.

StudioLab's pedagogy moves people transversally in three ways and provides critical design frames all along the way. On a first, spatial level, students in a StudioLab course, workshop, or even a single, 3-hour class meeting might begin with a hands-on studio installation, then shift to seminar discussion, lab for software training, and conclude with open workshop or field work. To help students articulate these transversal thresholds, we introduce the CAT design frame (Conceptual-Aesthetic-Technical), which maps onto seminar, studio, and lab activities. Conceptual work follows traditional critical thinking methods – reading, discussion, and written synthesis of textual and other materials – supplemented with dramaturgical and media approaches: students generate notes, conceptual spreadsheets comparing different methods, and intellectual dialogues that gather and dramatize ideational arguments. Aesthetic studio work focuses on the transmediation of discursive and material practices, mixing arguments with physical, visual, aural, and environmental media while drawing on fields of performance, graphic design, cinematography, installation, experience design, etc. Tactical media here include objects, storyboards, mood boards, user scenarios, posters, installations, and prototypes. CAT's technical dimension unfolds in computer lab space, with students learning and using digital software and hardware to support the conceptual and aesthetic activities. It is important to note that seminar, studio, and lab activities each have their own conceptual, aesthetic, and technical dimensions and they come to the fore in different ways. Over time, StudioLab's iterative process blends these dimensions precisely by incorporating their elements into the unfolding project. Students use CAT to both analyze and create, for it enables them to abstract and evaluate conceptual, aesthetic, and technical issues at any time in the creative process. In all cases, at this first level, student bodies are reshaped by transversal movement through distinct learning environments: seminar, studio, lab, field.

At a second, existential level, StudioLab's next design frame, UX or user experience, draws on fields of rhetoric, design, and performance to teach students ways of transforming people internally by moving them spiritually, conceptually, imaginatively, emotionally, sensually, and/or viscerally – experiences that unfold in schools, museums, churches, community centers, theme parks, or online environments. StudioLab's UX frame focuses on *experience design* or the crafting of experiential interactions, *information architecture* or the spatiotemporal structure of these experiences, and *information design* or the look-and-feel at any moment of their unfolding. Using the UX frame both analytically and synthetically, *students design transformational experiences for multiple stakeholders: community collaborators, target audiences, the general public, and themselves.* To this end, they learn how early ACT-UP members transformed their own anger and fear into love and action using social activism and tactical media, creating direct actions designed in turn to transform the feelings, thoughts, and actions of their target audiences and the wider general public. In our "Transform a Paper into an App, Service, or Social Movement" project, students scale up their intimate bureaucracies toward collective assemblages of enunciation where transformations of larger social systems become possible. At this second level, students use the UX frame to engage internal, "experiential architectures" of different stakeholders. These experiential architectures form the building blocks of the emerging heterotopias and provide the platform for micro-transvaluations of value.

At a third, sociotechnical level, StudioLab's critical design pedagogy moves students transversally across different social fields as they connect and engage people across disciplines, institutions, and communities. We draw on design thinking to tackle intractable, "wicked problems", using social activism and tactical media to connect students to community, culture, and history. In a recent

"Museum of Interactive Media" project, teams researched and proposed activist installations for an under-utilized space in the Wisconsin Institute of Discovery, a transdisciplinary research center at the University of Wisconsin-Madison. The center is built on the former site of Rennebohm's Pharmacy, known for the storytelling of founder Oscar Rennebohm, who later served as state Governor. Inspired by Reverend Billy's Earthellujah project, the KAMG student design team composed of Miranda Curry, Aaron Hathaway, Keegan Hasbrook, and Grace Vriezen interviewed current and potential WID visitors and aligned their research with the university's own legacy of environmental research and art activism. Their proposed reCLAIM Cafe offers a post-apocalyptic experience for both reclaiming personal space and measuring one's extension into ecological systems: at the VR Bar, patrons can view impacted environments and download a mobile app to track their waste habits, energy consumption, and water usage, while Trash Chutes visibly recycle consumer objects all around them.

Figure 3: "Rennie's Corner" redesign

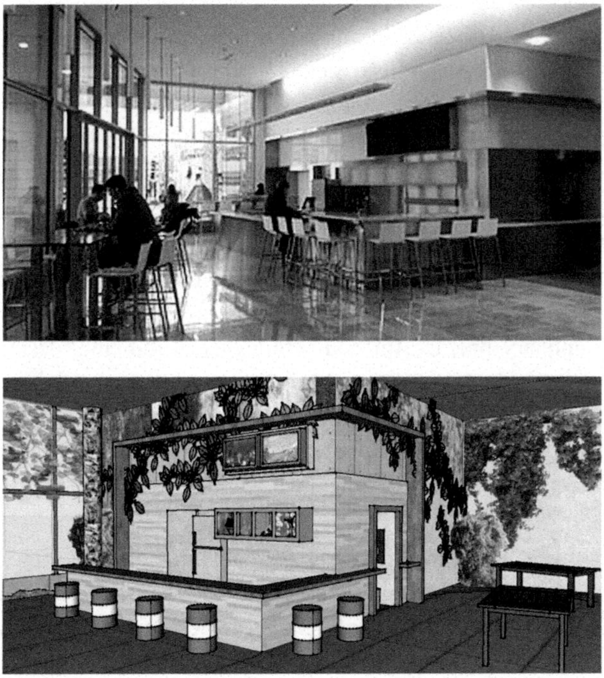

Credit: Miranda Curry, Keegan Hasbrook, Aaron Hathaway, Grace Vriezen

In StudioLab, ideas function as the means rather than the ends, entering an open, iterative process where collaborative problem-solving and innovation unfold via shared media and the posing of counter-factual possibilities and alternative worlds. Ideas become collective thought-action figures by moving from virtual to actual across different spaces as teams apply DT's transdisciplinary process of empathy, definition, ideation, prototyping, and testing.

An essential element of StudioLab's critical design approach to democratizing digitality is digital media itself, especially the production of *smart media*, emerging scholarly genres such as video essays, theory comics, and multimedia presentations which supplement traditional media forms of books and articles. Thought-action figures take shape via the circulation and sharing of smart media, whose genres mashup instruction and entertainment, *logos* and *mythos*, *eidos* and *imagos*, *episteme* and *doxa*. Everyday media forms such as public presentations, posters, and YouTube videos carry powerful communicative force, while search engines, wikis, and other tools have transformed knowledge discovery and empowered communities to connect locally and globally. At their very best, even the most derided of media forms, such as PowerPoint, can produce intelligent, sensitive effects for audiences intimate and massive: one thinks of Al Gore's 2006 *An Inconvenient Truth*, effectively an Oscar-winning PowerPoint presentation, or Chai Jing's 2015 *Under the Dome*, a powerful, censored documentary downloaded by hundreds of millions of viewers. StudioLab's critical design approach uses smart media to forge connections across spaces, disciplines, and communities. Yet while TED talks, digital storytelling, and similar media forms have become ubiquitous in the early 21st century, what is lacking is a *language* for analyzing them and a *practice* for creating them in saleable, sustainable ways. Together, the CAT, UX, and DT frames provide a transmedia language and transdisciplinary practice for combining critical thinking, design thinking, and tactical media at both intimate and infrastructural scales.

CODA

To teach the unteachable, to learn the unlearnable, the body becomes a test site of moiré patterning, the pulsating intersection of two circuits composed of impulses and markets, desiring machines and sociotechnical systems, idiosyncratic performances and general performativity. The fields of affect theory, experience design, consumer behavior, and micro-marketing all attest to the contemporary urgency of this vast yet discrete test site. As we have seen, performative digitality can itself be figured as the onto-historical overlaying of orality and literacy, ritual and theater, repertoire and archive, of two massive *dispositifs* for conducting these circuits' alternating currents through generations upon generations of bodies. StudioLab's overlaying of seminar, studio, lab, and field spaces attempts to democratize emerging modes of digitality by combining critical thinking, design thinking, and tactical media in order to tap into these circuits and intervene in the contemporary performative matrix.

Learning StudioLab's design frames through sustained project work can be transformational, empowering students and communities to bring critical design perspectives to other situations, including career and life decisions. The CAT frame enables students to augment conceptual making with aesthetic and technical making and thus redesign bodies of knowledge. The UX frame provides a language and practice for making such experiential transformations at intimate, interpersonal levels, while the DT frame provides a formal, ready-made process for attuning values of economic viability/efficiency and technical feasibility/effectiveness to those of human desirability/efficacy, as well as scaling up micro-transvaluations to the macro-valorizations of collective assemblages of enunciation. Moreover, DT's crowd-sourced, transdisciplinary ideation process is post-Platonic, making it a powerful force for democratizing digitality. Displacing the lone figure of the Romantic genius, StudioLab operates through intimate bureaucrats whose means and media of transformation are both idiosyncratic and common, impulsive and infrastructural. Critical design thinking produces not simply arguments or artistic expressions or technical objects as in traditional siloed learning spaces, but rather cognitive-perceptual-affective constellations of thought-action generated and arrayed in proposals, presentations, diagrams, prototypes, objects, apps, and other tactical media. At stake is not just critical analysis but creative making, and not just media-making but the building of transformative experiential architectures whose performance design extends from the internal dynamics of intimate bureaucracies to those of collaborating groups and communities. Emerging from seminar, studio, lab, and field spaces, from past, present, and future time zones, such experiential architectures give concrete form to the heterotopias envisioned by Foucault and provide intimate and common platforms for the transvaluation of performative values.

REFERENCES

Bardzell, Jeffrey/Bardzell, Shaowen (2013): "What is 'critical' about critical design?" In: CHI '13 Proceedings of the SIGCHI Conference on Human Factors in Computing Systems, New York: ACM, pp. 3297-3306.

Castanet, Hervé (2014): Pierre Klossowski: The Pantomime of Spirits (A.R. Price, trans.), Oxford: Peter Lang.

Critical Art Ensemble (2000): Digital Resistance: Explorations in Tactical Media, Brooklyn: Autonomedia.

Dunne, Anthony/Raby, Fiona (2007): "Critical Design FAQ." April 1, 2016 (http://www.dunneandraby.co.uk/content/bydandr/13/0)

Klossowski, Pierre (2007[1963]): Such a Deathly Desire (R. Ford, trans.), Albany: SUNY Press.

Lyotard, Jean-François (1984 [1979]): The Postmodern Condition: A Report on Knowledge (G. Bennington/B. Massumi, trans.), Minneapolis: University of Minnesota Press.

McLuhan, Marshall/Fiore, Quentin (1967): The Medium is the Massage: An Inventory of Effects, New York: Bantam Books.

Ong, Walter (1982): Orality and Literacy: The Technologizing of the Word, London: Routledge.

Saper, Craig J. (dj readies) (2012): Intimate Bureaucracies, Brooklyn: Punctum Press.

Smith College (2016): "The Design Thinking Initiative." May 15, 2016 (http://smith.edu/design-thinking)

Spicer, André/Alvesson, Mats/Kärreman, Dan (2009): "Critical performativity: The unfinished business of critical management studies." In: Human Relations 62, pp. 537-560.

Taylor, Diana (2003): The Archive and the Repertoire: Performing Cultural Memory in the Americas, Durham/London: Duke University Press.

Ulmer, Gregory L. (2002): Internet Invention: From Literacy to Electracy, New York: Longman.

Wickert, Christopher/Schaefer, Stephan M. (2015): "Towards a progressive understanding of performativity in critical management studies." In: Human Relations 68/1, pp. 107-130.

Notes on contributors

Marie-Luise Angerer is professor of Media Studies at the Department for Art and Media, University of Potsdam, and was previously professor of Media and Cultural Studies at the Academy of Media Arts Cologne. She has been a visiting fellow and guest professor in the US, UK, Canada, and Australia. Currently, she is member of the European Network *How Matter Comes to Matter* (2014-2018) and of the research network *Affective and Psychotechnology Studies* (DFG 2015-2017). The focus of her research is media technology, affect and neuroscientific reformulations of desire, sexuality, and the body. Her most recent publications include *Desire After Affect* (2014), *Timing of Affect* (with Bernd Bösel and Michaela Ott, 2014), *Choreography, Media, Gender* (with Yvonne Hardt and Anna-Carolin Weber, 2013), and numerous articles in books and journals on affect, art, and media theory.

Timon Beyes is a professor at the Department of Management, Politics and Philosophy, Copenhagen Business School (Denmark), and at the Centre for Digital Cultures, Leuphana University Lüneburg (Germany). Recent publications include *Social Media – New Masses* (with Inge Baxmann and Claus Pias, 2016), *The Routledge Companion to Reinventing Management Education* (with Martin Parker and Chris Steyaert, 2016), "Colour and Organization Studies" (*Organization Studies*, forthcoming), "Adorno's Grey, Taussig's Blue: Colour, Affect, Organization" (*Organization*, forthcoming).

Scott deLahunta is co-director of Motion Bank (with Florian Jenett) and Senior Research Fellow in partnership with Coventry University (UK) and Deakin University (AUS). He has worked as writer, researcher and organizer on a range of international projects bringing performing arts with a focus on choreography into conjunction with other disciplines and practices.

Herbordt/Mohren, Melanie Mohren and Bernhard Herbordt, have been creating interdisciplinary projects since 2000. In 2012, Herbordt/Mohren began work in different formats and media on institutions and their actualizations. Their spatial and sound installations, performances, exhibition projects, radio plays, stage plays, and musical theater works have been presented in a wide variety of international settings, and have received numerous prizes. Both have been members of the Young Academy at the Berlin-Brandenburg Academy of Sciences and Humanities and the German National Academy of Sciences, Leopoldina. Both graduated from the Institute for Applied Theatre Studies in Giessen.

Margarete Jahrmann is an internationally exhibiting artist and lecturer on activism, urbanity and play. She has received major media arts awards, such as the Prix Ars Electronica in interactive arts (2003) and the software arts award, Transmediale Berlin (2004). In 2006, she founded the Ludic Society and has been editor of the Ludic Society magazine since then. From 2010 to 2013, she was principal investigator of the EU funded research project "Play & Prosume" on Exhibition Game Design, with an exemplary Alternate Reality Exhibition at Kunsthalle Vienna in 2013. In 2016, Jahrmann and Max Moswitzer edited and presented the "VOID Book" at Cabaret Voltaire, Zürich. In 2016 she participated in "Entropy Opera" in Vienna – experimental mise-en-scene of 2nd order play and brain scan data.

Florian Jenett is an artist and currently Professor of Media Informatics at the design department of the Hochschule Mainz, University for Applied Sciences. He is co-founder of the basis studio houses and art space and a longtime contributor to the Processing project. In recent years he has been researching for the Motion Bank, which he has co-directed since 2014 (with Scott deLahunta).

Susan Kozel is a professor at the School of Arts and Culture of Malmö University, Sweden. She teaches the Interaction Design program, and is currently Project Leader of the interdisciplinary research project, *Living Archives*. She has an active artistic practice. She works at the convergence between philosophy, dance and digital technologies and writes on topics from performance to ubiquitous technologies to electronic music. Sole-authored books include *Closer: Performance, Technologies, Phenomenology* (2007) and *Mobile Choreographies: Affect and Encryption in Urban Spaces* (in progress).

Ann-Christina Lange is an assistant professor at the Department of Management, Politics and Philosophy, Copenhagen Business School, Denmark. She is part of the 'Crowd Dynamics in Financial Markets' research project, where her work focuses on high-frequency trading. She obtained her PhD from the Department of Sociology, Goldsmiths, University of London.

Martina Leeker is senior researcher at Digital Cultures Research Lab (DCRL), Leuphana University Lüneburg, and was previously Assistant Professor for Theatre and Media at University of Bayreuth. She has been guest professor at Bauhaus University Weimar and Berlin University of the Arts, and a research fellow at Morphomata, University of Cologne. The focuses of her research are digital cultures, digital methods, media anthropology, art/performance and technology, artistic research. Publications include *McLuhan neu lesen: Kritische Analysen zu Medien und Kultur im 21. Jahrhundert* (Ed., with Derrick de Kerckhove, Kerstin Schmidt, 2008), *Experiments&Interventions. Methods and Critique in Digital Cultures* (web publication, since 2014), and numerous book contributions on art/performance and technology.

Oliver Leistert currently works at the Chair of Media Cultures at Leuphana University Lüneburg and is post-doc on the research project "Complexity or Control? Paradigms for sustainable development". He was previously a member of the research training group "Automatisms" at Paderborn University (PhD 2013, winner of the Surveillance & Society book award 2014). His research focuses on: social and mobile media, algorithms and affect, protest media and surveillance, technological capture of relationality. Recent publications include *Critical Perspectives on Social Media and Protest. Between Control and Emancipation* (co-edited with Lina Dencik, 2015) and "Social bots as algorithmic pirates and messengers of techno-environmental agency" (*Algorithmic Cultures*, Eds. Robert Seyfert, Jonathan Roberge, 2016).

Jon McKenzie is Dean's Fellow for Media and Design and Visiting Professor of English at Cornell University. He is the author of *Perform or Else: From Discipline to Performance* (2001), which theorizes cultural, organizational, and technological performance in post-disciplinary societies. He is co-editor of *Contesting Performance: Global Sites of Research* (2009), as well as founder and former director of DesignLab. McKenzie has produced a number of experimental video essays and gives workshops on performative scholarship.

Sigrid Merx is Assistant Professor at the Department of Media and Culture Studies at Utrecht University where she coordinates the BA program Media and Culture. She is involved in the MA Contemporary Performance, Dance and

Dramaturgy and the minor Creative Cities. She is currently artistic co-director of Platform-Scenography. Her research focuses on performative interventions in public space and on the imagination of the future in performance practices.

Imanuel Schipper is a dramaturge, theater and performance studies scholar and curator. He is an appointed lecturer in Transdisciplinary Studies at Zurich University of the Arts (Switzerland), Dramaturgy at Free University Berlin, Ludwig Maximilian University Munich and Hochschule für bildende Künste, Hamburg. He is currently a research fellow at the Center for Digital Cultures and conducts PhD research on 'relational dramaturgies' at Leuphana University Lüneburg (Germany), and is collaborating as a dramaturge with the internationally-known theater collective Rimini Protokoll on a tetralogy on post-democratic phenomena, *Staat 1-4,* a coproduction with Haus der Kulturen der Welt (Berlin) and four theaters in Germany and Switzerland (2106-2018).

Jens Schröter is Chair for Media Studies at the University of Bonn. He was previously Professor for Multimedial Systems at the University of Siegen. He has been a guest professor in China and senior fellow in Hungary and Germany. He was director of the graduate school "Locating Media" (DFG) in Siegen and (with Lorenz Engell) director of the research project "TV Series as Reflection and Projection of Change" (DFG, 2010-2014). He is speaker of the research project "Society after Money" (since 2016). His main research topics are: theory and history of digital media, theory and history of photography, theory and history of three-dimensional images, intermediality, copy protection, media theory in discussion with the critique of value, TV-series. Recent publications include: *3D. History, Theory and Aesthetics of the Transplane Image* (2014), (ed.) *Handbuch Medienwissenschaft* (2014).